BEEKEEPING FOR BEGINNERS

A Complete Guide to Building Your Own Beehive, Colony Management, Honey Harvesting, and Turning Your Passion into Profit | + BONUS: Hive Inspection Checklist

MICHAEL YORK

YOUR FREE GIFTS!

As a beekeeper, you know that attention to detail makes all the difference. That's why I'm excited to offer you two exclusive bonus contents to enrich your beekeeping journey. The first is a meticulous **hive inspection checklist**, crafted to ensure that no detail is overlooked, from the smallest bee to the furthest corner of the comb. It's your step-by-step companion for flawless inspections.

But why stop there? Embrace the natural essence of beekeeping with a **comprehensive guide to the Top Bar Hive**, included as your second bonus. This trending hive type offers a bee-centric approach that could revolutionize your practice.

Both of these invaluable resources can be yours. Simply scan the QR code provided, and you're on your way to mastering both traditional and innovative beekeeping methods. Let's make your beekeeping experience as rewarding as it is productive.

SCAN THE QR CODE BELOW TO DOWNLOAD THE CHECKLIST AND THE TOP BAR HIVE GUIDE

TABLE OF CONTENTS

INTRODUCTION

Beehives/Credit: Radovan1(www.shutterstock.com)

If you've ever thought about buying a cow, you've likely discovered that they don't come cheap. Or perhaps you contemplated getting chickens and constructing a coop? That's quite a hefty investment too. A coop also needs a lot of space, which doesn't often work if you live in the city – it also won't charm your neighbors when the hens inevitably make their cacophony of sounds at all hours!

By comparison, bees aren't that costly. They also don't take up much space or disturb the neighborhood with an orchestra of noise throughout the day.

Perhaps money and space issues aren't your concern. Maybe the time factor is? Well, I'm here to inform you that beekeeping doesn't consume nearly as much time as you might imagine. While you will need to invest some time, particularly in the early stages of setting up your hive; it becomes less demanding once you get into the swing of things. You will soon discover that bees are impressively self-reliant creatures requiring little direct supervision.

Should you be holding this book, you've likely given up on that initial idea that piqued your interest—raising chickens. Your neighbors will thank you! What´s more likely is that you see yourself as something of an eco-warrior, producing honey from your own beehives and positively impacting your local ecosystem. Rest assured, when you do embark upon a new life that includes industrious bees you will not look back. Beekeeping is profoundly satisfying.

As you navigate through *Beekeeping for Beginners* you'll learn that this hobby or business can seamlessly blend into your daily routine without taking over. I'll even teach you how to overcome the fear of bee stings!

I will walk you through, step by step, the process of starting and maintaining a flourishing hive. We'll begin by empowering you with knowledge of bees' important role in your environment and many factors you need to consider before you begin.

The more you read, the more fascinating the world of bees will become! That is exactly what happened to me.

Bees, like all pollinators, are the lifeline for plants and help them thrive even when the odds are against them. If a plant faces the threat of extinction due to weather changes, diseases, or pest attacks, pollinators step in to assist their reproduction. Everything in our food chain relies on something; losing even one seemingly small link is all it takes to disrupt the balance. Bees and other pollinators are that crucial link. And being part of that precious and critical cycle, as a beekeeper, is immensely gratifying.

When you become a beekeeper, you'll realize how true the term, "liquid gold" is, as you unlock the door into the world of honey, beeswax, and even their medicinal uses. And as a bonus, you'll never be short of a gift at dinner parties, with ample liquid gold to exchange for other local produce.

Yet before we get ahead of ourselves, it's essential to say to you that the one thing I won't do in this book is pretend there are no potential obstacles to beekeeping. You may have read books or website articles that make beekeeping seem rather straightforward, but in reality, it's more like an elusive blend of art, science—and a dash of magic.

Always remember that the realization you don´t know *everything* is a vital part of the learning process. Every visit to your bee garden will teach you something new, or reveal that your understanding of beekeeping needs improvement, implying there's more to learn. That will never change. Not in the beginning, and not years down the road.

Beekeeping for Beginners helps you recognize the gaps in your knowledge and offers ample actions and information to fill in the blanks so that you are well-informed before you begin (and during) your journey. We'll touch upon important subjects like pest control, a vital aspect of ensuring your hive's health and longevity. We'll also introduce you to climate control, a frequently neglected but critical aspect of beekeeping.

For many, scalability is also an appealing aspect of beekeeping as it's a hobby that evolves with you. As you gain more confidence and expertise, you may decide to broaden your venture and actually market your honey. In the book's later sections, we'll discuss elevating your beekeeping game and address topics like marketing and expanding your honey range.

The first and best beekeeping fact to remember is that your location is of little significance, depending on local regulations, of course. Some people manage beehives in confined spaces in suburban areas. Some city dwellers keep beehives on apartment rooftops, contributing to the much-needed pollination in urban spaces. You can set up pretty much anywhere; the main ingredient to beginning this venture is ensuring that where you live is home to flowering plants, trees, or shrubs.

Before you know it, you will be more attuned to the seasonal cycles, as every season will bring something new for you and your bees. Weather conditions change—chilly springs, harsh winters, and rainy summers, all of these alter the availability of nectars and pollens, influencing colony growth. Your bee colony will react by swarming sooner, later, or usually when you least expect it!

Your experience with bees will bring you more in tune with the comings and goings of migratory birds and the blossoming of trees. Much of this awareness will be subconscious, aided slightly by jotting down observations of your beekeeping progress.

Beekeeping is a remarkable journey. One that offers an essential "grounding" if your typical week is spent commuting endlessly and working in a chaotic environment. The more you begin to understand the biology and behavior of your bees, the more you learn to appreciate the science behind beekeeping.

For example, if you live near a lake, you'll discover bees are not fans of flying for long distances over large bodies of water. The reflective lake surface provides inadequate visual cues for their retinas, compelling them to fly nearer and nearer to the surface to gauge speed and distance. The result leads to an unexpected swim, which is unfair to our winged friends.

You will find this book engaging and full of action-driven troubleshooting tips, providing practical advice that you can immediately put to use in your beekeeping adventure. There is also a great responsibility in the role you play as a beekeeper, so it is important to emphasize the need to always be mindful of your actions and understanding how your decisions can impact your bees and the broader environment in general.

However, *Beekeeping for Beginners* isn't just a book of instructions. It's a detailed guide aimed at unraveling the mystery of beekeeping, making it accessible and achievable for us all. With an extensively detailed chapter on hive inspection and a checklist of all those common "pain points" when it comes to hive inspections, I have you covered!

Whether you're a professional searching for a gratifying weekend activity, a retiree on the hunt for a fresh pastime, or a businessperson scouting for an eco-friendly business venture, this book offers something for you all.

The seasonal rhythm of beekeeping is ever-evolving; spring colony growth, queen breeding, honey gathering, preparing them for winter, honey bottling … and then the cycle restarts.

From one season to the next, it is never the same. But, of course, if you prefer the same routine week in week out, you can always opt to raise chickens!

Book Structure Overview

Beekeeping for Beginners serves as a comprehensive beginner's manual to the intriguing realm of beekeeping, specifically crafted for those who are fresh to the concept, or have minimal experience.

This book uncovers the blend of art and science that is beekeeping, primarily focusing on suburban and backyard beekeeping. With this guide, you will peer into the world of bees, acquire a knowledge of their behaviors, and learn about the essential equipment needed to establish a beehive.

Whilst city beekeeping is certainly covered in this book, our primary goal is to guide you in converting your backyard into a bustling bee sanctuary. You'll get to unravel the complexities of a beehive and learn the ropes of caring for bees throughout the changing seasons. This book also provides useful information for those considering turning their beekeeping hobby into a mini-scale business, including valuable insights into honey collection and its applications.

It is commonly regarded that Langstroth hives are the go-to for most beekeeping novices; therefore a significant portion of the content is based on the assumption that you will likely start with this type of hive. Information on alternative hive options is also provide however, guaranteeing that you'll be armed with a wealth of knowledge, whatever your choice of starting point.

Let's take a brief look at what you may expect:

- **Introduction to Beekeeping:** We'll start by exploring the incredible world of beekeeping. Beyond just the sweet allure of honey, there's a whole universe of benefits waiting for you—from playing a part in environmental conservation, to experiencing a deep connection with, and appreciation of nature. But, like any new venture, knowing what you're diving into—before you dive—is essential. So, we'll chat about what to think about before you get started.

- **Essential Equipment and Tools:** Ever wondered what tools make a beekeeper tick? We'll cover the essential equipment you need, ensuring you're well-prepared and confident.

- **Understanding Our Buzzing Friends:** Arm yourself with knowledge of these incredible creatures! We'll get up close and personal with beautiful bees, understanding their anatomy and helping you choose the right bee type for your goals. Your interest in them will increase as you learn more about them!

- **Setting Up and Stepping Out:** Ready to get your hands a little sticky? We'll help you set up your hive and acclimate your bees to their new environment. And if you're eyeing that golden honey, we've got you covered with a step-by-step guide on honey extraction.

- **Navigating Challenges—Bee a Problem Solver:** Every journey has its bumps. From managing unexpected swarms to keeping those pesky pests at bay, we'll arm you with strategies to tackle challenges head-on, ensuring your hive thrives.

- **From Passion to Profession:** Feeling a buzz and thinking of turning this into a full-blown business? We'll guide you through the transition, ensuring you're set up for success.

This isn't just a book; it's your companion on your exciting beekeeping adventure. With a little dedication and the insights from this guide, you're on the path to beekeeping success!

CHAPTER 1
Benefits of Beekeeping

As we set sail on this journey into the enchanting world of beekeeping, let us take a moment to appreciate the symphony of benefits this practice brings. From the tangible rewards of honey and the several other bee products, to the intangible benefits of mindfulness and connection with nature, beekeeping is a practice that enriches our lives in countless ways. Let's examine these advantages in more detail to see how beekeeping can sweeten our lives!

The Golden Harvest

Ah, honey! The primary allure of beekeeping, undoubtedly, is the harvesting of honey. This sweet, viscous food, created by our industrious little friends is a delight to our taste buds and a testament to the marvel of nature. Several variables affect how much honey you may anticipate gathering. The colony's strength, the location of your hive, and even the amount of rainfall your region receives will all play a role. A robust and healthy colony in an area abundant with flowering plants can yield a substantial amount of honey. However, remember that bees, like us, are at the mercy of Mother Nature. For example, heavy rainfall or drought season will impact the nectar flow and honey production.

The Honey Bees' Vital Role in Our Food Production as Pollinators

Honey bees are not merely honey producers—but also nature's most industrious pollinators. Their role in global food production systems is so critical that it's difficult to picture a viable world without them. As they flit from flower to flower collecting nectar, bees unintentionally spread pollen from plant to plant, fertilizing the plants and enabling them to produce seeds and fruit. Having a hive in your backyard means your garden will have its very own team of pollinators. You'll notice an improvement in your garden's yield and the quality of your fruits and vegetables as well as the variety of plants in general. It's a win-win situation; you provide the bees with a home, and they reward you with a bountiful garden and delicious honey.

Re-establishing the Honey Bee Population

In recent years, the honey bee population has seen a worrying decline. Factors such as habitat loss, the use of pesticides, and the advent of diseases have led to a decrease in their numbers. Backyard beekeeping is a small but significant step towards rebuilding the honey bee population. By providing a safe habitat for a colony, you're contributing to the conservation of this vital species.

Production of Healthy Food Other Than Honey

The benefits of beekeeping extend beyond honey and pollination. Bees produce a range of products that have significant health benefits. Honey and propolis are known for their antibacterial properties. Royal jelly, a substance secreted by worker bees, is rich in vitamin B and is used as a dietary and fertility stimulant. Bee pollen has a high protein content and is often used as a homeopathic remedy for seasonal allergies to pollen. Even bee venom has its uses, including in apitherapy, to treat patients who have arthritis and other inflammatory conditions. Let's also not forget that beeswax, a natural wax that honey bees produce, has many practical uses, from candle making to cosmetics.

A hive is a treasure trove of natural, healthy products. By embarking on this journey of beekeeping, you're not just taking up a hobby; you're stepping into a world that brings you closer to nature, rewards you with sweet treats, and contributes to the well-being of our environment. It's a lovely, symbiotic relationship that enriches our lives—and the planet.

A Natural Remedy for Allergies

Beekeeping offers a unique advantage for those who struggle with allergies. Pollen, a fine powder produced by flowers and collected by bees, is a powerhouse of nutrition. It contains up to 35% protein and a variety of other nutrients, including sugars, carbohydrates, enzymes, minerals, and vitamins such as A, B1, B2, B3, B5, C, H, and R. Paradoxically, consuming small quantities of pollen daily can help alleviate symptoms of pollen-related allergies. This is a form of natural inoculation; the key is using pollen harvested from your local area. If you have your hive, you can collect pollen from your bees and add a small amount to your breakfast cereal or yogurt, similar to how you'd add wheat germ. However, you don't necessarily need to collect the pollen yourself. Raw, natural honey contains traces of pollen, so every spoonful of honey you consume brings with it the benefits of pollen.

Consuming local honey daily can help mitigate the symptoms of allergies related to pollen, provided the honey is harvested within a 50-mile radius of your residence or from an area with similar vegetation to your community. Therefore, if you're an allergy sufferer, having your hive could be the very natural remedy you've been seeking. Not only will you have a steady supply of fresh, local honey, but you'll also have a tasty, natural method to manage your allergies. This is another reason why beekeeping is such a fulfilling activity!

The Therapeutic Dance with Bees

Engaging with nature through beekeeping is not just about the tangible rewards. It's also a dance in nature that soothes the soul and heals the mind. Yes, there might be a sting or two along the way, but the tranquility from tending to your bees is worth every bit of it. Imagine standing by your hive, engrossed in the hum of activity, watching the bees as they go about their day. It's a meditative experience that evokes mindfulness and melts away stress.

The routine of hive checks, the focus required during honey extraction—it's a rhythm that brings such a sense of calm and clarity. But the bee dance is more than simply a brain game. It's also a physical one. Lifting heavy boxes, bending, kneeling, and spending time under the open sky—it's a gentle workout that strengthens the body and invigorates the spirit.

In our modern and fast-paced world, beekeeping is a welcome pause. It's a moment to slow down, breathe, and connect with nature's rhythm. It's a dance that teaches patience, resilience and offers busy 21st century people a unique sense of achievement.

A Hive of Knowledge for the Young Minds

For youngsters, beekeeping offers a treasure trove of learning. It's a hands-on, experiential classroom where children can learn about the biology of bees, their role in pollination, and their importance to our food system. It supplements their science education—a practical lesson that brings textbooks and scientific theory to life. But the lessons from the hive go far beyond science.

Beekeeping teaches responsibility, instills a sense of care for the environment, and fosters a love for nature. It's a beautiful way to spark children's curiosity about the natural world and nurture their budding interest in science.

So, as you can see, the benefits of beekeeping are manifold. It's not *just* about the honey, though that is a pretty sweet perk! It's also about playing a part in nature's grand design and contributing to the survival of a species that plays a *vital* role in our food production. It's about the joy of watching your garden flourish under the diligent work of your resident pollinators.

The benefits of beekeeping are also about the satisfaction of knowing that every jar of honey, every beeswax candle, and every spoonful of royal jelly is the fruit of your labor and the labor of your bees.

We will examine these aspects in further detail in the chapters that follow. We'll guide you through setting up your hive, choosing your bees, and harvesting your honey. We'll share tips and tricks to help you become a content, dedicated and successful beekeeper.

CHAPTER 2

Key Factors to Ponder Before Diving into Beekeeping

Before you embark on the rewarding journey of beekeeping, it's essential to consider several factors affecting your decision to take up the practice. This chapter will provide an overview of the main aspects you should consider before deciding to become a beekeeper.

Climate Compatibility: Environmental Factors in Beekeeping

Contrary to what you might think, bees are incredibly adaptable creatures. They can thrive in various climates—from areas with long, cold winters, to tropical rainforests. You can raise bees as long as there are blooming flowers in your part of the world. So, whether you live on a sunny beach or in a snowy mountain town, beekeeping is a viable hobby.

Space Exploration: Is Your Backyard a Bee Haven?

You might be surprised to learn that you don't need a vast expanse of land to keep bees. In fact, many beekeepers manage their hives in urban environments, such as rooftops or terraces. The only space requirement is enough room to accommodate the hive itself. Bees can travel up to three miles from their colony to gather pollen and nectar, covering an area as large as 8,500 acres.

Legal Labyrinth: Navigating the Rules and Regulations of Beekeeping

Before you set up your first hive, it's crucial to check any local ordinances that might affect beekeeping. Some areas may impose limits on the number of beehives you can have, or they might demand that you register your beehives with the relevant authorities. Always check with your local bee clubs, town hall, or state's Department of Agriculture first to ensure you comply with local regulations.

The Art of Diplomacy: Neighbor Considerations

When you decide to bring bees into your backyard, you're not just making a decision for yourself—but for your community as well. It is essential to make sure your neighbors are at ease with your new hobby. A policy of open, honest communication, educating others about the behavior and benefits of bees—simply being a considerate neighbor will foster a harmonious relationship between you, your bees, and those living around you. You might find the subject of bees bring you happy interactions with your community, and a jar of honey for neighbors is a timeless sweetener!

Balancing the Books: Evaluating the Financial Aspects

Do remember that this fascinating endeavor comes with its initial expenses. The primary costs you'll encounter are related to the setup phase. This includes acquiring a hive kit, the necessary equipment, and the bees. While these might seem like substantial expenses at the outset, they are largely one-time investments. Also remember the potential return can be significant, especially from honey production.

Let's break it down a bit. The first year of your beekeeping adventure could see you spending between $400 and $1,500. This range depends on whether you choose basic or high-end equipment. The costs encompass your beekeeping education, tools, a bee suit, a 10-frame hive, a hive stand, and a bee package, or nucleus colony. You'll also need to account for consumables such as smoker pellets and sugar.

Now, let's talk about returns. Once your colony is established, which will likely take until the second year, you can start harvesting honey. The amount of honey a hive produces can vary from year to year, depending on factors like weather, nectar availability, and the overall health of the colony. However, each hive has the potential to produce between 30 to 60 pounds of honey each year. Given that natural, locally produced raw honey can fetch up to $10 per pound. This could translate to a return of $300 to $600 per hive per year from honey sales alone.

This simple calculation demonstrates that while beekeeping involves some upfront costs, it can be profitable—especially if you sell your honey at a premium price. However, it's important to remember that, like any business, the profitability of beekeeping can be influenced by various factors. These include market demand and pricing in your local area, the time and effort you can invest, your marketing and sales strategies, and the health and productivity of your bees. Therefore, it's crucial to thoroughly research and plan your beekeeping operation to maximize your chances of success.

Later in this book, we'll go into much more detail about the business case for beekeeping. We'll provide an analysis of the costs and potential profits, considering various scenarios and factors. This will assist you in making an informed decision about whether this rewarding hobby could also be a profitable venture for you.

The Timekeeper: Understanding the Commitment

A commitment to beekeeping is not just about the financial investment but also the investment of time. However, the beauty of this hobby lies in its flexibility. The time commitment for beekeeping can be tailored to fit your lifestyle and schedule.

The time you dedicate to your bees will vary, but a common estimate among beekeepers is approximately one hour every two weeks. This estimate, however, is not set in stone. The time you spend with your bees can fluctuate depending on the season. During the spring and summer months, when flowers are in full bloom and bees are at their busiest, you might check on your hives weekly, or even twice a week. In contrast, leaving the hive undisturbed during winter is best, reducing your beekeeping duties.

To give you a rough idea, checking on your bees every other week would equate to 26 visits to your hive in a year. This is how I estimated 26 hours per year for one colony; however, this is a flexible guideline, and the time spent can vary based on individual circumstances and preferences.

When managing more than one hive, the time commitment doesn't necessarily double. This is because some tasks are shared across all hives, such as preparing sugar syrup or cleaning equipment. On the other hand, hive-specific tasks, such as inspecting each frame for signs of disease or checking the queen's health, will increase with each additional hive.

To estimate the time commitment for multiple hives, you can use the following formula: 26 hours (for the first hive) + 13 hours for each additional hive. This rough time estimate considers the shared and hive-specific tasks.

The time you invest in your bees will be directly proportional to the results you'll feel and see. The more time you spend understanding and caring for your bees, the more rewarding your beekeeping experience will turn out to, well … *bee!* (could not resist, sorry!)

In a later chapter, we will delve deeper into the time commitment required for beekeeping, providing a more detailed breakdown of the tasks and time involved in each season.

Allergy Alert: Assessing Your Sting Tolerance Before Joining the Bee Brigade

It's important, before you get close to our little fuzzy, buzzy mates, to consider potential allergies. While good beekeeping practices will minimize the chances of being stung, it will occasionally inevitably happen. If you're uncertain about potential allergies to bee stings, you should check with an allergist before starting beekeeping. A blood test can measure your body's response to bee venom, so if you are unsure, have a blood test with this allergy under investigation.

In the following chapters, we'll explore these considerations in more detail to help you decide whether beekeeping is the right hobby for you.

Choosing Your Path: Deciding on Your Approach to Beekeeping

As you stand on the threshold of your new life as a beekeeper, determining the approach you wish to take is one of the most significant decisions you'll face. This decision will shape your beekeeping practice, influencing everything from the day-to-day management of your hives to the broader philosophy that guides your interactions with your bees.

Beekeeping is not a one-size-fits-all endeavor. It's a complex, nuanced practice that can be tailored to align with your personal beliefs, resources, and the specific needs of your bees. There are several paths you can choose—each with its own philosophy, methods, and considerations.

In this section, we'll explore four of the most common approaches to beekeeping: Medicated Beekeeping, Natural Beekeeping, Organic Beekeeping, and a Combined Approach. Each of these approaches offers a unique perspective, with different strategies for maintaining the health and productivity of your colonies.

The Traditional Route: Medicated Beekeeping

Historically, beekeepers have relied on various medications and chemical treatments to maintain their colonies. This approach, known as medicated beekeeping, involves a routine protocol of treatments administered throughout the year. While these methods have been widely used for generations, the rise in bee health issues and the potential overuse or misuse of these treatments have led many to reconsider this approach.

Back to Basics: Natural Beekeeping

Natural beekeeping aims to care for bees in a way that aligns more closely with their natural behaviors and needs. This approach addresses pests, illness, and possible starvation *without* using artificial diets, antibiotics, or synthetic pesticides. However, it's important to note that natural beekeeping *doesn't* mean minimal hive inspections—routine and regular inspections are crucial to understanding the needs of your bees and ensuring their survival.

Pure and Simple: Organic Beekeeping

Organic beekeeping is more than mere avoidance of synthetic chemicals; it's a comprehensive approach that prioritizes the health of the bees and the environment. Stringent standards guide this method of beekeeping and necessitate a high level of commitment and vigilance to ensure the honey produced is pure, natural, and created in a bee-friendly manner.

To be recognized as an organic beekeeper, you must adhere to a rigorous certification process and follow specific guidelines. These include using natural hives, positioning hives in organic or wild areas, and employing organic treatments for Varroa mites. The organic approach also extends to the bees' diet. Organic beekeepers ensure their bees forage from organic flora or wild areas where there is no risk of exposure to substances not allowed in organic farming.

One of the key aspects of organic beekeeping is also strict record-keeping. To be compliant with organic certification, beekeepers must keep detailed records of their beekeeping practices, including the treatment of any diseases, the sources of their bees, and the location of their hives. This documentation is crucial for the certification process and for maintaining transparency and traceability in the organic honey production chain.

The certifying body plays a significant role in maintaining the integrity of organic beekeeping. They conduct unannounced visits to ensure compliance with organic standards and require beekeepers to undergo an annual audit to maintain their certification. This rigorous process ensures that when you buy organic honey, you have a product made with the utmost care for the bees and the environment.

The entire chain, from beekeeper to seller, must be traceable to ensure the integrity of the honey. Every step in the process, from the hive to the store shelf, is documented and can be traced back to its origin. This level of transparency gives consumers confidence in the product and holds everyone in the production chain accountable for maintaining organic standards.

Organic beekeeping is not just about producing honey; it's also about fostering a sustainable and healthy environment for bees. It's about ensuring that our practices are in harmony with nature and that we're contributing to preserving the health of our precious bee populations.

In conclusion, organic beekeeping is a rewarding and fulfilling approach that aligns with a commitment to environmental sustainability, protecting our precious ecosystems and the welfare of bees who play such a fundamental role in it. However, it requires a significant commitment and adherence to strict standards. If you're considering this approach, be prepared for a rigorous—but rewarding—experience.

I would like to suggest that this approach might not be the best fit for beginner backyard beekeepers due to the additional costs and higher level of expertise required.

Reaping Dual Benefits: A Combined Approach

Finally, some beekeepers opt for a combined approach, blending elements from the medicated, natural, and organic methods. This approach allows for flexibility and adaptability, enabling beekeepers to respond to the specific needs of their colonies without strictly adhering to one philosophy, or set of practices. This might involve avoiding using chemicals as a preventative measure, only resorting to treatments when necessary, and when other non-chemical options have proven ineffective.

Your approach will depend on your way of thinking, your resources, and the specific needs of your bees. As you gain experience and knowledge, you may find that your approach evolves, reflecting your growing understanding of beekeeping and the unique requirements of your hives.

I recommend leaning towards as *natural* an approach as possible, resorting to chemical interventions only when necessary. This approach promotes the health and well-being of your bees and contributes to our environment's sustainability.

As I previously hinted, we will now go into some of the key considerations you need to ponder in more detail, before setting off on your backyard beekeeping journey!

Embracing the Sting: Overcoming Your Fear

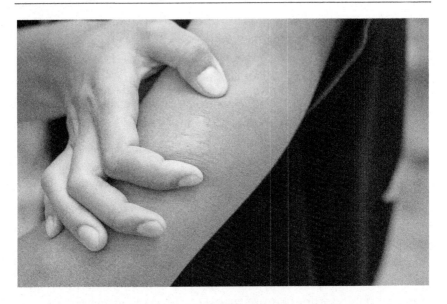

Bee Sting/Credit: Wirachaiphoto(www.shutterstock.com)

Beekeeping is a practice filled with wonder, learning, and a few inevitable stings. The fear of being stung is a common misgiving for new beekeepers. However, it's essential to understand that honey bees are generally docile creatures, especially when they are away from their hive foraging for nectar and pollen. Unless they perceive a danger to their colony, they are not likely to sting. After all, a honey bee dies after stinging—so it's not something they do lightly.

You will likely experience a few stings each season in your beekeeping journey. This is a normal part of beekeeping and is often a result of unintentional mistakes or carelessness on our part. Perhaps you suddenly moved? Or were rushing and not paying attention to the bees' behavior? These instances can lead to stings, but they also provide valuable lessons on interacting with your bees.

Understanding Bee Stings: The Sting, Symptoms, and Reactions

A bee sting is a wound inflicted by a bee deploying its stinger which is a barbed, thorn-like organ at the end of its body. The stinger carries venom, which triggers symptoms of pain and swelling when injected into your skin. As mentioned, bees are unlikely to sting unless they sense a threat to their colony.

While bee stings are generally harmless to most people, they can provoke different reactions, ranging from temporary discomfort to severe allergic reactions. The severity of the response can vary from person to person and doesn't necessarily predict the severity of future reactions.

- **Mild Reactions:** Most bee sting reactions are mild, with a red welt, a little amount of swelling, and immediate, intense, sharp pain at the sting site. These symptoms usually subside within a few hours.

- **Moderate Reactions:** Some individuals may respond more severely to bee stings, exhibiting acute swelling and redness at the sting site that progressively worsens over a day or two. These moderate reactions typically resolve over five to ten days. If you consistently react moderately to bee stings, it is recommended to consult your doctor about treatment and prevention options.

- **Severe Allergic Reactions:** A severe allergic reaction known as anaphylaxis is a potentially life-threatening condition requiring immediate medical attention. Skin responses, including hives and itching, breathing issues, throat and tongue swelling, a weak, quick pulse, nausea, vomiting, diarrhea, dizziness, fainting, and in extreme instances, loss of consciousness, are all signs of anaphylaxis. After a bee sting, if you have any of these symptoms, call for emergency medical attention right away. This happens in approximately 4 out of 1,000 children.

Bees are typically not hostile and only sting to *defend* themselves, but sometimes a human may disturb a hive and get several stings. A toxic response from several stings might result in symptoms including nausea, vomiting, headache, vertigo, convulsions, fever, disorientation, or fainting.

In particular, several stings may constitute a medical emergency for kids, older people, and those with respiratory or heart issues.

Tips to Avoid Stings

While stings are part of the beekeeping experience, there are several steps you can take to minimize your chances of being stung:

- **Understanding Bee Behavior:** Bees are generally docile creatures, especially away from their hive. They sting only when they feel threatened. So, the key to avoiding stings is to ensure you don't threaten them.

- **Wearing Protective Gear:** A veil and gloves are essential, and depending on your comfort level, you may also choose to wear a jacket or a full suit. Ensure that your suit or jacket's zippers are entirely closed, your veil has no holes, and your pants are tucked into your socks.

- **Using a Smoker:** To distract honey bees from their pheromones, the molecules they use to communicate, beekeepers use smoke. Puffing some smoke into a hive before opening it up lets the bees know you're coming in and keeps them docile. If you get stung, it's also helpful to puff smoke on the sting site to cover up the smell of the pheromone and prevent other bees from becoming agitated.

- **Timing Your Inspections:** The best time to check on your bees is on a nice day, usually between 10am and 5pm, when most bees are out foraging. Avoid inspecting your hive during cold, windy, or rainy weather as bees can be more defensive.

- **Moving Calmly Around the Hive:** Your physical presence can influence the bees' behavior. Move calmly and avoid sudden movements; bees can be startled by quick, jerky actions. Maintain a good grip on the frames to avoid dropping them, which can agitate the bees.

- **Avoid Swatting at Bees:** If a bee lands on you, it's usually just exploring. Be careful not to swat at bees as this could agitate them. Instead, just gently brush it aside.

- **Consider the Location of Your Hive:** Place your hive where people are not often walking. A spot with partial shade in your backyard is usually a good bet. Avoid locations where you must walk past the hive to get to your car or other frequently accessed areas. Never stand in *front* of your hive while inspecting it; instead, always stand *next to or behind it.*

While stings are part of the beekeeping experience— this doesn't mean they have to be frequent! Following these tips will *significantly* reduce the likelihood of you getting stung, and give you pain-free enjoyment of peaceful and rewarding beekeeping.

What to Do If You're Stung

Be aware you could still be stung, despite your best attempts. If that occurs, first remove the stinger calmly and smoke the area to cover up the odor of the chemical alarm left behind. This scent can stimulate other bees to sting. You can remove the stinger from your skin with your fingernail.

Apply a cold compress once the sting has been removed, and take an antihistamine pill to lessen swelling, itching, and pain. Some beekeepers swear by home remedies like baking soda and water poultices, however medical professionals generally recommend over-the-counter antihistamines.

If bees have swarmed you and you have multiple stings, seek prompt medical care. Also, schedule a visit with your doctor if the effects of a bee sting don't fade within a few days or if you have any signs of an allergic reaction to a bee sting, like breathing problems, nausea, or flushed or pale skin.

Preparing for Allergic Reactions

While most people experience mild reactions to bee stings, a small percentage of individuals can have severe allergic reactions, including severe swelling, shortness of breath, or even loss of consciousness. It's essential to have an EpiPen on hand in such circumstances.

EpiPen: A Lifesaver in Your Pocket

An EpiPen is a tool designed to provide the body with epinephrine automatically, sometimes referred to as adrenaline. Epinephrine is a hormone that can quickly reverse the symptoms of a severe, life-threatening allergic reaction known as anaphylaxis. It works by narrowing blood vessels and opening airways in the lungs, helping to restore normal breathing and heart rhythm.

However, it's important to understand that administering an EpiPen does not replace receiving emergency medical attention. It is a short-term solution that allows you to reach a hospital or medical facility for further treatment. Therefore, if you or someone else uses an EpiPen, you should immediately call for emergency medical help.

While EpiPens can be a lifesaver for those with severe allergies, they are not without their complications. They are expensive and require a prescription from a doctor. Additionally, there can be liability issues when injecting another person, so it's essential to consult your doctor or lawyer before deciding to keep an EpiPen on hand.

Building Tolerance: The Silver Lining of Stings

Interestingly, some beekeepers *look forward* to the first few stings of the season! There is, however, method in their madness. Regular stings can help build up a tolerance to bee venom. While the sting still hurts, the side effects, such as swelling and itching, tend to decrease with repeated stings. Some even believe that bee venom has health *benefits*, a concept that forms the basis of bee sting therapy.

Embrace the Sting, Embrace the Journey

In conclusion, while the fear of being stung can be a significant hurdle for new beekeepers, it's a fear that can be managed and even overcome with knowledge, preparation and a little bit of courage. Remember, beekeeping is a journey of learning and growth. Every sting is a lesson, and every interaction with your bees is an opportunity to understand them better.

Navigating the Legal Landscape: Understanding Beekeeping Laws and Regulations

Another factor to check before you begin beekeeping: understanding the rules and legislation that apply to beekeeping where you live is essential. Checking if beekeeping is permitted in your city is the first step. Most cities in the U.S. for example do allow beekeeping, but they have ordinances that must be followed. These ordinances can include restrictions on the number of hives you can have, the location of your hives, and the requirement for regular inspections.

In the U.S., each state's Department of Agriculture manages many state apiary inspection programs. These programs were created to inspect honey bee colonies for diseases like American foulbrood. The services offered by these programs can vary widely from state to state. Some states, like Florida, have robust apiary inspection programs with many dedicated inspectors. Other states may have only one or two inspectors, and their time may be divided between apiary inspection and other duties.

Regardless of the program's size, state apiary inspectors play a crucial role in maintaining bee colonies' health and ensuring beekeepers follow the necessary regulations. They can also be a valuable source of information and assistance for beekeepers.

In some states, registering your bee colonies with the State Department of Agriculture or similar authority is *mandatory*. In others, it's *voluntary*. Even if it's not required, registering your colonies can be beneficial. It shows that you're making an effort to comply with regulations—and can also provide you with access to important resources and information.

It's also worth noting that beekeeping might not be permitted in all areas, even if it's legal in your city or state. For example, your local homeowner's association may have rules against beekeeping. So, checking *all relevant regulations* before setting up your hives is important.

In conclusion, while navigating various laws and regulations might seem a bit daunting, it's essential for responsible beekeeping. Understanding and complying with these regulations ensures that your beekeeping practice is successful, sustainable, and beneficial to your local environment and community.

Building a Bee-Friendly Community: Addressing Your Neighbors' Concerns about Beekeeping

In the practice of backyard beekeeping, it's not just the bees you'll be dealing with—but also your neighbors! Remember that your decision to keep bees impacts your community, and it's only fair to consider their concerns. Here's how you can ensure a harmonious relationship with your neighbors while enjoying your beekeeping hobby:

- **Limit the Number of Hives:** Start with one or two hives. This allows your neighbors time to acclimatize and offers you the time you need to learn beekeeping without the burden of having to take care of more bees than you can manage. You could have a more profound challenge however if you're dealing with someone allergic to bee stings. It's a tough decision in such cases, and there is no right or wrong answer here, but honest and open engagement with your neighbors is usually a good place to start!

- **Consider Hive Placement:** Ensure your hives are not pointing towards your neighbor's driveway, house entrance, or any pedestrian traffic way. When bees leave the hive, they fly up and away; and once they are around 15 feet away, they are well above head level. It's also good to put your hive where neighbors can't easily see it. This can help to avoid unnecessary attention and potential concerns.

- **Blend with the Environment:** Place your beehives where they won't stand out too much. Keeping your hobby low-key in a densely populated urban setting could sometimes spare you from an opportunistic complainer. Additionally, consider painting or staining your hives to blend into the environment.

- **Provide a Nearby Source of Water for the Bees:** Providing your bees with a fresh water supply, such as a bird bath, will help them develop into excellent neighbors themselves. You don't want your bees sipping out of someone else's favorite pet dish or taking regular swims in their pool. Tell your neighbors that you are installing your hive including the bees´ own water source.

- **Invite Your Neighbors:** When broaching the subject of beekeeping topic, take the time to speak one-on-one with neighbors. Mention the benefits of having a group of pollinators nearby for each neighbor's garden. At this stage however, your major objective isn't promoting the virtues of honey bees—it is to pay attention and listen to the concerns of your neighbors. You'll find that if you take the time to listen and directly address any concern with a creative approach; that might just sell the idea of beekeeping—without coming across as pushy. People often like knowing what happens inside a hive; inviting them to participate to an inspection can also make them more comfortable with the activity and even feel more in tune with nature.

- **Share Your Harvest:** Nothing says "Thank you" better than a honey gift! When it's time to harvest your hive's honey, share some. There is no better way to express gratitude to your neighbors than to let them sample honey produced from nectar partly gathered in their yards!

- **Ask Them to Use a Bee-Friendly Product in Their Gardens:** If you get along well with your neighbors, you may advise them to use a bee-friendly product in their gardens, but remember that you might be asking them to abandon a brand they have a strong attachment to.

Being a good beekeeping neighbor involves communication, consideration—and a bit of honey! By taking these steps, your beekeeping hobby will be a source of joy for you and your entire neighborhood.

Deciding Where to Place Your Hive

Beehives/Credit: M9K(www.shutterstock.com)

The placement of your hive is critical for the health and productivity of your colony. This chapter will guide you through the factors you need to consider when deciding where to position your hive.

When you embark on the beekeeping journey, you'll quickly realize that the location of your hive isn't just a matter of convenience for you—it's a matter of survival for your bees. The ideal location for a hive is made from a delicate balance of several factors: drainage, sunlight, wind, accessibility, water, and the availability of floral sources.

Drainage

First and foremost, consider drainage. Bees, like us, prefer a dry home. Placing your hive on stable, dry ground will prevent it from becoming mired a quagmire. Additionally, the hive should be level from side to side, with the front slightly lower than the rear. This slight tilt allows rainwater and condensation to drain *out* of the hive rather than *into* it. Make sense right?

Sunlight

Next, consider sunlight. Bees are early risers, and a hive facing southeast will catch the early morning sun, encouraging your bees to start their day of foraging. However, bees must also regulate the hive's temperature while appreciating the sun's warmth. Therefore, a location with dappled sunlight, rather than full sun, is ideal. This will prevent the colony from working too hard to cool the hive on hot days.

Wind

Wind is another factor to consider. While good ventilation is essential for a healthy hive, too much wind can be detrimental. Protect your hives from harsh winds with a windbreak, such as trees or a fence. This is particularly important in climates with cold winters. At the same time, avoid locations where the air is too still and damp, as this can lead to problems with mold and disease.

Accessibility

Accessibility is a practical consideration for the beekeeper. Position your hive to be easily accessible for every activity, from routine inspections to the heavy work of honey harvesting. Carrying heavy loads of honey up a hill in the heat is not something you want to do. Also, consider the maintenance around the hive. Mulching around the hive can prevent grass and weeds from blocking the entrances.

Water

Providing your bees with a reliable water source is paramount. Bees use water for various purposes, from diluting honey to cooling their hive. However, finding a suitable water source can be challenging for them, especially in urban and suburban areas where there is much habitat loss. To help your bees thrive, you can create water sources for them. You may work on the following projects:

The Simple Bee Waterer

Bee Waterer/Credit: Vanessa Becker-Miller(www.shutterstock.com)

This project is straightforward and requires minimal materials. All you need are some rocks, a shallow dish, and water. Here's how to set it up:

1. Thoroughly rinse the rocks and dish to remove any dangerous chemicals and pesticides. Wash them with vinegar or a mild soap, then rinse well.

2. Place the rocks in the dish and add just enough water to almost cover them. The tops of the rocks should remain exposed and dry, providing a safe landing spot for the bees.

3. Place the dish near a location where you've observed significant bee activity. If you haven't spotted many bees in your yard, position the dish next to a food source, like flowers, ideally in a shady area.

4. Regularly check the water level in the dish. If it's too high after heavy rain, pour some water out. If it's running low, add more.

5. Allow the waterer to get a bit dirty. Bees can locate water sources quickly by smell and benefit from the added nutrients in slimy water.

The Natural Bee Watering Station

This project takes a more natural approach, using materials you can find on the ground outside or even in your garden. The idea is to create a watering station that feels like home to the bees. Here's how to do it:

1. Gather whatever materials you can find outside on the ground, in your garden or around and under trees. This could include small twigs, leaves, and pebbles.

2. Arrange these materials in a shallow dish, to provide a safe and natural refuge for the bees.

3. Fill the dish with water, ensuring plenty of dry spots for the bees to land.

4. Place the watering station in your garden, preferably near flowers that bees find delectable.

5. Keep an eye on the watering station to ensure it doesn't go dry.

Below are other options that you can consider.

- **Pie Dish with Gravel:** Use a standard kitchen pie dish with gravel inside, then cover it with water for a quick and easy solution. This setup allows bees to land on the gravel and drink the water without the risk of drowning. It's a cost-effective solution that can be easily set up in your backyard.

- **Chicken Watering System:** Another ingenious solution is to use a chicken watering system. These devices are designed to provide a steady water supply for chickens, but they work equally well for bees. Fill the tray with gravel or tiny stones to stop bees from drowning. Chicken watering devices are readily available at farm supply stores.

- **Outdoor Tap with a Slow Drip:** If you have an outdoor tap, you can adjust it to have a slow drip. This constant water source will be appreciated by your bees, especially during the hot summer months. However, be mindful of water conservation and any local water restriction regulations that may be in place and ensure the drip is slow and steady.

- **Hive-top Feeder Filled with Water:** A hive-top feeder typically provides bees with syrup but can also be filled with water. This can be particularly useful during times when natural water sources are scarce.

- **Clay Pot Pond:** This project involves flipping over a clay pot and filling the base with water. The inverted pot provides a stable and shallow water source for the bees. Plus, the clay keeps the water cool, which can be a relief for the bees on hot days.

- **Pet Bowl:** A self-filling pet water bowl can be repurposed as a bee watering station. These bowls are designed to automatically refill when the water level gets low, ensuring a constant water supply for your bees.

- **Hummingbird Feeder:** Repurposing a hummingbird feeder is another creative way to provide water for your bees. These feeders are designed to attract hummingbirds with liquid, which can just as quickly be water for your bees. The feeder's small feeding ports are perfect for bees, allowing them to drink without the risk of drowning.

Regardless of how you provide water, remember that bees can't land on the water's surface, so it's essential to provide landing pads for them to drink from safely.

Remember, bees are creatures of habit. They will repeatedly return to a reliable water source once they find one. Therefore, it's crucial to maintain your water source, ensuring it's always available for your bees. By providing a reliable water source, you're supporting your bees and contributing to the overall health of your local ecosystem. Also, the key is ensuring the water source is close to the hive and safe for the bees. Bees are excellent foragers and will find the water source, but having it nearby reduces their workload and allows them more time for other essential tasks.

In conclusion, selecting a location for your hive is difficult and requires careful evaluation of several criteria. However, with careful planning and some flexibility, you can find a location that meets your and your bees' needs. A healthy, productive hive is well worth finding the perfect location.

Bee Water Feeder/Credit:Dovzhykov Andriy(www.shutterstock.com)

Local Floral Sources

Your honey's flavor is primarily determined by the floral sources from which your bees gather nectar. Like different instruments in a symphony, each flower adds a distinct tone to the overall composition and flavor profile of the honey produced.

Imagine for a moment a field of clover. Bees fly around collecting nectar from clover flowers. The honey this nectar produces will have a distinct clover flavor—light and mildly sweet. Now, picture an orchard of orange trees in full bloom. The honey from this floral source will have a different character altogether, with a citrusy tang that reflects its origin.

That is the beauty of honey—it's a snapshot of a particular time and place captured in liquid form. Each jar tells the story of the landscape, the weather, and the flowers in bloom. It's a story told by the bees, but interpreted and enjoyed by us.

But what if you want to tell a specific story? What if you want your honey to have a particular flavor? This is where the art of hive placement comes into play. You can influence your honey's flavor by positioning your hives amidst specific floral sources. Want a dark, robust honey? Place your hives near a stand of buckwheat. Are you looking for a light, delicate flavor? A field of acacia might be just the ticket.

However, it's important to realize that this level of control is generally more suited to commercial beekeepers. As a beginner, it's best to let nature take its course. After all, the beauty of beekeeping lies in its unpredictability—you never quite know what you'll get, and that's part of the fun!

There is one type of honey that's particularly well-suited to beginner beekeepers: wildflower honey. As its name suggests, wildflower honey is produced naturally from a combination of nectars from many floral sources. It's a bit like a mixed bouquet with many flavors and aromas. It's also a great way to get a taste of the local flora, as the composition of wildflower honey will vary from place to place. So, consider the local flora when deciding where to place your hives. Not only will it influence the flavor of your honey, but it will also provide your bees with a diverse range of nectar sources, which is good for their health.

Starting Your Beekeeping Journey: Timing is Everything

Setting off on your beekeeping journey is exciting, but timing is crucial. When to start your beekeeping project largely depends on where you live. Generally, a few months before the blooming season is an ideal time—when the flowers begin to bloom, providing a rich source of nectar for your bees.

The beekeeping season officially kicks off in the United States in early spring. This is when bee breeders, primarily in southern states, have package bees ready for sale. However, it's essential to avoid waiting until the last minute.

The winter months should be used to *order and assemble* the necessary equipment, with the *delivery of bees* reserved for early spring.

During these preceding months, it's also a good idea to read up on beekeeping and bees, familiarize yourself with your equipment, and join a bee club. Many clubs offer special training programs for new beekeepers, affectionately known as "Newbees." These programs often include hands-on weekend workshops that provide practical experience and insights into beekeeping.

Finding a mentor during this time can also be incredibly beneficial. Having someone to call upon to answer questions and provide guidance as you get started will make the process less daunting—and more enjoyable.

When it comes to installing your bees, early spring is the best time. Where you live will determine the precise start of spring, but the objective is to align your start date with the first early-season flowers and only a few weeks before the fruit bloom. Your colony won't be able to develop well enough for its first season if you start in the summer.

It's crucial to have everything ready before the arrival of your live bees. But don't worry, I will cover the list of equipment and hives you'll need for this new adventure in detail in the following chapters of this book.

CHAPTER 3

The Right Hive for You: Making an Informed Choice

One of the first decisions you'll make as a new bee beekeeper is choosing the type of hive that best suits your needs. If you are asking, "What's the best type of beehive for me?" you'll find the answer isn't as simple as you may expect. There are several types of beehives, each with unique features and benefits.

In this chapter, we'll explore the different types of beehives that a beginner backyard beekeeper can choose. From the traditional Langstroth hive, which is highly recommended for beginners due to its ease of use and efficiency, to the increasingly popular Top Bar Hive, each type of hive offers a unique beekeeping experience.

I advise new beekeepers to start with the Langstroth hive. This hive type is widely recognized for its practicality and efficiency, making it an excellent choice for those just starting their beekeeping journey. As you gain more experience and confidence, you might explore other types of hives, such as the Top Bar Hive, which is gaining popularity among beekeepers for its natural approach.

Remember that the kind of hive you choose might significantly affect your beekeeping experience. So, take your time, consider all your options, and make an informed decision. After all, beekeeping is not merely about harvesting the liquid gold honey; it's about creating a nurturing environment for your bees to thrive.

Langstroth Hive: The Perfect Hive for Beginners

Langstroth Hive/Credit: Geoffrey Kuchera(www.shutterstock.com)

Let's look at the Langstroth Hive, the most popular and recommended hive for beginner beekeepers. This hive, named after its inventor, the American apiarist L. L. Langstroth, was created in 1852. The Langstroth hive is often what people imagine when they think of beehives. Its design, which has remained relatively unchanged since its inception, is based on the "bee space" principle. This principle ensures that the frames within the hive are neither glued together nor filled with burr comb (honeycomb built by the bees in unintended places), making them easy to remove, inspect, and replace without harming the bees.

The Langstroth hive is a modular, expandable beehive that provides convenient and easy access for the beekeeper. It involves stacking rectangular boxes with detachable frames. The boxes are available in shallow, medium, and deep heights, and the beekeeper may stack them as high as desired. As for width, you can choose between eight frames and ten frames. The medium-depth, eight-frame beehive would be a great choice for beginners. It isn't as heavy compared to a bee box with ten frames. The interior frames within a Langstroth hive maintain a precise spacing of 3/8-

inch, ensuring the optimal "bee space". This hive is customizable, with many options available, making it the most widely used type of beehive today. While the conventional design of a Langstroth hive accommodates ten frames per box, numerous suppliers now offer a variant with eight frames.

Of course, the Langstroth hive has its advantages and disadvantages. It is suitable for large colonies and contains a lot of honey, there are several customized options and the beginner beekeeper has access to a wealth of resources and materials. However, a Langstroth hive can be pretty heavy, and the boxes can be a bit of a handful when loaded with honey, so you need to take care.

The Langstroth hive is however best for beginners due to its flexibility and ease of use, so I will focus on this type of hive in this book. As mentioned, when you gain more experience, you may explore other types of hives, such as the increasingly popular Top Bar Hive. But let's continue with the tried-and-true Langstroth hive for the time being.

Let's distill the essence of this hive type into a concise list of its pros and cons to consider:

Pros:

- **Universality:** The Langstroth hive has become the standard in many parts of the world, making it easier for beekeepers to find resources, equipment, and advice tailored to their needs.

- **Interchangeability:** Beekeepers can easily exchange frames with others, a feature particularly useful in managing and growing colonies. This interchangeability also extends to the hive's components, with a wide range of accessories and tools designed specifically for the Langstroth hive.

- **Community Support:** The popularity of the Langstroth hive has led to a wealth of knowledge and community support. Whether facing a problem, seeking advice, or wanting to share experiences, a large community of Langstroth hive beekeepers is ready to help.

- **Versatility and Ease of Use:** The Langstroth hive is often recommended for beginners due to its flexibility and ease of use. Its design is based on the "bee space" principle, ensuring that the frames within the hive are easy to remove, inspect, and replace without harming the bees.

- **Customizability:** The Langstroth hive is highly tailorable, with many options available, making it adaptable to various beekeeping needs and preferences.

- **Capacity:** As the colony expands and honey output rises, you may add additional medium or shallow honey supers to the Langstroth hive since it is modular. The capacity of the hive is virtually unlimited.

- **Suitable for Large Colonies:** The Langstroth hive is good for large colonies and can contain a lot of honey.

Cons:

- **Weight:** The Langstroth hive can be heavy, especially when loaded with honey. This can make the boxes tricky to move around, potentially challenging some beekeepers.

- **Potential for Overwhelming Options:** While the customizability of the Langstroth hive is generally seen as a benefit, the vast amount of options and accessories available could be overwhelming for beginner beekeepers.

- **Less Natural:** Some beekeepers feel that the Langstroth hive, with its highly managed and structured design, is less natural than other hives. This can be a downside for beekeepers that like to choose a more naturalistic approach.

Before exploring other hive types, let's take a moment to delve into two innovative adaptations of the traditional Langstroth hive currently on the market. These variants can be seen as enhancements to the traditional Langstroth setup, each bringing unique advantages. However, it's worth noting that these advancements often come with a heftier price tag than their traditional counterpart.

The Apimaye Insulated Hive: A Modern Take on the Langstroth

Apimaye Hive

The Apimaye hive is a modern, innovative variant of the Langstroth hive designed to address beekeepers' challenges. Originating from a desire to make beekeeping more accessible and manageable, the Apimaye hive has integrated features that help bees cope with extreme weather conditions and pests.

The Apimaye hive, like the Langstroth, stacks boxes vertically. However, it distinguishes itself with its insulated walls made from food-grade, UV-resistant plastic. This insulation offers six times more protection than traditional wooden hives, mimicking the insulating properties of a thick tree trunk. This feature is particularly beneficial for bees in regions that experience extreme winters or summers, as it helps moderate the hive's internal temperature.

The hive also has a powerful ventilation system that fosters air flow. Air enters through the screened bottom board, rises through ducts, and exits through louvers in the hive top cover. This mechanism reduces unwelcome humidity and prevents the development of mold or yeast.

The Apimaye hive comes fully assembled, saving beekeepers a significant amount of time. The boxes are made from durable, food-grade plastic and have latches that allow them to be securely attached. This makes the hive resistant to strong winds and predators.

The frames in the Apimaye hive are designed to increase productivity. They can be separated easily, allowing foundation sheets to be inserted without nailing frames or embedding wax. These frames are also compatible with honey harvesting and uncapping machines, making them appealing for beekeepers working with multiple hives.

However, the Apimaye hive does have some limitations. Although the kit includes additional components you wouldn't receive from a standard hive, the initial prices might be higher. It may not be cost-effective for large-scale operations. Frames could block the front vents of Apimaye hives. When doing inspections, removing the feeder might be problematic if it's filled with sugar water. Additionally, natural beekeepers may choose a Top Bar Hive since it is less artificial.

The Flow Hive: Revolutionizing Honey Harvesting

Flow Hive/Credit:Brett Holmes(www.shutterstock.com)

The Flow Hive, created in Australia by beekeepers Stuart and Cedar Anderson, is a revolutionary development in Langstroth beehives. The state-of-the-art design of this beehive allows honey to be drained straight from the hive without the need for honey extractors. With a simple lever turn, the Flow Hive provides honey—actually on tap!

A Langstroth-style beehive, The Flow Hive has wooden foundations, frames, and boxes. The Flow Hive's brood box is identical to that of any other Langstroth hive. However, the special Flow frames and artificial foundations are made from BPA and BPS-free food-grade plastic. The Flow frames fit into a standard-sized Langstroth super. Flow's super has observation windows and an opening for honey collection.

The foundations in the Flow frames are shaped into partially formed honeycomb cells. The bees finish constructing the cells and then fill them with honey. You can check when the frame is full of honey by looking in the observation window. This causes the honeycomb cells to split in half and turn into channels for the honey to flow down. No honey extractors are needed. The honey just falls out of the frame, due to gravity.

The Flow Hive is more expensive than a regular Langstroth hive, ranging from $499 for the Flow Hive Hybrid to $800 for the Flow Hive 2+. However, it's important to note that you do not need to purchase a honey extractor if you have a Flow Hive. The Flow Hive is also made of superior Western Red Cedar, naturally resistant to pests and rot. It has a built-in pest management system, including a screened bottom board and tray.

The Flow Hive's unique design has advantages and, of course, disadvantages. It makes honey harvesting much easier and lessens the stress for the bees. There's no need to open the hive and remove the frames, which can be disruptive and stressful for the bees. The Flow Hive also allows honey to be harvested frame-by-frame so that you can enjoy different honey flavors throughout the season.

However, the Flow Hive also has its drawbacks. The biggest one is the cost. Some beekeepers may find the Flow Hive prohibitively pricey since it is substantially more expensive than conventional hives. Additionally, while the Flow Hive makes honey harvesting easier, it removes some of the hands-on aspects of beekeeping. Some beekeepers feel this can lead to a lack of understanding and connection with the bees.

The Flow Hive also requires regular maintenance and cleaning to ensure the honey extraction system works appropriately. The plastic frames need to be cleaned after each harvest to prevent the build-up of wax and propolis (a resin-derived substance used by the bees to coat the walls of their hive). This can be a time-consuming process, and if not done correctly, it can lead to issues with the hive.

In the natural world, bees build their wax comb, a necessary process for the hive's health and the bees' lifecycle. In a Flow Hive, however, the bees are given plastic frames to build upon. This deviation from their natural behavior has raised concerns among beekeepers and enthusiasts.

Some argue that plastic frames may not provide the same comfort or flexibility for the bees as natural wax combs. Bees have been known to be selective about where they lay their eggs and store their honey, and some beekeepers have observed that bees may be less inclined to use plastic frames.

The plastic frames are also uniform, which doesn't allow for the natural variation in cell size that bees would typically create in a wax comb. This lack of variation could potentially impact the bees' behavior and the overall health of the hive.

Lastly, there's the environmental aspect to consider. While the plastic frames are durable and long-lasting, they are simply not biodegradable. If discarded, they contribute to plastic waste, an issue of growing global concern.

In conclusion, while the Flow Hive offers many conveniences, it's essential to weigh these against potential issues (like the use of plastic frames). As always, the best choice of hive will depend on your circumstances, goals, and values as a beekeeper.

Having explored the Langstroth hive and its notable variants, it's time to turn our attention to other hive types that have gained popularity among beekeepers.

The Kenyan Top Bar Hive: A Natural Approach to Beekeeping

Kenyan Topbar Hive/Credit:Jonas Sjoblom(www.shutterstock.com)

The Kenyan Top Bar Hive, (often referred to as the Top Bar Hive), has been steadily gaining popularity, particularly among backyard beekeepers. This hive design offers a unique, natural, and user-friendly approach to beekeeping, making it top choice for many.

The Top Bar Hive was not introduced recently. Its design traces back to ancient Greece, making it one of the oldest hive designs in beekeeping. The idea probably started as sticks placed across a simple cage, an improvement over the original skep hives. (A skep is an upturned straw basket under which the bees form their honeycomb. When honey is collected the bees are made homeless!) A practical option for beekeepers, the bars may be taken off for inspections and left intact after honey harvesting.

One of the most appealing features of the Top Bar Hive is its resemblance to a natural hive. Bees seem to appreciate this design because it closely mimics their natural environment. Inspections are also less disruptive and easier on the beekeeper. Each top bar laden with honey weighs just three to seven pounds as opposed to the large, heavy frames and boxes of the Langstroth hive.

A single box, or hive body, houses all of the Top Bar Hive's parts. A peaked roof with hinges is characteristic of this hive design. The hive sits on its legs, allowing the beekeeper to adjust its height for comfort. The design is simple, with the main components being the legs, the box, and the top.

The legs of the hive serve to elevate the entire structure to a convenient waist-high level, making the hive easily accessible for the beekeeper. This ergonomic design reduces the physical strain often associated with beekeeping, as there is no need to bend or crouch to inspect the hive.

Kenyan Top Bar Hive/Credit:Beth Anne Soares(www.shutterstock.com)

The box is the heart of the hive, where all the action happens! It's a single, elongated structure that houses the top bars from which the bees build their comb. The top bars are simple sticks laid across the box's top. These bars may be removed for inspections and left intact after honey collection, minimizing the disruption to the bees. Some beekeepers employ top bars with a little "comb guide," providing the bees with a place to start while drawing comb. Those that use natural beekeeping methods prefer a foundationless approach.

A viewing glass that runs the length of the box is a typical, entertaining feature included with many Top Bar hives. This window allows for a non-intrusive quick scan of the bees and their activities, adding an educational aspect to the beekeeping experience.

The hive's top has a hinged construction to shield it from the weather. It shields the hive from rain and wind, ensuring the bees have a safe and stable environment to thrive.

A unique feature of the Top Bar hive is a follower board. This piece of wood segments off a portion of the box. The board's other side entrances are blocked so no bees can enter. The follower board may be moved within the box as the colony grows to provide the bees additional room. Eventually, it is removed. This characteristic ensures that the bees start in a limited space and gradually expand it as the colony grows.

Some notable differences exist when comparing the Top Bar Hive to the Langstroth Hive. The Top Bar Hive is less physically demanding, making it a good choice for those who may struggle with the heavy lifting involved in managing a Langstroth Hive. However, the non-standardized parts of a Top Bar Hive can make it difficult to find local mentors or compatible equipment. The Top Bar Hive also produces less honey and requires a specific bar handling technique.

Despite these differences, the Top Bar Hive offers a unique and natural approach to beekeeping that many find rewarding. It's a hive that brings you closer to nature's bee life, making it a popular choice for those seeking a more natural beekeeping experience.

Let's delve deeper into the pros and cons of the Kenyan Top Bar Hive:

Pros:

- **Natural Beekeeping:** The Kenyan Top Bar Hive is preferred for beekeepers who like a more natural approach since it resembles hives in nature.

- **Ease of Inspection:** Inspections are less disruptive and easier to perform with a top bar hive. Since each top bar loaded with honey only weighs three to seven pounds, you can skip lifting heavy frames and boxes.

- **Simplified Honey Harvesting:** You won't need a large, pricey extractor to put the honey in jars. Since the top bar comb is foundationless, you only need buckets and filters to get started.

- **Physically Less Demanding:** The physical demands on the beekeeper are significantly reduced with top bar hives. You may take up one bar at a time instead of removing whole portions. Because these hives are on legs, the beekeeper may change their height to suit their comfort level.

Cons:

- **Non-Standard Equipment:** If you also plan to have Langstroth hives, none of the equipment is interchangeable between Top Bar and Langstroth hives. This can be a disadvantage for beekeepers who want to use both types of hives.

- **Honey Harvesting Process:** The comb must be destroyed to gather the honey. You must use the crush and squeeze technique, as there aren't any frames to spin around. As a result, the bees will have to put in more effort while constructing the comb following each harvest.

- **Less Honey Per Hive:** Less honey is typically extracted from each hive. Each frame is much smaller without the huge stacks that Langstroth hives have.

- **Not Ideal for Large-Scale Beekeepers:** Most large-scale or commercial beekeepers wouldn't choose these hives. They're far more suited for backyard amateur beekeepers who enjoy caring for their hives and giving their family and friends beautiful honey.

The Warré Hive: A Naturalist's Choice

Warre' Hive/Credit: www.shutterstock.com

The Warré hive, also known as the "People's Hive," is a beekeeping structure that has gained recognition for its unique design and naturalistic approach. This hive was developed by Emile Warré, a French monk who sought to create a hive allowing bees to build their comb as they would in nature. Warré's design, which he detailed in his book *Beekeeping for All* was a response to the more industrial methods of beekeeping that were becoming popular in the early 20th century.

The Warré hive is a vertical top bar hive, designed with bars instead of frames, allowing the bees to build their comb naturally. The hive typically comprises several boxes stacked vertically, with the top bars placed across the top of each box. The bees build their comb from these bars, starting from the top box and working their way down. This significantly differs from the Langstroth design, where bees are encouraged to build horizontally across frames.

One of the most distinctive features of the Warré hive is its quilt box, a unique component filled with absorbent material such as wood shavings or straw. The quilt box regulates the hive's temperature and humidity, creating a more comfortable environment for the bees. The hive also includes a roof for protection against the elements and a floor with a small entrance for the bees.

Warre' Hive/Credit: Bernhard Heuvel(www.shutterstock.com)

The Warré hive's design encourages minimal intervention from the beekeeper, aligning with Warré's philosophy of "Beekeeping for all." The hive's vertical design allows the bees to regulate their space, expanding downwards as the colony grows. This approach reduces the need for regular inspections and the potential stress they can cause to the bees.

Like any other hive design, the Warré hive has advantages and disadvantages. Let's delve deeper into these:

Pros:

- **Natural Beekeeping:** The Warré hive is designed to mimic the natural living conditions of bees. It allows bees to build their comb, a more natural process leading to healthier bees.

- **Ease of Management:** The Warré hive is designed to be low maintenance. Minimal beekeeper involvement minimizes stress for both the bees and the beekeeper. This hive design encourages bees to manage their own space and resources, which can lead to a more resilient colony.

- **Efficient Use of Space:** The vertical design of the Warré hive allows for efficient use of space. The bees can move up and down the hive as needed, leading to better temperature regulation and resource management.

- **Cost-Effective:** The Warré hive can be less expensive to set up and maintain than other hive types. This might make it a fantastic option for individuals just starting out in beekeeping.

- **Sustainable Honey Production:** The Warré hive is designed for sustainable honey production. The beekeeper only harvests the honey the bees can spare, leading to healthier colonies and more sustainable beekeeping practices.

Cons:

- **Non-Standard Equipment:** The Warré hive uses non-standard equipment, making it difficult to find replacement parts or compatible equipment. This can also make local mentors or resources harder to find when you need help.

- **Comb Destruction During Harvest:** Harvesting honey from a Warré hive involves cutting and crushing the comb, which is more labor-intensive and disruptive for the bees.

- **Lower Honey Yield:** The Warré hive typically produces less honey than other hive types. This is due to the smaller size of the hive and the fact that the bees are allowed to manage their own space and resources.

- **Not Ideal for Large-Scale Beekeeping:** The Warré hive is not typically used in commercial or large-scale beekeeping operations. It is better suited for small-scale, backyard beekeeping.

- **Requires Specific Handling techniques:** Managing a Warré hive requires specific handling techniques. For example, the hive boxes must be lifted and manipulated carefully to avoid damaging the comb. This requires a learning curve for newbee beekeepers.

In conclusion, the Warré hive offers a unique approach to beekeeping that prioritizes the natural behavior of the bees. While it may not be the best choice for those seeking high honey yields or a standardized design, it can be an excellent option for beekeepers seeking a more naturalistic and hands-off approach to their practice. As always, the choice of hive will depend on your individual needs and philosophy as a beekeeper.

Nucleus Hives

Nucleus Hives/Credit:speedshutter Photography(www.shutterstock.com)

Drawing from rich traditions of beekeeping wisdom, let us now explore into the world of nucleus hives, or as they are more commonly known, "nucs." These small-sized hives, housing modest colonies of bees, are the unsung heroes of the apiary, playing a pivotal role in the management of every beekeeping operation. Their utility is as diverse as it is indispensable, from disease and pest management to solving queen problems.

The history of nucs is intertwined with the evolution of beekeeping itself. As beekeepers sought to optimize their operations, they discovered the benefits of maintaining smaller colonies alongside their full-sized hives. These nucs, often holding between two to five full-sized frames, became a versatile tool in the beekeeper's arsenal.

The Nuc hive, akin to a miniaturized Langstroth hive, accommodates just five deep frames, a feature that lends its compact size and distinct functionality. The Nuc hive's design is reminiscent of the Langstroth hive, albeit on a smaller scale. It houses five deep frames, a characteristic that gives it its compact form and unique functionality. Despite its smaller size, the Nuc hive serves multiple purposes and might just be a hive you favor.

Now, why should one consider investing in a nuc? The reasons are manifold. Firstly, nucs are instrumental in swarm control. By creating a nuc from a full-sized colony, sometimes called "splitting," beekeepers can alleviate swarming tendencies in the parent colony. This is particularly useful in early spring when colonies grow in strength with the increased availability of nectar and pollen.

Secondly, nucs can be used to strengthen production colonies. As backup colonies for their producing hives, many beekeepers retain spare nucs. Beekeepers may maintain the health and productivity of their hives by taking brood (eggs, larvae and pupae) and grown bees out of the nuc and placing them in the producing colonies.

As with all things, there are pros and cons to using nucs.

Pros:

- **Universality:** Using Langstroth-style frames makes finding the right size foundation for this hive easy.
- **Requeening:** Nucs can be a lifesaver when it comes to requeening. If a colony loses its queen, it doesn't have to wait for a new queen to be ordered or for the colony to produce its own. The problem can be solved almost instantly by using a queen from a nuc. This is

particularly useful during times of the year when queens are not readily available, such as winter.

- **Strengthening Weak Colonies:** Nucs can bolster a weak or sick colony by providing bees and brood. A colony that is too weak to live in a full-size hive body may be transferred to a nuc hive body, which is simpler to maintain.

- **Expanding Your Operation:** Nucs offer a cost-effective way to expand your beekeeping operation. With extra foundation frames, a healthy nuc may be put into a full-size hive body to establish a new hive. This is a quick, easy, and inexpensive way to increase the number of production colonies.

- **Selling Bees:** Producing and selling nucs can be a lucrative income stream. The demand for bees has never been higher due to the increase in new beekeepers. There was a 47% increase in bee colonies worldwide between 1990 and 2020. Finding customers interested in buying nucs is not too difficult.

Cons:

- **Management Frequency:** Nucs require more frequent attention than full-size colonies. The bees often become more numerous than the equipment can handle, which increases the likelihood that they may swarm, particularly in the spring.

- **Supplemental Feeding:** Nuc hive bees can rapidly deplete food resources, particularly during the winter. They need to be checked on at least once a month to see if they have enough food, and if not, they should be fed with cane sugar syrup, the safest and most reliable nectar substitute.

- **Pest and Disease Control:** Compared to full-size colonies, nucs could be more vulnerable to illnesses and pests. For example, small hive beetles appear more likely to harm nucs. Additionally, medication doses for diseases/pests are often tailored for full-size colonies rather than nucs. As a result, beekeepers must carefully watch for pests and diseases in Nucs and respond with the appropriate medication dosage.

- **No Honey Production:** Due to its limited capacity, no honey will be harvested from this hive.

With its unique features and challenges, the nuc hive offers a different perspective on beekeeping. It may not be the first choice for beginners, but as one gains experience, the nuc hive can be a valuable tool in the beekeeper's toolkit.

Choosing the Right Hive

As we move deeper into the art and science of beekeeping, we must understand that choosing a hive is not a one-size-fits-all decision. It's a decision that should be guided by your primary objectives and philosophy as a beekeeper. If you're a novice backyard beekeeper, any of the Langstroth styles of hives are your best bet. They offer a solid foundation for learning about bees and managing them. You may wish to attempt any of the other hives listed in this chapter, such as the Top Bar, Warré, or Nuc hive, after gaining a year or two of experience. Many excellent resources are available for keeping these other sorts of hives, each demanding distinct approaches for managing your colonies.

If your main objective is harvesting honey, you can harvest from most of these hives except for the nuc. The Kenyan Top Bar and Warré hives both yield good honey. However, the Langstroth is the hive for you if you're after an abundance of sweet, gooey honey. With its modular construction, you may add as many honey supers as the season demands, and it will hold the largest colony of bees actively making honey. The Langstroth is, without a doubt, the best honey producer.

On the other hand, any of these hives will be beneficial if your main goal in keeping bees is to increase plant pollination. The size of the pollinating colony increases with the size of the hive. Moreover, you will have more work to do the larger the hive is. Therefore, if you want to maximize pollination, think about using the Kenyan, Warré, Flow, or Langstroth types of hives. If you don't want to deal with the extra work that comes with bigger hives, a small five-frame nuc hive put in the corner of your garden will do a good job of pollinating.

In conclusion, the choice of hive should align with your objectives as a beekeeper. Whether you're interested in honey production, garden pollination, or simply learning about bees, there's a hive out there that's just right for you. As you gain more experience, you may consider exploring other types of hives. But for now, let's stick with the tried and true. Happy beekeeping!

CHAPTER 4
The Langstroth Hive

Langstroth Hive Main Components/Credit:Meister
Photos(www.shutterstock.com)

In this chapter, we further explore the hive that is our primary focus throughout this book—the Langstroth hive. This hive, a brainchild of the American apiarist Lorenzo L. Langstroth, has been a pillar of modern beekeeping since its inception in 1851. The design, rooted in the principle of "bee space," has withstood the test of time. Its durability over the past century is evidence of its usefulness.

The Langstroth hive is often the first choice for those dipping their toes into the world of beekeeping. Its user-friendly design and the ready availability of its components make it an ideal choice for novices. While building your hive from scratch is undoubtedly available, most beekeepers find solace in the convenience of a kit. These kits, which come precut and ready for assembly, significantly simplify the process. Some suppliers even go a step further, offering pre-assembled hives, thus easing the initial setup even more.

The Langstroth hive has two common variants: the eight-frame and the ten-frame hives. Both variants have unique merits, and your choice will largely hinge on your requirements and capabilities as a beekeeper. The ten-frame version, being the original design, offers maximum honey production. However, it can be cumbersome, especially when the frames are filled with honey. On the other hand, the eight-frame version is lighter and easier to handle, making it an increasingly popular choice among bee people.

The design of the Langstroth hive is meticulously crafted to cater to the needs of both the bees and the beekeeper. The ideal "bee space" is provided by the hive's interior parts, which are spaced exactly 3/8 inches apart. This spacing keeps the bees from 'gluing' components with propolis or filling too many spaces with burr comb. It also allows the beekeeper to freely inspect and manipulate the frames of comb, a revolutionary feature at the time of the hive's invention.

In the following sections, we will explore the components of the Langstroth hive, discussing its design, dimensions, and purpose in detail. As we progress, you will gain a comprehensive understanding of the Langstroth hive, equipping you with the knowledge you need to begin your amazing beekeeping journey.

Langstroth Hive: Understanding its Architecture

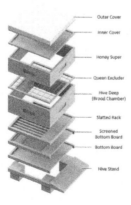

Hive Components

The Langstroth hive is traditionally a wooden structure. The parts arrive precut, ready for assembly. It's a bit like a jigsaw puzzle, each piece fitting neatly into the next. The use of wood not only ensures durability but also provides a natural environment for the bees. It's a home, a sanctuary, a bustling city of activity.

We'll carefully go through each component of the Langstroth hive in the following sections. Each piece plays a crucial role in the hive's operation and the overall well-being of the bee colony. It's a fascinating journey, and I'm thrilled to be your guide on this incredible path!

The Hive Stand: Elevating Your Beekeeping Game

The hive stand is the foundation, the base that supports the entire hive. It's typically made from cypress or cedar, wood known for resilience against rot. The hive stand's job is to lift the hive off the ground. This elevation is more important than you might think. It improves circulation around the hive, reducing dampness that could lead to unfavorable conditions like mold growth. It also lifts the hive above the grass, ensuring nothing obstructs the bees' entrance and exit routes. Plus, it brings the hive to a more convenient height for inspection, making your job as a beekeeper a little easier.

Three rails and an inclined landing board make up a typical hive stand. The bees land on this landing board when returning from their foraging trips.

Assembling the hive stand requires a bit of precision, especially when attaching the landing board. It's best to follow the assembly instructions to the letter and to assemble the stand on a level surface to prevent instability.

The Bottom Board: The Hive's Sturdy Foundation

Bottom Board/Credit:Sheri Howell(www.shutterstock.com)

The bottom board is typically crafted from resilient woods like cypress or cedar. It's the platform that the rest of the hive stands on, but it's more than just a base. It's also the main entrance and exit for our industrious little fuzzy friends, the bees.

Beekeepers commonly use two main types of bottom boards: solid and screened. Each has its own set of advantages.

Solid bottom boards are like the cozy hearth of a home during winter. They help keep the hive warm, which can encourage earlier brood rearing. Plus, they help keep the bees' pheromones inside the hive, aiding their communication. But there's a downside. Solid boards can often fail to provide enough ventilation when the weather warms up.

On the other hand, screened bottom boards are like a breath of fresh air. They allow for ventilation, preventing condensation buildup inside the hive. They're also handy for monitoring and controlling pests, particularly the varroa mite, a common nuisance in bee colonies. However, screened bottom boards will force the colony to work harder in colder climates.

The Entrance Reducer: The Hive's Security Gate

Entrance Reducer/Credit:Super8(www.shutterstock.com)

Let's turn our gaze to the entrance reducer, a seemingly simple yet crucial component of the Langstroth hive. This humble piece of wood is often overlooked and vital to the hive's security and overall health.

The entrance reducer serves as the doorkeeper of the hive, controlling the size of the hive's entrance. This is very helpful when establishing a new colony. The young bees, still finding their wings, can more effectively guard against robber bees when the entrance is smaller. It's like having a single door to guard instead of a wide-open gate.

But the entrance reducer isn't just about security. It also plays a vital role during the winterization of the hive. When the entrance size is reduced, unwanted pests have more difficulty entering the hive. It's like adding an extra lock to your door during the colder months.

However, as with most things in life, there's a trade-off. The reduced entrance can lead to overcrowding, mainly when set to its smallest setting.

This can cause a bit of a traffic jam during peak foraging times, potentially slowing down the bees' comings and goings.

Hive Bodies: The Heart of the Langstroth Hive

Hive Bodies/Credit: Egor Valeev(www.shutterstock.com)

Let's now take a look at the hive bodies, the heart of the Langstroth hive. These rectangular boxes are the living quarters for the bees, where they build their comb and go about their daily tasks.

The deep-hive body, typically designed to accommodate eight or ten honeycomb frames, is a practical and efficient hive component. The frames fit neatly into the box, providing a structured space for the bees to build honeycomb. You'll require two deep-hive bodies stacked atop the other, much like a two-story house. The lower deep functions as the nursery, where the bees nurture their young, while the upper deep acts as the pantry, where they store honey and pollen.

Although the inside dimensions of these boxes are standard, there may be variations across brands and nations. Depending on the materials chosen, the exterior dimensions may also change. For instance, boxes made of wood will be smaller than those made of polystyrene foam.

The three hive body heights are shallow, medium, and deep. Deeps or mediums are frequently positioned at the hive's bottom, on top of the bottom board. The bees will raise their young in this location. For storing honey, medium and shallow boxes work best because deep ones can get quite heavy when filled with honeycomb. "Supers" are the boxes used to store honey. In a later section of this book, I will devote a section to them.

Assembling a hive body is a straightforward task. It is constructed from four precut wood planks that fit together to form a box. The four planks are matched up, and to keep the box square, a single nail is hammered into the center of each of the four intersections. Before driving the last few nails, check that everything is level with a carpenter's square. After being put together, the bottom board supports the hive body. If it wobbles, smooth out any high spots with a plane or gritted sandpaper. The hive stand must snugly fit the hive body and bottom board.

The Queen Excluder: The Hive's Selective Doorway

Queen Excluder/Credit: ClimbWhenReady(www.shutterstock.com)

A typical piece of equipment many backyard beekeepers use is the queen excluder. It is crucial in the hive's structure—between the honey supers and the deep food chamber.

The preassembled queen excluder is made of a wooden structure holding a metal wire grid or a punched plastic sheet. As the name suggests, this component keeps the queen from accessing the honey supers and depositing her eggs. This is significant since once a queen lays eggs in the supers, it tempts bees to bring pollen inside, potentially compromising the purity of the honey you intend to harvest. The honey supers are spaced apart in the grid so smaller worker bees can access them and fill them with honey.

When honey supers are placed on the hive and bees bring nectar in and turn it into honey, the queen excluder can be used. It is thus a unique piece of woodenware for honey production. It shouldn't be used if you aren't collecting honey. Additionally, it should never be applied during the winter as it may prevent the winter bee cluster from accessing vital honey reserves.

Because using a queen excluder can hinder bees' ability to produce honey, many seasoned beekeepers decide against using one. Some even suggest it may contribute to swarming. However, determining when it's appropriate to forego using a queen excluder takes one or two seasons of practice. I advise using the queen excluder in your first one or two seasons to be safe. Then, try not using it when you install the honey supers, which are timed to occur during an important nectar flow.

The Honey Super: The Hive's Sweet Repository

Let's shift our focus to the honey super, a vital component of the Langstroth hive that plays a significant role in honey production. The honey super is positioned atop the hive, serving as a storage unit for the sweet nectar the bees collect.

The honey super comes in two standard sizes: shallow and medium. The choice of size largely depends on the beekeeper's strength and preference. A medium super filled with honey can be heavy, making handling challenging. For this reason, many beekeepers prefer to use shallow supers for honey storage.

In accordance with the size of your hive, the honey super may hold eight or ten frames. These frames provide a structured space for the bees to construct their honeycomb. When the bees return nectar to the hive, they store it in the honeycomb cells within these frames. Over time, they transform the nectar into honey, which they cap with a layer of wax for preservation.

You should add to the hive the honey supers only eight weeks after placing your bees or for second-year beekeepers when a variety of spring flowers bloom. During this time, the colony's population is at its peak, and the bees can fill multiple supers with honey. Once the nectar flow season ends, the honey supers are removed, and the honey is harvested.

Due to their reduced depth, the supers are simple to handle during the honey harvest. A shallow one with ten frames of honey weighs approximately 40 pounds; a medium super with ten frames full of honey weighs about 55 pounds; while a deep-hive body filled with honey weighs about 80 pounds or more. That is a heavier load than you probably want to carry!

As the bees gather more honey, you can stack more honey supers on top of each other and add them to the hive. For your first season, I recommend you purchase a couple of honey supers (medium or shallow).

Frames and Foundations: The Hive's Architectural Blueprint

Frame/Credit: Lukasz Wrobel(www.shutterstock.com)

Let's shift our focus to the building blocks of the Langstroth hive—the frames and foundations. These components are the backbone of the hive, offering a structure for our industrious bees to construct their comb and carry out their daily routines.

As we have seen, the Langstroth frames come in various sizes to suit the box size they occupy. The standard sizes are deep, medium, and shallow, with corresponding frame heights of 9 1/8", 6 1/4", and 5 3/8". The choice between wooden or plastic frames often comes down to personal preference. Wooden frames, typically constructed from pine, appeal to many beekeepers due to their natural charm. Conversely, plastic frames are lightweight, durable, and immune to rot, although they can warp under high temperatures.

Foundations/Credit: kosolovskyy(www.shutterstock.com)

The foundation is a wax or plastic layer that fits precisely within the frame. It features a molded hexagonal pattern that guides the bees in building their comb. This guidance not only ensures a straight comb, avoiding the mess of cross comb, but also determines the size of the cells. Wax is often put on plastic foundations to stimulate the bees to create cells.

The decision to use foundation, or go foundationless, is a significant one for the beekeeper. Each approach has advantages and challenges; the choice often hinges on the beekeeper's experience and level of comfort with each option.

Beeswax Coating/Credit: Lindasj22(www.shutterstock.com)

The wax used to coat the foundation often originates from large-scale commercial beekeeping operations. Pesticides used by professional beekeepers to treat mites, and pesticides connected to the crops the bees have been pollinating may be present in various amounts in this wax.

Another issue is that bees can only use one cell size due to the pre-formed hexagonal cell pattern. For instance, drone cells are bigger than worker bee cells, and cells designed to store honey can be of a different size.

Allowing the bees to construct the comb with the size of cells they choose and need is one of the benefits of using foundationless frames. An increasing number of beekeepers are moving toward "natural beekeeping". A frame without a foundation enables the bees to construct what they naturally require.

Going foundationless enables honeybees to create the size cells they require as they develop various-sized cells for different functions. Foundationless frames allow bees to build comb any way they like. Bees can build the size cells they need without exposure to the chemicals commonly associated with wax-coated foundations.

However, this "bee freedom" comes with challenges for the beekeeper in the form of a cross-comb. An artificial foundation guides the bees to build a straight comb down the length of the frame. Without it, the bees frequently switch between frames, making removing a frame for inspection challenging without damaging the natural foundation.

A visit to the hive is often necessary every three days for beginner beekeepers starting new colonies in foundationless hives—to address cross-comb before it becomes a serious problem. This can be a daunting task for someone just starting, and there are risks associated with it. Huge pieces of organically produced comb that fall off the frame when the frame is taken from the hive is an unpleasant experience that many newbee beekeepers have experienced. Nothing is more disappointing, especially considering how hard it was for the bees to build that comb. When this happens, it can also potentially kill or harm the queen. The quantity of drones produced by foundationless frames is another potential problem. While seasoned beekeepers will be able to handle it, it may present another challenge for novices.

One possible tactic is alternating foundation and foundationless frames. The foundation-filled frames will direct your bees to create a straight new comb, preventing the cross-comb problem while minimizing the quantity of foundation needed in the hive.

The Langstroth hive is generally used with foundations, but it doesn't have to be. Foundationless beekeeping is worth considering. It has several benefits, not the least of which being that bees may live more naturally. However, for new beekeepers, the focus should be on understanding what happens in the hive. One of the worst things that can happen is "foundation collapse" with a fragile comb.

For this reason, I advise newbee Langstroth beekeepers to begin with foundation frames before considering foundationless. It's not necessary to do this, though—there are many options in beekeeping (as with everything). Many novice beekeepers have had success using foundationless frames.

As a beekeeper, it's important to maintain a degree of independence. Take advantage of every opportunity to learn in the early years of your practice. You can choose the best beekeeping methods when you can incorporate your personal experiences with what you've heard from others and read.

The Inner Cover: A Breathable Barrier for the Hive

Inner Cover/Credit: Lindasj22(www.shutterstock.com)

Let's focus on the inner cover, which might seem inconsequential but significantly affects the hive's health and functionality. The inner cover, typically crafted from durable woods like cypress or cedar, serves as a breathable barrier at the hive's top. It maintains the correct "bee space" and provides essential ventilation, contributing to the hive's overall well-being.

The inner cover's design is simple yet effective. It's a flat, framed plank with a hole cut in the center. Some models feature a ventilation hole, a small cut-out that further enhances the hive's airflow. When placing the inner cover, ensure the "tray" side faces up, and if there is a ventilation hole, position it towards the front of the hive.

This component's role is more than just a physical barrier. It helps regulate the hive's internal environment, ensuring the bees have optimal conditions for their daily tasks. Whether it's a high-quality wooden model or a budget-friendly pressboard version, the inner cover is a testament to the intricate and well-thought-out design of the Langstroth hive.

Note that you cannot use the inner cover when the hive is equipped with a hive-top feeder. The hive-top feeder replaces the inner cover.

The Outer Cover: The Hive's Weather Shield

Outer Cover/Credit: milart(www.shutterstock.com)

Let's now cast our eyes on the outer cover, the hive's weather shield. This component, also known as the top cover, is the final layer of protection for the hive and is perched on top of the inner cover, protecting the hive from the weather. Its design is such that it overlaps the edges of the hive, preventing any rainwater from seeping in.

The telescoping outer cover is a favorite among seasoned beekeepers. This type of cover, typically made from wood, features a thin metal sheet on top. This metal surface reflects the hot sun and allows rainwater to slide off easily, providing additional protection against the weather.

To secure the cover and deter potential predators, it is a good idea to place a heavy object, such as a rock or brick, on top of the outer cover. This is useful as the cover could be blown away during windy or stormy weather.

A telescoping outer cover can be an excellent asset for those in colder climates. In the winter, a wrap can be placed inside the cover's rim, providing an extra layer of insulation for the hive. The outer cover, while simple in design, plays a crucial role in maintaining the integrity of the hive and protecting our industrious little black and gold friends, the bees.

Beyond the Basics: Exploring Additional Components of the Langstroth Hive

As we travel further into the captivating realm of beekeeping, we must remember that the components we've covered are the bedrock of a Langstroth hive. These foundational elements—the hive stand, bottom board, entrance reducer, hive bodies, queen excluder, honey super, frames, inner cover, and outer cover—are the heart and soul of a thriving hive. They create the perfect environment for our hardworking bees to flourish and produce the golden honey we cherish.

But here's the exciting part: beekeeping isn't a one-size-fits-all endeavor! While the essential components of the Langstroth hive are indispensable, a world of additional components can be integrated into your hive to boost its functionality and productivity. These aren't just bells and whistles; they can make your beekeeping life more rewarding and less challenging. In the next part of this book, we'll explore the roles and benefits of additional hive components, and how they can make your hive a buzzing success.

The Frame Rest: A Handy Companion for Beekeepers

Frame Rest/Credit: Sobolevskyi_Vadym (www.shutterstock.com)

The frame rest, often referred to as a frame perch, or frame holder, is a nifty device that attaches to the side of your beehive. It is a secure and accessible spot to hang your frames during hive inspections. It is a temporary parking bay for your frames, keeping them off the ground and within easy reach.

The frame rest is a model of simplicity. It hangs on the exterior of the hive box, with two bars jutting out. These bars act as a resting place for the frames, holding them just as they would inside the hive. It's a simple design, but its benefits to your beekeeping practice are substantial.

One of the key advantages of using a frame rest is that it keeps your valuable frames off the ground. While it's not catastrophic if your frames touch the ground, it's not ideal. Frames on the ground risk toppling over, squashing bees, damaging the comb, and getting dirty. If the queen bee were to wander off the frame and onto the ground, finding her would be like finding a needle in a haystack!

Another perk of the frame rest is its non-intrusive nature. It allows you to handle your frames with minimal disruption to the bees, contributing to a more tranquil and productive hive. It's a small detail, but one that can significantly impact the mood of your bees (and you!)

Lastly, a frame rest helps keep your frames in order during inspections. It's easy to lose track of which frames you've inspected and the sequence they should be placed back in the box. A frame rest solves this problem as a temporary storage space that keeps your frames organized and accessible.

When selecting a frame rest, opt for a robust, durable material. It should support the weight of your frames, which can sometimes be quite hefty. Some frame rests come attached to a hive stand, which can be handy if you need a new stand. However, a standalone frame rest can be used with multiple hives, making it a versatile tool in your beekeeper's kit.

The Slatted Rack: A Valuable Addition to Your Hive Arsenal

Slatted Rack

The slatted rack is a few inches deep and shares the exact dimensions of the hive boxes. The slats are thoughtfully arranged to run parallel to the frames in the boxes above, a design feature that's not made just for aesthetic reasons, but serves a specific purpose.

One of the key benefits of a slatted rack is its contribution to hive ventilation. Air, a poor conductor of heat, forms an insulating layer beneath the brood box when trapped within the slatted rack. This feature is a boon in both summer and winter. Bees can use the area in the slatted rack to fan air through the hive during the summer, reducing congestion. Come winter, the insulating layer helps shield the hive from the cold air.

Another potential advantage of the slatted rack is its role in reducing swarming, which occurs when bees don't have enough space. By expanding the bees' hangout area, the slatted rack may decrease the likelihood of swarming.

When used with a screened bottom board, the slatted rack also aids in mite management. The slats, running parallel with the frames above, allow mites to fall directly on the bottom board, making it easier for beekeepers to assess mite levels.

The design of the slatted rack includes a larger piece of wood at one side, which should be positioned facing the hive's front. This design feature helps moderate the airflow at this critical hive area. Additionally, it's important to note that the less deep side of the rack should be oriented upwards. This arrangement helps deter worker bees from constructing comb from the slatted rack up to the bottom edge of the brood chamber.

Lastly, the slatted rack may positively influence the queen's egg-laying pattern. Without a slatted rack, the queen bee may cease egg-laying at a specific level above the hive entrance, a behavior aimed at preserving the temperature of the brood. The thermal barrier created by the slatted rack motivates the queen to lay eggs nearer to the bottom edge of the brood box frames, thereby increasing the space for egg deposition.

Your Guide to Beehive Shopping

You might wonder, "Where can I buy a beehive?" Don't worry; we've got you covered.

The Local Route

Let's start with the traditional, in-person approach. You might think, "I'll just pop into my local store and pick up a beehive." Well, it's not that simple. Beehives aren't typically found on the shelves of your local supermarket. But don't let that discourage you!

There is a whole community of beekeepers out there, and many members would be more than happy to help a newbee. Reach out to a local beekeeper or an apiary near you. They might have the perfect hive for you, and you'll gain a valuable local resource for your beekeeping journey.

However, a word of caution: buying used beehives can be risky. They could carry diseases that might harm your future bee colony. So, when you're starting, it's safer to go with new equipment.

The Online Marketplace

Now, let's talk about the wonders of the internet. It's a treasure trove for beekeepers, both new and experienced. Websites like Amazon offer many beehives and accessories. Additionally, they offer quick, free shipping and a reliable return policy.

If you're interested in specific brands like Apimaye or Flow Hive, it's worth considering purchasing directly from their respective websites. By buying directly from the Apimaye or Flow Hive websites, you can ensure that you get genuine products and take advantage of any warranties or customer support they offer. These websites often provide comprehensive product details, user guides, and even tutorial videos to help you get the most out of your hive.

Choosing Your Perfect Hive

Now that we've covered where to buy, let's discuss *what* to buy. Choosing a beehive may seem daunting, but don't fret. Here are a few things to think about:

- **Assembly:** Do you want a ready-to-use hive or a DIY project? Assembled hives save time, but unassembled ones can be a fun, hands-on experience.

- **Paint:** Some hives come pre-painted, but why not paint your own if you feel artistic? You could match it to your house or garden or create a unique design.

- **Wax Coating:** Wax-coated hives are durable and waterproof. Plus, they're non-toxic and beneficial for the bees.

- **Material:** Look for solid and durable materials like pine, cedar, or fir. Your bees deserve the best!

- **Design:** A good hive design will protect your bees from the elements and allow them to thrive.

- **Honey Harvesting:** How do you plan to harvest honey? Traditional methods use a honey extractor, but hives with a tap are gaining popularity.

- **Budget:** Beehives range from $100 to $1,000. Choose one that is within your means.

- **Shipping:** Check the shipping policies. Free shipping is always a bonus, but some retailers may have restrictions based on size, weight, or location.

Your Beehive Journey: From Ordering to Assembly

Placing Your Order: The First Step

When ordering your hive, you'll find that most manufacturers use sturdy woods like cedar, cypress, or pine. While the bees won't mind the type of wood, the quality can significantly affect how easy your hive is to assemble and how long it lasts. So, go for the best your budget allows.

You will find various beekeeping supply stores online, ready to deliver to your doorstep. But here's a pro tip: Avoid placing your order at the last minute. If you plan to start beekeeping in the spring, placing your order a few months beforehand is advisable. This way, you can avoid the spring rush and ensure your hive arrives quickly.

Starter Hive Kits: The All-in-One Solution

Consider a starter hive kit if you're overwhelmed with all the components and tools. These kits offer everything you need in one package. They usually include the hive body, honey supers, frames and foundation, assembly hardware, a veil and gloves, a smoker, a hive tool, and a feeder. These kits often come at a discounted price, making them an excellent option for newbees.

Setting Up Your Beehive: A Fun and Rewarding DIY Project

So, you're ready to set up shop for your beehive? But where do you start? Fear not! Read on!

Finding Your Perfect Workspace

First things first, let's find you a workspace. You might think, "I need a huge space, right?" Not at all! A small corner in your garage, basement, or kitchen will do just fine. And if you can get your hands on a worktable, even better. It's all about making the space work for you.

Tools of the Trade

Now that you've got your workspace, it's time to gather your tools. Of course, you'll need your hive components, (or "woodenware," as we beekeepers refer to it), and their accompanying instruction manuals. But what about tools?

Well, a hammer is a must. But there are a few other tools that will make your life a lot easier:

- Pliers are great for removing nails that bend instead of going in straight.

- Brad driver with ¾-inch, 18-gauge brads: This little tool can speed up the installation of your wax foundation.

- All-weather wood glue: A little glue before nailing can strengthen your hive and aid longevity.

- Carpenter's square: This will help ensure your hive doesn't wobble when assembled.

- Grit sandpaper: Perfect for smoothing out any rough spots.

- Hive tool: This is a beekeeper's best friend. It works well for removing wedge strips from frames and prying out nails.

Assembling Your Hive: The Adventure Begins

With your workspace and tools ready, it's time to assemble your hive. It's best to start from the bottom and work your way up, so you can ensure everything fits together perfectly.

Remember that the components aren't nailed together if you're using a Langstroth hive. They're stacked on top of each other, like pancakes. This design makes opening your hive and lifting boxes during inspections quite easy.

Painting Your Beehive

Beehive Painting/Credit: Lukasz Wrobel(www.shutterstock.com)

Honeybees aren't overly concerned about the color of their homes. As long as the structure is sound, they're content. However, beekeepers often opt to paint their hives and the reason for this is more practical than aesthetic. The primary purpose is to preserve the wooden parts of the hive. Most woods used in hive construction aren't naturally resistant to weathering. Painting the hive helps protect the wood and extend its lifespan.

There are several compelling reasons why beekeepers paint their hives:

- **Preservation:** Painting the hive shields the wood from water, bacteria, and fungi. This is particularly crucial as beehives are usually stationed outdoors, exposed to these elements. The paint acts as a waterproofing agent and may also possess antimicrobial properties. Dry wood is less prone to rotting.

- **Bee Navigation:** Honeybees employ various cues to navigate around their surroundings. In the open, they utilize a combination of landmarks and color cues to locate foraging fields and find a route to return to their hives. In a sizeable beekeeping operation where hives are closely packed, painting individual hives in different colors assists bees with navigation. The bees use landmarks to reach the apiary and color coding to locate their respective hives. Honeybees can navigate using additional cues—such as the direction in which the beehive entrance faces. When using beehive painting as a navigational aid for bees, it's important to remember that honeybees cannot see the color red, so it should be avoided.

- **Spotting and Identification:** A painted hive can be easier to spot in large spaces if it contrasts with its surroundings. In addition to aiding in spotting a beehive, painting a beehive assists in identifying it, among others. You can also write a name or code while painting the beehive for easier identification.

- **Camouflage:** Apiaries in remote areas present difficult-to-overcome security challenges. Beehives that aren't painted may be more visible and are simple to locate. This can attract thieves and wild animals who might steal or attack the beehive. Giving your beehive a natural-looking paint job can lessen the likelihood of this happening. Painting a beehive in camouflage colors doesn't require the same rigorous techniques and patterns as in the military! A single, continuous color is often sufficient for the job. If the "hidden" beehive is their home, bees—who are excellent navigators—will find it. They employ various homing techniques, including beehive odor, color, and landmarks. Even if the beehive is camouflaged, the bees will not get lost or fail to locate their home hive.

- **Temperature Control:** Paint can assist bees in controlling beehive temperatures. Use light colours to prevent the beehive from overheating in hot climates. Dark paint will help the beehive retain heat and warm up in cold climates. In many parts of the USA and worldwide, beekeepers use this technique to help their bees conserve energy. Bees cooling a beehive could use their energy for other things, like foraging. Similarly, bee activity involving heating a beehive uses much energy and drastically shortens each bee's life span. Helping to regulate temperature by painting the hive frees up bees so they can use their energy on other hive tasks, resulting in high yields of hive supplies from your beekeeping operation.

Knowing What to Paint

The golden rule for painting your beehive is straightforward: paint the exterior, leave the interior alone. The outside of your hive needs that extra layer of protection against the elements, while painting on the inside could negatively impact your bees and the honey they produce.

Before opening that paint can, ensure your hive is well-assembled and sturdy. A well-built hive is the foundation of a long-lasting paint job.

Certain parts of the hive should *never* see a paintbrush. These are the inner cover, screened parts of the bottom board, the frames, and the entrance reducer.

Below is a list of the parts that do require painting:

- **Hive Stand:** The hive stand doesn't house your bees, so let your creativity flow here. This part of the hive must withstand a lot, including wind, rain, temperature changes, grass, and other vegetation. It must also withstand any mud or snow accumulating throughout the year.

- **Bottom Board:** The wooden surfaces of your bottom board can be painted with water-based paint. However, if your bottom board has a screen, avoid painting it. Bees will climb the screen and could come into contact with the paint. But don't worry about the unpainted screen being an eyesore—it's invisible.

- **Hive Boxes:** The hive boxes are the body of your hive, and you can let your creativity run wild here! Take care not to paint the interior of your hive boxes. Some beekeepers decide to paint the hive boxes' top and bottom edges, while others feel that in warm weather, this may make the boxes stick together. The choice is yours. The most important thing is to protect the exterior from the elements.

- **Outer Cover:** While the inner cover should remain paint-free, coat the outer cover. Just avoid the inside and underneath of the cover and the metal top. Focus your painting efforts on the exterior surfaces and the top and bottom ends of the cover.

The Color Spectrum: It's Not Just About Looks

The color of your beehive isn't merely a matter of artistic taste. It plays a crucial role in managing the hive's temperature. For instance, white is a popular beehive paint choice, particularly in warmer climates because white reflects more light than darker colors, reducing heat absorption and helping to maintain a comfortable temperature for your bees.

In contrast, if you're in a colder region, it's recommended to go for a darker color but steer clear of black. Dark green and blue hues are preferred. These colors absorb heat, helping the hive stay warm during the chilly winter. Even with minimal sunlight, a dark-colored hive will stay warmer than a light-colored one, saving your bees energy they would otherwise use to heat the hive. On occasion, you want your beehive to blend in with its surroundings. In such cases, dark green is a good choice, especially if your hives are outdoors amidst greenery. However, you're free to choose any color that suits your needs, especially if you have multiple hives, and use color to help bees identify their respective homes. Remember to *avoid black*, which can cause overheating, and red, as bees have difficulty seeing this color.

The Paint Selection: More Than Just Colors

As we have seen, painting your beehive is not just about picking your favorite color. The composition of the paint is also a crucial factor. You need to select a paint that won't harm your bees but will protect your hive. Remember, you should only paint the exterior surfaces of the hive, leaving the interior untouched, so your bees don't contact the paint directly.

Decoding VOCs in Beehive Paint

VOCs, or Volatile Organic Compounds, are found in water- and oil-based paints. These compounds evaporate from the paint as it dries, giving off that fresh paint smell. The VOC levels in paint are usually indicated on the paint's container. When choosing paint for your beehive, aim for the one with the lowest VOC levels. This way, you minimize the amount of potentially harmful chemicals that could affect your bees.

Regarding the best paint for beehives, aim for a VOC level of 50 or below. If you can find paint with a VOC level of zero, that's even better. Here are some top contenders:

- **Milk Paint:** This eco-friendly paint is mineral-based and free from VOCs. It comes in powder form, mixed with water to create a usable paint. Once applied, it gives a matte finish.

- **Water-Based Latex Paints:** These paints are a great choice for beehives due to their low VOC levels and ability to waterproof the wood. They are durable, readily available, and easy to apply. If you notice the paint peeling off, you can easily touch it up. You can protect the latex paint with a clear varnish for added durability.

- **Chalk Paint:** This mineral-based paint is odorless and dries quickly. However, it doesn't provide much waterproofing, so you must apply fresh coats periodically.

Other Key Considerations When Choosing Beehive Paint

When selecting paint for your beehives, keep the following factors in mind:

- **Base:** Paint comes in two types: water-based and oil-based. While oil-based paint traditionally offers better wood preservation, advancements in paint technology have led to high-quality water-based paints that offer similar levels of protection.

- **Main Components:** Some paints contain chemical elements and compounds that could harm your bees or affect you with long-term exposure. Choose paints that are safe for both you and your bees.

- **Durability:** Opt for long-lasting paints. High-quality paint may be more expensive but lasts longer than lower-quality options.

- **Light Reflectance Value (LRV):** The amount of light reflected from the paint can affect the bees and the temperatures inside the hive. Paints with a high LRV can confuse bees, so it's best to check the paint's LRV before making your final decision.

Beyond Paint: Other Protective Measures

While painting is a common method to protect your beehive's wood, it's not the only option. Here are some other great alternatives you might consider:

- **Wax:** Waxing the wood of your beehive can extend its lifespan by 15–20 years. Wax is a natural substance that bees are familiar with. It keeps moisture out of the wood and you don't need to often reapply. Coat the wood with hot wax. After drying off the excess, the hive component is ready. Remember to take safety precautions to avoid fire hazards when using hot wax.

- **Tung Oil:** Tung oil is another alternative to painting. It's clear, odorless, and contains no volatile compounds that could harm bees. Tung oil can be applied either by itself or over milk paint. Plus, it doesn't hide the wood's natural grain, giving your beehive a beautiful, natural look.

- **Varnish:** Varnishes and clear coats are waterproof substitutes for painting. They shield the wood. Varnish gives the wood color and improves its appearance. However, VOCs are present in some clear coats and varnishes, which require long drying periods and could contaminate your hive products, so be careful and check the contents before applying.

Feeding Your Bees: The Importance of Adding Feeders to Your Hive

So, you've got your beehive set up and ready to go. That's fantastic! But wait, there's one more thing you need to consider: feeders. Yes, those handy devices that help you nourish your bees when nectar is scarce. Let's dive into the world of bee feeders!

The Benefits of Feeding: A Well-Fed Bee is a Happy Bee

Feeding your bees goes beyond just ensuring their survival—it's about helping them thrive. In the spring, feeding sugar syrup can stimulate the queen to lay more eggs, expanding the colony. In the fall, feeding helps your bees store food for the winter, keeping the colony strong.

And let's not forget about food supplements. There are plenty of all-natural options available that can boost your bees' nutrition. Adding these to your feeding routine can help keep your bees as healthy and strong as possible.

Remember, feeding your bees is a crucial part of beekeeping. So, take the time to find the right feeder and create a feeding schedule. Your bees will thank you for it!

The Feeding Schedule: Timing is Everything

You might be wondering, "When should I feed my bees?" If you've just installed a new colony, it's feeding time *immediately*. For established colonies, consider the early spring and fall as your feeding seasons. This schedule ensures your bees have the nutrients they need to thrive all year round.

Choosing Your Feeder: One Size Doesn't Fit All

You will find several choices of feeder available, each with special benefits and drawbacks. I will provide a comprehensive overview in the following pages. Exploring these options and finding a feeder that aligns with your requirements, and those of your buzzing friends, is crucial. Always remember, the ideal feeder isn't a one-size-fits-all solution—but one that perfectly suits you and your bees. Let´s explore the world of bee feeders together!

Hive-Top Feeder

Top Feeder/Credit: shoot4pleasure(www.shutterstock.com)

Have you considered using a hive-top feeder? Also known as a Miller feeder, this handy device could be a game-changer in your beekeeping life.

The Hive-Top Feeder sits snugly on your hive's upper deep brood box, right under the outer cover. It has a reservoir with a three-gallon syrup capacity. Yes, you heard that right—three gallons! And the best part? Your bees can access this feast from below thanks to a screened entrance. That's the magic of a hive-top feeder.

You might ask, "Why should I choose a hive-top feeder?" Well, there are several reasons:

- **Less Refilling, More Relaxing:** With a large reservoir, you won't need to refill the feeder more than a few times a month. That's a lot of saved time!

- **Sting-Free Refilling:** Thanks to the screened bee access, you can refill the feeder without worrying about stings. The bees are on the other side of the screen, after all.

- **Peaceful Bees:** Refilling a hive-top feeder doesn't require you to open the hive completely. That means less disturbance for your bees, and more peace for you.

- **Medication Made Easy:** If your bees receive medication, the syrup in a hive-top feeder isn't exposed to the sunlight. That means the medication stays effective.

While hive-top feeders are fantastic, there are a few things to consider:

- **Feeding Frenzy:** In their excitement, some bees might slip off the screen and end up drowning in the syrup.

- **Level Matters:** For a hive-top feeder to work effectively, your hive must be on level ground, or almost level.

- **Inspection Time:** When it's full, a hive-top feeder can be a bit heavy and awkward to take away for regular inspections.

For urban beekeepers, a hive-top feeder can be an excellent choice. Its large volume is perfect for situations where access to the hives is less frequent. With ample syrup, your bees can stay healthy and productive.

Hive-top feeders come with different price tags. Generally, you can expect to invest between $20 and $60 for a quality hive-top feeder.

Entrance Feeder

Entrance Feeder/Credit: Jennifer Wallace(www.shutterstock.com)

Among the various types of feeders, one that often pops up is the entrance feeder, also known as the Boardman feeder. But is it the right choice for you? Let's find out.

Picture a small inverted jar of syrup nestled in a contraption right at the entrance of your hive. Simple, right? That's the beauty of an entrance feeder. It is a well-favored option due to its simplicity and price, and it is often included in many hive starter kits.

While entrance feeders are easy to use, there are a few things you should keep in mind:

- **Unwanted Guests:** The feeder's location at the entrance might invite bees from other hives to help themselves to your syrup and honey. Not exactly the neighborly sharing you had in mind!

- **Sun and Medication Don't Mix:** Planning to medicate your syrup? An entrance feeder might not be the best choice. The sun can degrade the medication, making it less effective.

- **Spoilage:** Speaking of the sun, it can spoil syrup quickly. Not the best treat for your bees.

- **Refill, Rinse, Repeat:** With a small jar, you'll refill the feeder often, sometimes even daily.

- **Springtime Woes:** Bees gather at the hive's top in the spring. An entrance feeder at the bottom might not get much attention.

- **Sting Alert:** Refilling the feeder at the hive entrance might get you some unwanted attention from guard bees. Ouch!

While entrance feeders have their place, these considerations suggest they might not fit every beekeeper best. I don't recommend you apply an entrance feeder to your beehive.

Entrance feeders come in a range of prices. Generally, you can expect to shell out anywhere between $5 and $20 for a basic entrance feeder.

Pail Feeder

Pail Feeder

Imagine a one-gallon plastic pail with a friction top closure. Now, picture several tiny holes drilled into the top. Fill it up with syrup, snap the top into place, invert it, and put it over the inner cover's center hole of the hive. Voilà! You've got a pail feeder. It works like a water cooler, with the syrup held in by pressure. Your bees can feed by sticking their tongues through the small holes.

While pail feeders are easy to use, there are a few things you should consider:

- **Refilling:** To refill the feeder, you'll have to open the hive placed within an empty deep-hive body. This leaves you open to potential stings.

- **Bee Disruption:** Typically, refilling the feeder requires smoking bees and upsetting the colony.

- **Capacity:** With a one-gallon capacity, you must refill the feeder once or twice weekly.

- **Feeding Limitations:** due to the restricted access to the syrup, only a handful of bees can feed simultaneously.

Now, let's talk about the cost. You can expect to pay anywhere from $5 to $15 for a basic pail feeder. However, if you're looking at a larger feeder or one with additional features, you might pay up to $20 or $25

Baggie Feeder

Baggie Feeder/Credit: Olexgood(www.shutterstock.com)

The baggie feeder is a one-gallon-size plastic baggie that contains about three quarts of syrup. It lies flat just above the top bars of the hive. An air bubble appears along the bag's top, and a few 2-inch-wide cuts are made using a razor blade. A gentle squeeze of the bag allows some syrup to seep through the slits, helping the bees find the syrup. The hive has an empty super and an outer cover to protect the feeder.

While baggie feeders are affordable and straightforward to use, there are a few things you should consider:

- **Handling:** To add new bags, you must open the hive and disturb the bees. This could be a little troublesome.

- **Maintenance:** After being razor-cut, the used bags cannot be used again. Plus, the bags have to be replaced relatively frequently.

- **Benefits:** They are cost-effective, reduce the likelihood of robbing, are easy to access for the bees, and prevent bees from drowning.

The price of a baggie feeder can vary based on the brand, materials, and where you buy it. Generally, you can expect to spend anywhere from $1 to $5 for a basic baggie feeder.

Frame Feeders

Frame Feeder

A frame feeder is a narrow plastic vessel like a standard frame. This vessel is inserted into the upper body of the Langstroth hive, substituting one of the frames and replacing one adjacent to the exterior wall. Fill it up with one or two pints of syrup, and just like that – you've got a frame feeder! With this feeder, your bees can access the syrup directly.

While frame feeders are easy to use, there are a few things you should consider:

- **Refilling:** The feeder's capacity is small, so you must refill it often.
- **Frame Usage:** When the feeder is installed, you will have one less frame of honey.
- **Bee Disruption:** Refilling the feeder usually involves opening the hive, disrupting the colony and potentially exposing you to stings.
- **Drowning Risk:** There's a risk that bees drown in the feeder.

A frame feeder generally ranges from $10 to $25.

Mastering the Fundamental Tools

When you start beekeeping, there are a few more essential tools you'll need to become familiar with. These aren't merely tools—they're your new best friends! They'll make your work easier, ensure your safety, and—most importantly—help keep your fuzzy, buzzing buddies happy and healthy! So let's learn more about them.

Bee Smoker

Bee Smoker/Credit: RossHelen(www.shutterstock.com)

The bee smoker is a device that generates smoke from a slow-burning material, often wood or paper. This smoke confuses the bees' communication signals, specifically the alarm pheromones they release when they sense danger. The result? A calmer hive that's easier to handle. It is a simple device, but it's cleverly designed. It consists of three essential parts: a fire chamber for burning the fuel, bellows to control the flow of oxygen and produce smoke, and a nozzle to direct the smoke where it's needed.

To use a bee smoker, you ignite the fuel in the fire chamber, then lightly blow smoke with the bellows over the bees you are working with, or into the hive entrance. The smoke helps to keep the bees calm, making your beekeeping tasks a breeze (well, a smoky breeze!)

Bee smokers come in two main categories, each with its ignition method: electric and charcoal.

- **Electric Smokers:** These are a favorite among many beekeepers for their convenience. They don't need a lighter or matches and are easy to operate. Just insert the rechargeable batteries, switch them on, and you're ready. Plus, they are transportable, so you can bring them along on your beekeeping adventures.

- **Charcoal Smokers:** These smokers heat charcoal briquettes until they're red hot, then you place the burning charcoal in the smoker's fire chamber. The result is a slow, steady stream of smoke. However, they can take a little longer to get going than other bee smokers.

Bee smokers can also be differentiated by the material used for their bellows. While leather was once the material of choice, today's bee smokers usually feature bellows made of vinyl or rubber.

When it comes to picking out a bee smoker, there are a few things to keep in mind:

- **Size:** The size of your smoker should match the size of your beekeeping operation. If you have a lot of hives, you'll need a larger smoker.

- **Material:** The material of your smoker can affect its durability and how well it works. Some materials are more effective than others regarding heat retention and smoke production.

- **Price:** Prices for bee smokers range widely, from about $30 to $200. Finding a balance between cost and quality is fundamental.

- **Mounting Hook:** A hook can be a handy feature, making it easier to hang your smoker while using it.

- **Heat Protection:** A heat-protective cage can prevent accidental burns.

In an upcoming chapter of this book, we'll explore how to use a bee smoker effectively. So, stay tuned for that!

Hive Tool

Hive Tool/Credit: Hakim Graphy(www.shutterstock.com)

The hive tool is like a Swiss Army knife for beekeepers. It's a multi-functional tool that you'll find yourself using repeatedly. Whether you're prying open your hive, moving around frames, scraping off excess wax and propolis, or adjusting loose nails or staples—the hive tool is your go-to gadget.

There is no standard direction for choosing hive tools since they come in different forms and sizes. It's wise to have a few styles to cater to various tasks. And let's be honest, hive tools often tend to go missing when you need them the most—so having a backup is always a good idea!

You might ask yourself, "How do I pick the right hive tool?" Consider factors like the blade's shape, size, and slope. Some hive tools feature a combination of shapes—a flat blade for prying and lifting, a curved blade for leverage and scraping, and hooks for pulling out a frame. The size is mainly down to personal preference and the task at hand. Typically, an all-around good size is between eight and ten inches long. The width of the blade is another consideration. A thinner blade can squeeze into small gaps between boxes, while a thicker blade provides more strength for prying.

Mastering the hive tool is an art form. The most important thing is to be gentle and disturb the bees as little as possible. Whether opening the hive, removing frames, or carrying out maintenance, the hive tool is your trusty companion. And don't forget, always clean your hive tool after use. This keeps the tool in tip-top condition and helps prevent the spread of diseases.

Frame Lifter

Frame Lifter/Credit: Sauce Reques (www.shutterstock.com)

Hive inspections are a vital part of beekeeping. During these inspections, you'll frequently have to remove a frame from the box to inspect the brood. A healthy brood pattern is a clear indicator of a thriving colony. But lifting frames isn't always a walk in the park! Frames can be weighty, and propolis can cause them to stick to the box. While a hive tool can help pry the frame out, a frame lifter offers a more streamlined solution.

So, what's a frame lifter? It is a tool for extracting a frame from a honey super or brood box. It allows you, the beekeeper, to securely hold a frame with one hand, freeing up the other hand to inspect the brood. When used, the tool clamps down and locks onto the frame. Springs in the handle enable the beekeeper to open and release the grip quickly. It's a highly effective tool that simplifies hive inspections and speeds up the process.

A frame lifter is arguably the easiest way to extract frames from the box. You can first loosen the frame using a hive tool, then use the frame lifter to lift it out, effortlessly. The secure grip means you don't have to be concerned about accidentally dropping frames, allowing the other hand to be free for inspection or performing other tasks.

When it comes to choosing a frame lifter, comfort is vital. Look for one with a comfortable handle. Some handles are crafted from wood, while others are made of steel. Also, ensure that the frame lifter is robustly constructed. They're typically made out of steel, and are very strong and durable.

Finding a frame grip in a regular hardware store might be a challenge. You might have better luck in a farm equipment shop. However, the internet is probably your best chance of purchase. The advantage of online shopping is access to the wide range of models available. Plus, to assist you in making a well-informed choice, take note of customer reviews.

Bee Brush

Bee Brush/Credit: Kzenon(www.shutterstock.com)

The bee brush is a real lifesaver when interacting with your bees, especially when you're not using other methods like fume boards. The bee brush is also your go-to tool when extracting honey from the supers, or when the bees cluster.

When you're in the market for a bee brush, there are three main aspects to keep in mind:

- Bristle Material
- Handle Material
- Brush Size

The bristle material is of utmost importance. Pig hair, horse hair, or synthetic materials are commonly used to make bristles. Horse and pig hair brushes are gentle, with horse hair brushes being the softer. On the other hand, synthetic bristles are soft, easy to clean, and long-lasting. They're not a risk for the bees and the hive, and many beekeepers have used them without any issues for many years.

The handle of the bee brush can be made from wood or plastic. Wooden handles have a stylish look and are biodegradable. Plastic handles, while not biodegradable, are durable and safe for the bees. However, brightly colored plastic handles might disturb the bees. Bees can't see red, so red would be a good choice if you prefer a brightly colored brush.

The size of the brush is also important. A typical bee brush is 14 to 16 inches long. A smaller brush might not effectively brush off the bees, while a long brush could be cumbersome.

Utilizing goose or turkey feathers is a preference of some beekeepers who want to keep things natural. However, brushing the bees off when honey sticks to the feathers can be difficult. Therefore, it's a good idea to have a gentle-bristled bee brush for your tasks, and you could always have a few feathers in your tool bag as a backup.

Beekeeping Protective Clothing

Beekeeping Clothing/Credit: 24K-Production(www.shutterstock.com)

It's time to turn our attention to a critical component in beekeeping—protective clothing! Let's face it, bees do sting. You might have seen videos of seasoned beekeepers on YouTube, managing their hives with minimal or no sting protection. But remember, these beekeepers have honed their skills over the years, learning the art of interacting with bees to minimize stings, recognizing when to retreat—and possibly even building immunity to bee venom.

It's wise to don protective gear until you've gained enough experience to handle bees effectively, minimize stings, and understand your body's reaction to bee venom. The protective clothing for beekeeping includes veils to shield your eyes and face, beekeeping suits and jackets to protect most of your body, gloves for your hands, and boots to cover your feet and ankles. The level of protective clothing you choose to wear will hinge on your comfort level and the nature of your interaction with the bees. One key piece of advice is not to leave the acquisition of your initial protective gear until the last moment. Before purchasing, you'll want to ensure the gear fits well and is comfortable. In the following sections, we'll look at each piece of protective clothing, providing insights and guidance to help you make informed decisions. So, let's get started!

Beekeeping Veils

This fine mesh head covering, made of wire, or fabric like tulle, is designed to shield your face and eyes from bee stings while causing minimal obstruction of your vision. As you grow more accustomed to your buzzing friends, you might feel the urge to interact with them without full protective gear. However, it's *always* a smart move to keep your veil on. Even though bee stings to the eye are rare, they can be quite dangerous. Why take the risk, right? Because your head and face are the most exposed areas, defensive bees are known to target them.

Now, let's explore the different types of veils you can choose from:

- **Round Veils:** Offering a panoramic view, these veils have at most one seam at the back. The 360° mesh ensures excellent ventilation. They are designed to be worn with a helmet or hat, usually sold separately. Some round veils have drawstrings or elastic at the bottom for a snug fit. Others have zippers that can be used to fasten them to bee suits.

- **Alexander Veils:** A variant of round veils, these come with an elastic headband and a cloth top. You don't need a separate hat or helmet, but many beekeepers prefer wearing a cap underneath for added comfort.

- **Square Veils:** Also known as folding veils, these fit over a helmet or hat. The multiple seams keep the veil away from your face, allowing a wide field of vision. Plus, they can be folded flat for easy storage.

- **Fencing Veils:** Also referred to as hooded veils, these attach to a bee suit or jacket, usually through a zip. The mesh section allows for front and partial side vision. However, they offer less airflow than other veils due to the lack of mesh at the back.

- **Pull-Over Veils:** These provide additional protection by combining the veil with a vest or shoulder covering.

Choosing the right veil is your personal decision. Rest assured, if you buy from a reputable supplier or manufacturer, you'll get a quality product, no matter what you choose. For beginners, wearing protection when working with hives is advisable. The most practical option would be a fencing veil attached with a zipper to a beekeeping suit or jacket. If you're more daring, a round or square veil with a helmet or hat could be a good fit. As you grow accustomed to the apiary, any of these veils will serve you well.

Beekeeping Suits and Jackets

When it comes to beekeeping, your safety is paramount. This is where beekeeping suits and jackets come into the picture. These protective outfits are designed to shield your body from potential bee stings, offering a layer of security as you interact with bees. With a wide array of styles and price points, finding the one that fits your needs and budget is essential.

A beekeeping suit is an all-in-one garment that provides full-body coverage from your ankles to your neck and wrists. It's like your personal suit of armor against bee stings. Conversely, a beekeeping jacket covers your upper body, offering a less comprehensive but often more convenient option. The choice between the two often comes down to personal preference and the intensity of your beekeeping activities.

Several factors must be considered when hunting for a beekeeping suit or jacket. The fabric should be sturdy enough to prevent a bee's stinger from reaching your skin yet flexible enough to allow easy movement. Suits and jackets of the highest quality are made from cotton or a cotton-polyester combination. For those hot summer days, ventilated suits and jackets made from layers of breathable materials like polyester or vinyl are a godsend.

Steer clear of cheap, flimsy cotton clothing that offers minimal protection. The wrists and ankles on suits, and the wrist and waist openings on jackets, should be snug, with Velcro or elastic closures to keep bees out! Thumb loops are a nifty feature that stops sleeves from creeping up your arm.

Metal zippers tend to outlast plastic ones, but they have a higher price tag. Check the manufacturer's sizing guide before ordering to avoid the hassle of returns. Your protective clothing should offer plenty of room for movement. Extra features like sealed pockets can be handy for carrying tools and other essentials.

The hood is another crucial element. It should feature a fine, non-glare mesh for clear visibility and enough space to keep the mesh away from your face. A Velcro-secured flap over the zipper ensures complete protection.

While top-quality protective clothing tends to come with a higher price tag, choosing more affordable gear is perfectly fine, make sure it offers sufficient protection.

I recommend kicking off with a full beekeeping suit for those just starting out as beekeepers. This will give you the confidence to work with the hives without disturbing the colony. A full beekeeping suit is non-negotiable if you're in an area known for Africanized Honey Bees, which are notably more defensive than typical Western Honey Bees.

If you choose a beekeeping jacket, pair it with jeans or overalls to protect your legs. Boots, Velcro, duct tape, or leg straps can help keep bees from venturing up your pant legs.

Beekeeping protective clothing is traditionally white, as light colors are cooler in the summer sun and less likely to provoke bees. However, more color options have become available over the years.

Beekeeping Gloves: A Must-Have for Every Beekeeper

Beekeeping is a hands-on activity, quite literally. Your hands are your primary tools, lifting, moving, and inspecting. But they're also the most exposed to potential bee stings during hive inspections. That's where beekeeping gloves come in handy.

You might think, "Great, I'll just get the thickest gloves I can find!" But here's the catch—the thicker the gloves, the harder it is to handle your hive tools and frames. It's a delicate balance between protection and dexterity. Some tasks might feel like trying to thread a needle while wearing mittens!

While many seasoned beekeepers are confident to work barehanded, I strongly advise beginners to start with gloves. As you acquire greater experience and feel more at ease with your bees, you may decide not to use them anymore.

So, what makes a good pair of beekeeping gloves?

First off, they should cover your forearm, not just your hands. You'll likely wear them with a suit or jacket, so ventilated extensions are a plus for comfort.

Secondly, they need to fit well. Unlike your suit or jacket, which should be roomy, your gloves should fit snugly to prevent them from sliding off.

There are a few different options in terms of materials. Cowhide leather gloves offer the most protection due to their thickness, but they can be clunky. Goatskin gloves, on the other hand, are thinner and more flexible, making them easier to use. Make sure they are still sufficiently thick to block a stinger, though.

Nitrile gloves are another option. While they're not thick enough to prevent a sting outright, they vcan deter bees from stinging. Plus, the gloves can prevent the stinger from embedding in your skin if a bee does sting. They're usually shorter, so make sure your wrists are covered. They offer the same agility as being barehanded, and keep your hands clean.

Boots for Beekeeping

Beekeeping is obviously not just about the bees and the honey—it's also about ensuring your safety, from head to toe. Now, let's talk about the "toe" part. You might wonder, "Why would bees be interested in my feet?" Well, under normal circumstances, they wouldn't be. However, imagine dropping a bee-filled frame unintentionally close to your feet. Suddenly, those buzzing critters might take an unexpected interest in your ankles!

So, what's the solution? Boots, of course! But wait, before you rush off to buy a pair of fancy, specialized beekeeping boots, let me stop you right there. You don't need them. Some boots are available in pristine white or adorned with adorable bee emblems, but they aren't necessary. It would be best if you had a pair of boots that are comfortable, practical, and suitable for outdoor work. Think along the lines of agricultural-type boots. For instance, we swear by muck boots. They're comfortable, durable, and perfect for a day out in the apiary.

But here's a little nugget of wisdom for you. Bees are curious creatures, and one might decide to explore the inside of your boot. Consider tucking your pant leg into your boots to prevent this unexpected visit. It's a small adjustment but can save you from a potential sting.

So, the next time you head out to your hive(s), remember to leave your sandals behind. Embrace your trusty boots, and step into the world of bees with confidence and the right protection.

The Beekeeper's Toolbox

Beekeeper's Toolbox/Credit: kosolovskyy(www.shutterstock.com)

As a beekeeper, you now know that preparation is key. You don't want to be caught short without a vital tool when you're out in the field, ready to approach your hive. This is where your beekeeper's toolbox comes into play.

This indispensable kit is packed with all the necessary items for a successful hive inspection, ensuring you're always ready for action.

Think of the beekeeper's toolbox as your treasure chest, filled with beekeeping essentials. The heart of the toolbox is occupied by the fundamental tools of the trade: a hive tool and a frame lifter. These are the bread and butter for any beekeeper, aiding in easy access to the hive.

The contents of the toolbox however do extend beyond the basics. You'll find matches safely stored in a waterproof container, ready to reignite your charcoal smoker when required. A small spray bottle filled with rubbing alcohol is also a handy addition. When conducting inspections, this can remove pollen or honey from your hands. Just remember—the bees should never be sprayed with this!

Another unexpected yet useful item is baby powder. Use it to clean your hands before inspections. It facilitates keeping hands clean, and the bees also appreciate the scent.

Disposable latex gloves can be a game-changer when the season is in full swing and propolis is abundant. Easy to find at any drugstore or supermarket, these gloves allow you to maintain dexterity while keeping your hands clean amongst the notoriously sticky propolis. However, bear in mind that they don't offer protection against stings.

A pencil with a notebook is also crucial for recording observations during inspections, noting completed tasks, and identifying what might need attention during your next visit. If you prefer, you can opt for one of the innovative new beekeeping apps.

A hammer and a selection of frame and hive nails are useful for quick repairs. A multipurpose knife with small pliers, screwdrivers, or blades can prove invaluable.

Lastly, don't forget to include reading glasses (if you need them) or a magnifier, and a flashlight. Spotting eggs can be a challenge without a bit of assistance.

Your Hive is Ready; What's Next?

Well, we've done it! We've described the intricate world of beekeeping equipment, dissected the complexities of the Langstroth hive, and introduced the essential tools that will be your trusty allies in this exciting practice.

By now, your beehive should stand proudly, a beacon of your dedication and hard work. It's a thrilling achievement, but remember, this is just the beginning. The real enchantment starts when your hive transforms into a bustling, lively home for your fuzzy, buzzing bees.

Here's a small pearl of wisdom for you to remember: timing is everything. Your beehive should be assembled, ready, and waiting to greet its new residents well before arrival. This foresight and preparation ensures that everything is in its rightful place and gives you plenty of time to tweak any last-minute details. As the saying goes, "Preparation is the key to success," and this couldn't be truer in beekeeping.

So, what's next? The bees, of course!

In the following chapter, we'll dive headfirst into the captivating world of bees. We'll guide you through introducing them to their new abode, caring for them, and ensuring they flourish in your meticulously prepared environment.

As we wrap up this chapter, take a minute to consider your signifcant progress. You've taken the initial steps into beekeeping life and are well on your way to becoming a seasoned beekeeper. The next chapter is set to be *even more* exhilarating, so let's continue this remarkable journey together!

CHAPTER 5

Unveiling the Mysteries of Bee Anatomy

This chapter will give you a good understanding of the intricate anatomy, societal hierarchy, and fascinating life cycle of these diligent little insects.

Firstly, we'll navigate through the physical features of bees, from their multifaceted eyes to their pollen-carrying corbicula. Each part of a bee's body serves a unique function, contributing to the survival and efficiency of their communal headquarters, the hive. Understanding such details will give us a profound appreciation for these incredible creatures.

Next, we'll meet the three distinct kinds of bees that inhabit a hive: the industrious worker bees, the male drones, and the all-important queen bee. Each of these types has responsibilities and physical traits that set them apart. We'll delve into the specifics of each caste, offering a detailed understanding of their unique roles within the hive.

Then, we'll journey through the captivating life cycle of bees. From the laying of an egg to the emergence of a fully-grown bee, we'll guide you through each stage of development, illuminating the miraculous metamorphosis within the hive.

Lastly, we'll uncover a bee colony's complex communication systems and work organization. Bees are sophisticated communicators, combining scent signals with intricate "dance" movements. We'll explore how such methods of communication contribute to the smooth running of the hive.

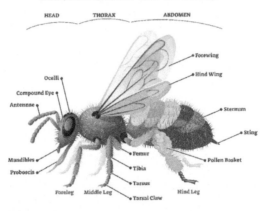

Anatomy of a Bee/Credit: VectorMine(www.shutterstock.com)

The head, thorax, and abdomen are the three major parts of a bee's body. Each section is a hub of activity, supporting the functions of the attached body parts. The head houses the eyes, antennae, and mandibles, serving as the bee's command center. The thorax, the middle part, is the powerhouse, supporting the legs and wings for movement and flight. The abdomen, the rear part, is home to the reproductive organs, wax glands, and stinger. The bee's body is encased in an exoskeleton, a kind of "external skeleton" covered in a layer of hair. This hair is not just for show—it aids in pollen collection and helps the bee regulate its body temperature.

The Bee's Head

Let's take a moment to appreciate the bee's head, an intricate hub of sensory and processing capabilities. This is the bee's command center, where all the essential decisions are made.

Antennae: The Bee's Multifaceted Sensory Tool

The antennae, those protruding stalk-like features on a bee's head, are nothing short of a sensory powerhouse. They are the bee's primary sense organs for taste, touch, and smell, as well as a special kind of hearing. Each antenna, segmented and featuring an elbow-like joint, is a marvel of nature's design. The antennae are equipped with mechanoreceptors, which respond to touch and the movement of air particles. This mechanism allows bees to detect sound, despite not having conventional ears as we know them. Moreover, the antennae are packed with odor receptors, providing bees with an incredibly refined sense of smell.

Compound Eyes: A Unique Perspective

The large, captivating eyes of a bee are known as compound eyes. Each of these eyes is composed of many units, known as ommatidia. These units each capture a separate image, which is then sent to the brain to be pieced together into a single, coherent image. This process also enables bees to see the world in polarized light, similar to the effect of sunglasses. Bees' distinctive vision helps them navigate and shields their eyes against the harsh glare of day.

Simple Eyes: Detecting the Invisible

Bees have three simple eyes in addition to their compound eyes. These eyes, each with a single lens, detect UV light. This ability to perceive UV light allows bees to spot the location of pollen, guiding them to their food source.

Proboscis and Mandibles: Essential Tools

The bee's tongue, or proboscis, is a soft and extendible instrument bees use to access flower centers and gather nectar. It also serves a grooming function. On the other hand, the bee's strong mandibles guard the remainder of the mouthparts. The mandibles of worker bees are smoothed to aid in wax production.

The Brain: The Command Center

Tucked away from view is the brain. The bee's brain can comprehend information and make decisions despite its diminutive size. Bee brains are less than two cubic millimeters in volume! The brain comprises a series of lobes and houses glands that produce secretions to create wax and royal jelly.

Thorax

The thorax of a bee, the middle segment of its body, is designed primarily for movement. Here, you'll find the bee's six legs and two pairs of wings, all controlled by the muscles housed within the thorax. These muscles are responsible for the very rapid, almost shimmering movement of the wings that we can see.

Guess what? A honey bee flies at a top speed of 15 miles per hour! This is all thanks to the bee's wings, arranged in two pairs. The larger forewings and the smaller hind wings work together to enable flight, with a propeller-like twist during the upward and downward strokes. Bees can travel up to five kilometers from their hive thanks to the fast-pulsating muscles in their thorax, which further increase their speed. This significantly expands their pollination area, making them invaluable contributors to our ecosystem.

Let's not forget about the bee's legs, divided into six segments for remarkable flexibility. Each leg has a unique function. The front legs are designed to clean the antennae, whereas the pollen basket part on the back legs is intended to collect pollen. The legs also have sticky pads to help the bee land on slippery surfaces, and claws for gripping. Interestingly, bees can taste with the tips of their legs, thanks to the presence of taste receptors.

The worker bee's back legs are a marvel in their own right. They come equipped with specialized combs and a pollen press to brush, gather, pack, and transport propolis and pollen to the hive. An intriguing feature on the bee's hind legs called the pollen basket is made up of hairs that enclose a concave area. A bee grooms herself as she visits a flower, brushing pollen from her body toward her legs. After that, the pollen is placed inside the pollen basket. Some nectar is mixed in to ensure the pollen stays together during flight. Finally, the pollen basket's hairs keep everything in place.

Abdomen

A bee's abdomen is a marvel of design, playing host to various functions vital to the bee's survival and the overall health of the hive. Its complex structure houses reproductive organs, wax glands, and the stinger, each with its unique role.

In the queen bee, the abdomen is the location of the spermatheca, a specialized organ that stores sperm collected during her nuptial flights.

Throughout the queen's lifespan, this sperm is utilized to fertilize eggs. The queen's ovaries begin to produce eggs when she is just 1–2 weeks old, and she continues to lay eggs until her demise.

The drones have a rather dramatic and fatal mating process. Their reproductive organ is only used once! After mating, the drone's reproductive organs are torn from his body, leading to his death. Interestingly enough, the drone's ejaculation is so forceful that the human ear can detect it!

In contrast, female worker bees have four scales that produce wax on the underside of their abdomen. These scales release liquid wax, which when exposed to air solidifies into thin scales. The responsibility of wax production within the hive falls to the younger worker bees, who can produce about eight scales in 12 hours. The colony must create approximately 1,000 such scales to produce just one gram of wax.

The stinger—the most infamous part of a bee's anatomy—is also in the abdomen. It's the bee's primary defense mechanism. Bees generally sting only when perceiving a threat since doing so typically implies their death. The stinger varies among worker bees, queens, and drones. Workers have a barbed stinger that, when lodged in human skin, results in the worker's death. Queens, however, have a smooth stinger and can sting multiple times without losing it, although queen bee stings are rare. Male drones, however, are harmless as they do not possess a stinger.

In the following sections, we will explore the specific roles and characteristics of worker bees, drones, and queen bees. Understanding these differences is critical to appreciating the intricate and efficient society that bees create within their societies, their hives.

How do Bees communicate?

Bees are not solitary creatures; they live in highly organized societies and must communicate effectively to survive and thrive. The following section will explore how bees interact, including using pheromones, a unique process called Trophallaxis, the famous waggle dance, and even acoustic signals. Each method of communication is crucial in the hive's daily operations and the colony's overall success.

Pheromones

In the buzzing world of bees, communication is a vital aspect of survival, and they've mastered this through the use of pheromones. These chemical signals are the secret language of the hive, used by every member—from the queen to the workers, drones, and even the developing brood. Pheromones are the invisible threads that weave the colony together, triggering behaviors and ensuring the hive operates like a well-oiled machine.

Pheromones are produced by several glands scattered throughout the bee's body. These include the Nasanov glands inside the abdomen, the mandibular glands in the jaws, and the Koschevnikov and Dufour glands next to the stinger. Even the tiny footprints that bees leave contain pheromones, thanks to the Amhart glands.

Among bees' myriad of pheromones, there are a few that stand out—such as the alarm pheromones, which are like the colony's emergency sirens. When a threat like a wasp or a hornet approaches the hive, guard bees release these pheromones, rallying their sisters to mount a defense. They spread the alarm by raising their abdomens, pointing their stingers outwards, and fanning their wings.

The queen uses a cocktail of pheromones to generate the "queen signal". This signal and other pheromones help maintain order in the hive, ensuring the worker bees carry out their tasks efficiently.

The Nasonov gland pheromone, produced by worker bees, also plays a crucial role in the hive's activities. It's used during swarming, recruiting foragers, and even selecting new queens. This complex chemical communication system is just one of the many ways bees collaborate.

Trophallaxis

Bees also have a unique communication method known as Trophallaxis. This might sound like a big, complicated word, but it simply means the process of transferring food and other fluids from one bee's mouth to another bee's mouth. It's a give-and-take scenario, with worker bees acting as the giver and the receiver. They share sustenance not only among themselves but also with the queen and the drones.

But Trophallaxis isn't just a food-sharing exercise. It's also a crucial form of communication among the hive. When worker bees engage in Trophallaxis, they're not just passing on food but also information. They share the contents of their crops and sometimes even the products of their head glands. This exchange is thought to inform other bees about the food situation in the hive, including the quality and quantity available. Also, they use it to transmit the colony's pollen requirements. So, in a nutshell, Trophallaxis is a dual-purpose process—it's about sharing food and exchanging vital intelligence.

Acoustic Signals

Picture a hive as a symphony orchestra, with each bee playing its part in creating a harmonious melody. The sounds they produce, such as piping, tooting, quacking, and even hissing, are not just noises. They're a complex language that aids in preserving peace and order inside the hive.

Like the conductor of this orchestra, the queen bee uses these sounds to manage her colony. For example, a newly emerged queen "toots" to announce her presence, while rival queens respond with "quacking". This acoustic dialogue is a sophisticated form of communication that signals the presence of a healthy and active queen.

The queen, however, isn't the only one making noise. Worker bees also use acoustic signals in various situations. Worker bees may start piping or hissing when the hive is threatened. This hissing serves as a warning to possible predators. Furthermore, worker bees use piping as a signal to swarm, encouraging their fellow bees to prepare for departure. They also use a unique "stop signal" —a short pipe or "beep"—to interrupt the waggle dance of a nestmate recruiting foragers to a nectar source.

These acoustic signals are a vital part of the intricate communication system that allows bees to work together as a highly efficient unit. So, the next time you hear the buzz of a hive, remember, it's not just noise—it's a conversation—many conversations!

"Waggle" Dance

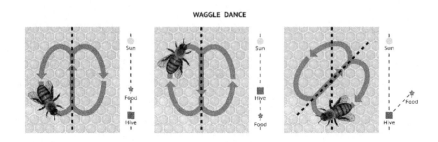

WAGGLE DANCE

Waggle Dance/Credit: J. Marini(www.shutterstock.com)

Yes, you heard it right! Bees, especially honey bees, are famous for their intricate dance moves. But these moves aren't just for show; they're a complex form of communication within the hive. This dance, often known as the "waggle dance," is a wonder of nature and a testament to the intelligence of these small, hardworking creatures.

Foraging worker honey bees use the waggle dance as a special means of communication. They use it to share vital information with their hive mates. This dance isn't a random burst of energy; it's a carefully coded message that provides accurate directions to a food source, a water source, or even a potential new home.

The dance routine involves a series of movements, including a straight run with the bee shaking its body in a lateral motion and a return run to the starting point. This sequence is repeated several times, with the bee often changing direction for each new run. The length of the waggle run is directly related to the distance to the food source or the new nest site. The more distant the target is, the more prolonged the waggle phase is.

The direction of the food supply in relation to the sun's position is indicated by the angle of the waggle run with respect to the vertical direction of the comb. If the bee runs straight up, the food source is in the sun's direction. If the run is at the right or left angle, the food source is the same angle to the right or left of the sun. How clever are our bees?!

Even more intriguing is the fact that bees consider the intensity of the wind to factor into their dance. For example, When there is a strong headwind, the bee will dance as if the food source is farther away. This level of detail in communication is quite remarkable and shows the deep complexity of bee society.

When a swarm is looking for a new home, scout bees perform the waggle dance on the swarm, walking over other bees while communicating the potential nest site's location. This collective decision-making process shows the power of the hive mind and the bees' spirit of cooperation. The most popular sites, indicated by the number of bees dancing, are usually chosen as the new home.

The waggle dance is a captivating aspect of bee communication, showcasing their incredible ability to convey complex information through movement.

The Intricate Society of Bees: Understanding their Roles and Life Cycles

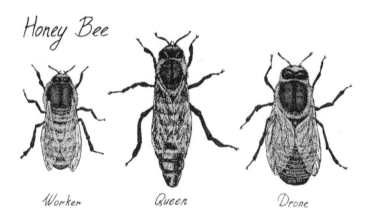

Bee Types/Credit: Artophoto(www.shutterstock.com)

Bees live in highly organized societies, each with a specific role to play in the survival and success of the hive. We will now explore the three main castes or types of bees that make up a colony: the worker bees, the drones, and the queen bee.

Queen Bee: The Beehive's Soul and Heart

The queen bee, the heart and lifeblood of the hive, is a creature of immense importance in the world of bees, and hence the planet. She's the largest bee in the colony, boasting a long, elegant body—she's the only female bee in the hive with fully developed ovaries. Her main roles? To emit chemical scents that help maintain the colony's unity, and lay eggs. And boy, does she lay eggs! She's a veritable egg-laying powerhouse, capable of producing over 1,500 eggs daily, each laid at 30-second intervals. That is more eggs than her whole body weighs!

The queen doesn't go about her duties alone—she's always accompanied by a group of attendant bees who cater to her every need. You see, the queen bee can't actually take care of herself. She cannot care for herself, groom, or even leave the hive more than the few times she flies out to mate with drones. Her attendants care for all her basic needs, allowing her to focus on her primary duty: laying eggs.

Now, you might be wondering about the queen's stinger. Yes, she does have one, but a queen seldom stings a beekeeper. The queen's stinger is primarily used to dispatch rival queens that might emerge or be introduced into the hive. The queen bee can live for several years, but many beekeepers replace their queens every year or two to ensure the hive remains the most productive and healthy.

But the queen's role isn't just about laying eggs—she's also crucial in maintaining the stability and unity of the (very populous and busy) colony. Her presence in the hive is always noticeable, with worker bees constantly attending to her. The queen produces a variety of pheromones that attract the workers and stimulate activities like brood-rearing, foraging, and comb-building. These pheromones, chemical signals, reassure the colony that all is well and the queen is present and hard at work. These pheromone levels decrease as the queen gets older, alerting the colony that the time has come to install a new, younger more productive queen.

Worker Bees: The Unsung Heroes of the Hive

Let's contemplate with appreciation the worker bees—the tireless toilers that form the backbone of the hive. These bees are all females, like the queen, but they are distinct in several ways. They have pollen baskets on their rear legs, allowing them to carry pollen back to the hive, and smaller, shorter abdomens. Interestingly, worker bees, despite being females, cannot lay fertile eggs because they never mate and therefore lack the sperm necessary to fertilize eggs. Although they are capable of laying eggs and have functioning ovaries, their eggs are infertile.

Worker bees are equipped with a unique stinger, which is three-shafted and barbed, much like a fish hook. This design ensures that when a worker bee stings a mammal, the stinger, venom sack, and a significant part of the bee's gut remain in the victim, a self-sacrificing act to protect the colony. However, when stinging other insects, the worker bee's stinger doesn't get stuck, allowing them to sting multiple times in defense of their home.

The lifespan of a worker bee is relatively short, typically six weeks during the active season. Yet worker bees may survive for four to eight months during the less busy winter. Rich in protein, these winter workers are sometimes called "Fat bees."

The phrase, "Busy as a bee" is a fitting description for worker bees. They are the definition of dedication and cooperation. They perform many tasks, and their roles change as they age, with more complex and demanding tasks gradually assigned to them. The tasks are usually set, but they can overlap, and a worker bee may switch roles if there's an urgent need within the colony.

The Life Cycle of Worker Bees: A Detailed Exploration

The story begins in a meticulously cleaned cell, the birthplace of our worker bee. The first three days of her life are spent in a flurry of activity as she takes on the role of a housekeeper. Her first task? Cleaning her birthplace, preparing it for the next cycle of life.

As the days pass, our worker bee transitions into the role of an undertaker, a role she will fulfill from the third to the 16th day of her life. This role is vital for the hive's health, as she removes deceased bees and disposes of them far from the hive, preventing the spread of disease.

From the fourth to the 12th day, she becomes a nurse, caring for her younger sisters. She feeds the larvae a nutritious blend of pollen, honey, and royal jelly, ensuring they grow strong and healthy. The duration of this role can vary, depending on the hive's needs and the urgency of other tasks.

Around the seventh day, some worker bees are chosen to serve the queen as royal attendants. They cater to her every need, from grooming to feeding and removing her waste. They also encourage the queen to continue laying eggs, ensuring the hive's future.

Our worker bee becomes a pantry stocker from the 12th to the 18th day. She collects nectar from returning foragers and stores it in designated cells. She adds enzymes to the nectar and fans the cells to evaporate the water content, turning the nectar into honey. She also packs pollen into other cells, creating a food source called "bee bread". She also helps control the hive's temperature and humidity during this period. She fans her wings to draw air into the hive, maintaining a constant temperature for the developing brood and aiding in the honey-curing process.

As her stay in the hive draws to a close, she assumes the job of a guard. From the 18th to the 21st day, she stands at the hive's entrance, checking each returning bee for a familiar scent. Only family members can pass, while intruders are bravely driven off.

Finally, as she reaches maturity, she ventures outside the hive to become a forager. This is her final role and perhaps the most dangerous. She collects pollen and nectar, risking her life for the colony's survival. Despite all the dangers and hardships, she works diligently until the end of her life. The spirit of selflessness and dedication defines the life of a worker bee.

The Intriguing Life and Role of Drone Bees

These bees, the colony's males, are often misunderstood due to their unique roles and characteristics. While they may be fewer in number compared to the industrious worker bees, their contribution to the hive is no less significant.

Drones are easily distinguishable from their counterparts. They are larger, with a stout, barrel-like shape, and their eyes are noticeably bigger, covering a significant portion of their head. This physical attribute often leads to misidentification, particularly among novice beekeepers. Unlike worker bees, drones do not have the equipment to gather food or contribute to the construction of the hive. They lack pollen baskets and wax-producing glands and don't have a stinger to defend the hive.

Despite these seemingly unproductive traits, drones play a pivotal role in the survival of bee species. When the current queen dies or has to be replaced, their main job is to mate with a fresh virgin queen from another colony. This mating ritual takes place in mid-air—at a 200 to 300 foot height—in a location known as the "Drone Congregation Area." This area can be far from the hive, often a mile or more. The drone's large eyes are instrumental in this scenario, helping them spot virgin queens on their nuptial flights.

However, the life of a drone bee is not all roses. Their primary function, mating, also signals their end. After mating, a significant part of their internal anatomy is torn away, leading to their death. This is because their sex organ fits into the queen like a key into a lock, ensuring effective sperm discharge.

As the seasons change and the mating season ends, drones are no longer welcome in the hive. Their large appetites would consume significant food during the challenging winter months. As the nectar-producing season ends in cooler climates, worker bees regularly remove drones from the hive. This expulsion marks the end of the beekeeping season for the year in areas experiencing cold winters.

The Cycle of Life: A Bee's Journey

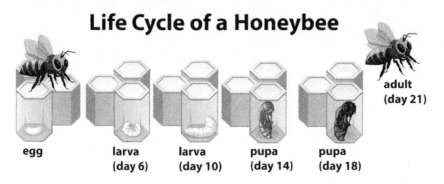

Life Cycle of a Honeybee

adult
(day 21)

egg

larva
(day 6)

larva
(day 10)

pupa
(day 14)

pupa
(day 18)

Credit: BlueRingMedia(www.shutterstock.com)

As winter's chill gives way to the warmth of spring, the hive stirs from its slumber. The queen, nestled safely within the cluster of adult bees, is fed a protein-rich substance known as royal jelly. This nourishment triggers the queen to begin laying eggs, setting the stage for the next generation of bees.

Honey bees undergo a four-stage life cycle: egg, larva, pupa, and adult. Interestingly, the time it takes for a bee to develop varies depending on its role in the hive. Queens emerge after 16 days, worker bees after 21 days, and drones, the males of the hive, after 24 days.

The journey begins with the queen laying an egg. These tiny eggs are barely 1.7 millimeters long. Worker bees carefully clean and prepare each cell where the queen lays an egg. The queen will either deposit a fertilized egg that will grow into a worker bee or an unfertilized egg that will turn into a drone, according to the size of the cell.

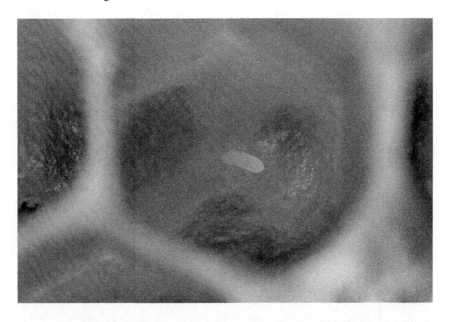

Bee Eggs/Credit: Kuttelvaserova Stuchelova(www.shutterstock.com)

The egg becomes a larva three days after being laid. These small, white larvae resemble tiny grubs curled up in the cells. They grow rapidly, shedding their skin five times as they consume a steady diet of royal jelly and later, a mixture of honey and pollen known as bee bread. Within five days, they grow to be 1,500 times their original size.

When the larvae reach the appropriate size, worker bees seal the cell with a capping of beeswax. The larvae subsequently enter the pupa stage by creating a cocoon around themselves. This is where the true transformation occurs, hidden from view under the wax capping. If you could peek inside, you'd see the pupa developing the familiar features of an adult bee, including legs, eyes, and wings. The bee's body develops fine hair, and the colour of its eyes shifts from pink to purple to black. After 12 days, the adult bee is ready to emerge and join the hive.

While most fertilized eggs become worker bees, some are destined for a different path. They develop into the queen bee. But that's a story for another time…

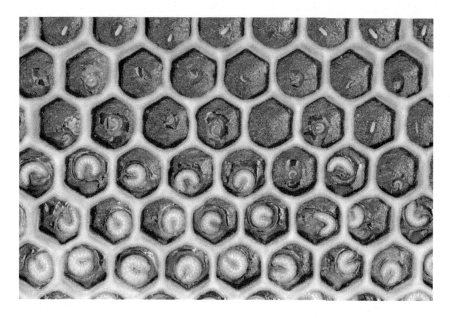

Bee Eggs and Larvae/Credit: Megan Kobe(www.shutterstock.com)

The Queen Bee: A Journey from Birth to Reign

The queen bee's story begins as a fertilized egg, hanging in a vertical egg cell built by the worker bees when the previous queen becomes weak. Upon hatching into a larva, she is nourished with huge amounts of royal jelly, a nutrient-dense substance produced by worker bees. Although all larval bees are fed some royal jelly, the queens develop functioning ovaries through consuming large amounts of royal jelly. This royal diet, which continues throughout her larval stage, sets her apart from her worker bee sisters and triggers her development into a queen.

The queen bee's transformation is swift, taking a mere 16 days, in contrast to the 21 days for a worker bee and 24 days for a drone. The initial two days see the egg standing upright at the base of the cell. By the third day, the egg hatches, and the larva begins to feast on the royal jelly. From the fourth to the eighth day, the larva continues to be nourished with royal jelly as the cell is extended and reshaped. On the ninth day, the queen cell is sealed, and the queen-to-be, now a pupa, consumes the stored royal jelly and spins a cocoon. Between the tenth and 14th day, the queen undergoes a metamorphosis into her adult form. It's vital during this time that the queen's cell is left undisturbed, as the queen is extremely delicate and could be harmed. By the 15th day, the queen is less vulnerable—and can be relocated to a queenless nucleus hive if necessary.

Finally, on the 16th day, the queen emerges from her cell. Environmental factors such as temperature can affect this timeline, potentially causing the queen to emerge a day or two later.

Once it emerges, the virgin queen needs just a few days to grow and mature. Her glands develop, and her wings enlarge and dry. She then spends a few more days flying and mating before settling down to lay eggs. Two to three weeks can pass between emergence and egg-laying.

The virgin queen bee's mating process is a unique spectacle. She mates in the air, with multiple drones in the drone congregation areas, and she then stores the resulting sperm in an organ in her abdomen known as the spermatheca. This organ nourishes the sperm, keeping it alive as long as the queen is productive.

Genetic variety is maintained in the colony by the queen bee's mating behavior. Since she mates with multiple drones, the bees in the colony are a mix of full and half-sisters. This diversity is critical for the survival and health of the colony, and ultimately the species.

If severe weather or other factors prevent the queen bee from mating, she will eventually start laying eggs. However, drones will be produced because these eggs are not fertilized. The hives of bees have created a system that fosters genetic variation and lessens the likelihood of inbreeding.

The queen travels significantly further distances to drone gathering locations than frequented by her drones, lowering the likelihood of her pairing with a drone belonging to her hive.

Bee Larvae and Pupae/Credit: bamgraphy(www.shutterstock.com)

CHAPTE 6
From Bee Selection to Hive Installation

Well, here we are! You've toured with us through part of the fascinating world of bee life, delving into their intricate anatomy and marveling at the complex social structure that underpins their colonies. Now, you're standing on the very threshold of an exciting new chapter in your bee journey—it's time to roll down your sleeves and prepare to welcome your buzzing fuzzy companions into their new abode!

In this chapter, we will cover some critical decisions and preparations to set the stage for your beekeeping venture. We'll start by exploring the diverse types of honey bees you might consider raising. Each type has unique traits and advantages; we'll help you understand these nuances so you can make an informed choice.

We'll also shed light on the various ways of acquiring your bees. Whether you're considering purchasing a package, opting for a nuc—or even daring to catch a swarm—we'll discuss it all.

And, of course, before your bees make their grand entrance, there's some groundwork to be done. We'll guide you through the essential steps to take and prepare for your bees' arrival. This includes setting up their new home, ensuring it's ready and a safe and comfortable haven for its new residents.

Finally, the moment of truth—introducing your bees to their new home. It might seem daunting, especially if you're brand new to beekeeping, but fear not! With our step-by-step guidance and a dash of patience and courage, this will transform into a truly rewarding experience!

Choosing Your Bees

Like dogs, chickens and horses, bees come in various breeds, each with unique traits. These traits include everything from temperament and productivity to disease resistance and color. While the environment can influence these traits to some extent, the genetic makeup of a bee colony is the primary determinant of these characteristics.

Beekeepers have known for centuries that different breeds of bees have unique traits that can either be a boon or a bane. Whether you're looking to maximize honey production, improve pollination, breed bees, or want a resilient colony, understanding these traits is crucial to achieving your goals.

So, what do we mean by "bee stock"? It's a term that describes a group of bees characterized by a specific combination of traits. These groupings can be divided based on race, species, geography, population, or, in a commercial enterprise, even a particular breeding line. Think of it as the bee equivalent of horse pedigrees, with lines of heredity that can be traced back hundreds of years.

It's important to note that while you can purchase bees from specific races, maintaining the "purity" of the stock can be challenging due to the nature of honey bee reproduction and queen mating.

When choosing a bee stock, there are four key characteristics: gentleness, productivity, disease tolerance, and adaptability to local weather conditions. In this chapter we'll explore these factors more, helping you decide the type of bees you'd like to raise!

Italian Bees: The Golden Standard of Honey Production

When it comes to honey bees, the Italian variety, scientifically known as *Apis mellifera ligustica* holds a special place in the hearts of many beekeepers. Originally from Italy, these golden-yellow beauties made their way to the United States in the mid-19th century and have become a favorite among hobbyists as well as commercial beekeepers. Their popularity stems from their prolific breeding habits, impressive honey production, gentle demeanor and low-swarming tendencies.

However, as with any breed, Italian bees come with their own set of challenges. While beneficial for honey production, their extended brood cycles can lead to rapid food resource depletion. This trait, coupled with their propensity to rob weaker hives, requires beekeepers to monitor their colonies fairly closely.

Furthermore, Italian bees are more susceptible to pests, leading to increased colony collapse rates. Despite these challenges, the Italian bee's overall productivity and availability make it an excellent choice for beekeepers at all levels of experience.

Russian Bees: The Hardy Survivors

We have the Russian honey bees on the other end of the spectrum. These bees, native to the Primorsky Krai region of Russia, were introduced to the United States in the late 20th century as a solution to increasing colony collapses due to parasites. Russian bees have demonstrated impressive resilience to varroa and tracheal mites, with studies showing significantly lower mite loads than other commercial stocks.

However, Russian bees are not without their quirks. Their brood rearing heavily depends on nectar and pollen flows, which can limit their productivity in less-than-ideal environments. Additionally, their availability is somewhat limited due to breeding constraints, making them a less accessible choice for novice beekeepers.

Russian bees also exhibit some unique behaviors. For instance, it's common to find a queen cell in a Russian bee colony at any given time, a trait not typically seen in other bee breeds. While Russian bees can be a bit more aggressive than their Italian counterparts, they offer a unique resilience to pests, making them an appealing choice for those willing to take on the challenge.

Carniolan Bees: The Gentle and Efficient Pollinators

Originating from the lush landscapes of Central and Eastern Europe, Carniolan bees (*Apis mellifera carnica*) have found a warm welcome among beekeepers across the United States.

One of the most striking features of Carniolan bees is their rapid spring buildup. This trait is a boon for beekeepers aiming to establish a strong colony in time for the summer bloom. Adding to their appeal is their gentle nature. They are known to be less defensive, making them a joy to handle, particularly for beginners in beekeeping.

Carniolan bees also have a long tongue. This allows them to access nectar from flowers like clover that other bee types might struggle with, broadening their nutritional range.

Their adaptability to colder climates is another feather in their cap. They form tight clusters during winter, conserving food and energy. However, their propensity to swarm due to their rapid early-year growth might require extra attention from the beekeeper. Nevertheless, their resilience in the face of fluctuating weather and harsh winters makes them a worthy choice for many.

Buckfast Bees: The Resilient Hybrids

The story of Buckfast Bees is a testament to the power of selective breeding. Born out of necessity at the Buckfast Abbey in Devon, United Kingdom, these bees answered a crisis caused by tracheal mites that decimated local bee populations in the early 20th century.

Buckfast bees are celebrated for resisting certain parasites and their exceptional foraging abilities. They are also less likely to swarm, a trait that makes them a bit of a rarity in the United States, and is appreciated by many beekeepers. However, they tend to inbreed over time, which can potentially reduce their resistance to pests.

Despite this, with careful management, a Buckfast bee colony can flourish for years without needing replacement. Their slightly increased defensive behavior is a small trade-off for their hardiness and longevity.

Caucasian Bees: Masters of Nectar Collection

Meet the Caucasian bees, known scientifically as *Apis mellifera caucasica*. These bees were once a favorite among American beekeepers, but their popularity has waned due to their lower honey production than other bee types. However, they still hold a special place in the hearts of some commercial pollinators, thanks to their unusually long tongues.

Like their Carniolan cousins, Caucasian bees are known for their gentle demeanor. They also have a slower colony buildup rate, which allows them to store honey more efficiently, filling one comb at a time. This trait can be a boon for beekeepers in colder climates, as it aids the bees in surviving the winter.

German Bees: The Resilient Pioneers

Next, we have the German bees, the European Dark Bee, or *Apis mellifera mellifera*. These bees were among the earliest bees introduced to the United States during colonial times and are native to Northern Eurasia. German bees are renowned for their resilience, often outlasting other bee types in harsh, cold winters. However, the popularity of this species has decreased due to their defensive nature and vulnerability to brood diseases including European and American foulbrood. Despite these challenges, some dedicated researchers and hobbyists are working to harness the hardiness of this subspecies through careful breeding and meticulous data tracking.

Africanized Bees: The Fearless Foragers

Finally, let's talk about the Africanized bees, often called "killer bees." Despite their African moniker, these bees were created in a lab in Brazil. The aim was to create a hybrid bee that was more resistant to pests and parasites and had higher honey production. Twenty-six experimental swarms, however, escaped confinement and spread throughout South America. Their presence is now reported also in Mexico and the Southern United States.

Despite their aggressive nature, Africanized bees have some redeeming qualities. They begin foraging earlier and usually generate more honey. Despite having a quicker reproductive rate, they maintain a lower colony size. Some beekeepers have worked successfully with these bees, capitalizing on their positive traits. However, the risks associated with handling such aggressive bees often outweigh the potential benefits, particularly for novice beekeepers. Even though Africanized bees might not significantly impact the beekeeping industry, beekeepers still need to be aware of them.

The Italian or Russian castes are recommended for those just beginning their beekeeping practice. These bees are known for their gentle nature, productivity, and adaptability to various climates, making them an excellent choice for newbees. However, aside from the Africanized bees, which require expertise and caution, all the bee strains we've discussed could be considered. Each bee type has unique strengths and characteristics; the choice ultimately depends on your needs, goals, and local environment.

Obtaining your bees

Now that we've looked at bee castes and you've hopefully pinpointed the one that's just right for you, it's time to move on to the next big and very practical adventure: bringing your bees home!

This part of the book will explore the four most popular ways to acquire bees for your hive. Each method has its benefits and considerations, and we will dissect each to help you make the best choice for your situation.

Firstly, we'll explore the ins and outs of ordering packaged bees. This method is a favorite amongst newbees thanks to its straightforwardness and ease. Next up, we'll look at buying a "nuc" colony. As we have seen, this is essentially a mini, fully-functioning colony that can give you a headstart in your beekeeping venture. We'll also talk about buying an existing colony if you wish to get started immediately. This complete, operational beehive can be moved right into your backyard!

And lastly, for those of you who love a good adventure—we'll dive into the exhilarating process of capturing a wild swarm of bees!

Acquiring Packaged Bees

Bee Package/Credit: Diane Garcia(www.shutterstock.com)

Ordering packaged bees is one of the most common and beginner-friendly ways to kickstart your life with bees. What actually are packaged bees? Simply put, they are bees that you can order by weight from a trusted supplier. These suppliers are typically based in the warmer regions of the United States, but they're usually more than happy to ship to any location within the continental U.S.

A package of bees is a small box made of wood or plastic. To promote airflow, the box features two sides that are either screened or ventilated. Inside this box, you'll find a queen bee housed in a small, screened cage—a similar size to a matchbox. Alongside the queen, there's a tin can filled with sugar syrup, which sustains the bees during their transit.

Around 10,000 bees are included in a typical box of bees, which is the ideal number for beginning a new hive. You should purchase a single package of bees, containing a queen, for each hive you intend to start. It's highly recommended to get a "marked" queen along with your parcel. A little dot is painted on the thorax of a marked queen. Although it comes with a slight additional cost, this marking makes it easier to locate the queen during hive inspections. It also verifies that the queen you're observing is the one you installed. If you spot an unmarked queen, it indicates that your original queen has been replaced. The dot's color also represents your queen's year of purchase—which is handy information as it helps you monitor the queen's age. It's good practice to replace your queen every few years to ensure optimal brood production.

When selecting a dealer, check they have a solid reputation for supplying healthy, disease-free packaged bees. Don't hesitate to request a health certificate from the vendor's state apiary inspector. Consider it a red flag if the vendor declines to offer this.

Buying a Nucleus Colony

If you want to begin your beekeeping journey with a bit of a head start, buying a nucleus colony, affectionately known as a "nuc," might be just the ticket. Picture this: a mini bee colony with a queen laying eggs and four or five frames buzzing with brood and bees. It's a compact, self-contained unit that you can quickly transfer into your hive. (Once the transfer is complete, you return the nuc box to the supplier.)

Finding a local beekeeper selling nucs might feel like looking for a needle in a haystack. Not all beekeepers sell nucs, primarily due to the work involved in setting them up. But if you manage to locate a local supplier, it's a win-win situation. The bees avoid the stress of shipping, and you obtain bees already acclimatized to your local environment.

They're familiar with the local weather, flora, and conditions, which gives them a better chance of thriving. Another perk of sourcing your bees locally is the potential for mentorship. Having a local supplier also means you have someone to turn to when you have questions or encounter problems. It's like having a personal beekeeping guru right in your neighborhood!

So, how do you go about finding a local nuc supplier? A good starting point is to do an online search for "beekeeping" along with your area code, city, or state. You could also contact your state's bee inspector or connect with local beekeeping clubs or association members.

Purchasing an Established Colony

Buying an established colony might seem attractive for those eager to jump into the thick of beekeeping. It's like purchasing a fully furnished house— everything is already functioning. However, as tempting as it might be to skip the initial steps, this approach isn't always the best fit for beginners, because an established colony presents challenges that may be overwhelming for someone starting out.

For instance, you'll deal with a significantly larger bee population than the 10,000 that come with a package or a nuc. These bees have already established their home and will be more defensive, which could increase the risk of stings. In addition, the huge number of bees makes inspecting the hive intimidating. Having been in operation for at least a season, the equipment may be more challenging as the bees would have sealed things with propolis, a sticky substance they produce.

By opting for an established colony, you might miss out on the valuable learning experiences of starting a hive from scratch. There's a unique sense of satisfaction and a wealth of knowledge to be gained from watching a new colony grow, seeing the bees construct fresh comb, and introducing a new queen.

If you're still keen on purchasing an established colony, it's essential to do so *responsibly*. Just as you wouldn't buy a used car without getting it checked by a mechanic, you shouldn't buy a colony without having it inspected by your state's apiary inspector, or a seasoned local beekeeper. This step is crucial to ensure the colony is disease-free, as existing diseases could spread and cause significant issues.

Capturing a Swarm of Bees

Bee Swarm/Credit: Tony Campbell(www.shutterstock.com)

While this method of starting your colony is undeniably cost-effective—after all, swarms don't come with a price tag—it does present its own unique set of challenges and uncertainties. It's not a path I'd recommend for those just dipping their toes into the world of beekeeping!

Capturing a wild swarm is a complex dance that requires a certain level of expertise and confidence. It's not a task for the faint-hearted or inexperienced. Therefore, getting some hands-on experience with beekeeping is very wise before you consider this option. One of the major uncertainties when capturing a wild swarm is the bees' unknown health, genetics, and temperament. When you order packaged bees or buy a nuc, you have some assurance of the bees' health and characteristics—but wild swarms are a bit like a mystery box. You won't know their health status or genetic traits until they're already part of your apiary, which could potentially introduce risks to your other colonies.

In certain areas, particularly in the southern parts of the United States, there's also the risk that the swarm you're trying to capture could be Africanized. As we have seen, these bees, also known as killer bees, are a more aggressive variant of honey bees that can pose significant challenges and dangers to beekeepers. It's crucial to be aware of this possibility and to take necessary precautions if you're in an area where Africanized bees are common.

Given these considerations, I advise newbees to hold off on the adventure of capturing a wild swarm until your second year or later. Observing an experienced beekeeper capturing a swarm can be incredibly beneficial before you attempt it yourself. This will give you a better understanding of the process and the potential challenges.

You might also be tempted to start your colony by transferring feral bees from a tree hollow or a building. While this might seem appealing and cost-free, I urge you to resist the temptation. Moving bees from an established nest site can be fraught with difficulties and potential problems. It's best to leave wild bees alone until you've gained more experience. Even then, I recommend observing an expert perform a transfer before deciding if you want to try it.

In my view, if you're starting out in beekeeping, ordering packaged bees will likely be your best bet. It's a method that offers a good balance of affordability, control, and simplicity, making it a great first step into this fascinating world. So, with that assumption in mind, we will now move forward on how to get started!

Starting Right—How Many Hives for a Beginner Beekeeper?

The answer isn't as straightforward as you might think. It's not a one-size-fits-all scenario, but the wisdom of seasoned beekeepers suggests that starting with 2–4 hives in your inaugural season strikes a good balance.

You might be tempted to play it safe and start with just one hive. However, this approach carries its risks. If your single colony fails, you lose your entire bee population. Conversely, managing more than four hives as a novice could be too much to handle. So, the recommended range of 2–4 hives balances risk mitigation and manageability.

It's important to remember that having *more* hives doesn't necessarily mean you'll get *more* honey! Quality trumps quantity every time. It´s a fact that a few well-tended bee colonies can yield more honey than eight neglected ones. So, focus on quality management rather than just increasing the number of hives.

Several factors can influence the number of hives you can effectively manage. These include your available time, the location of your hives, your physical health, level of motivation, purpose, and the quality of your beekeeping equipment. For example, if you're juggling a full-time job with a busy schedule, you might find it more challenging to manage multiple hives compared to someone who's retired and has plenty of time to spend on their bee practice.

Starting with just one hive might seem more straightforward, but you'll miss the advantages of having multiple hives. With more than one hive, you can compare and evaluate their performance. If one hive is flourishing while another is struggling, it could indicate a problem, such as a disease outbreak or a non-productive queen. With only one hive, it's harder to identify whether there's an issue with the hive itself, or external factors, like perhaps the lack of nearby nectar sources.

To sum it up, as a beginner beekeeper, starting with 2–4 hives provides a good balance of risk and reward. It offers a manageable workload, a safety net in case of colony loss, and a comparative basis to assess your hives' performance. You may progressively increase the number of hives you maintain as you build expertise and confidence.

Where to buy your bees?

We're now at a pivotal juncture: determining the best source for our bees. We have three primary avenues to explore: local beekeepers, distributors in your area, or online suppliers. Each option brings unique benefits and potential challenges; the optimal choice will hinge on your circumstances and requirements.

I'd lean toward local beekeepers if you're seeking a personal recommendation. Why, you ask? Well, these seasoned beekeeping veterans are treasure troves of knowledge and experience. Plus, as previously noted, they can offer bees already adapted to your local climate and conditions.

But what makes this option stand out from the rest? In this chapter, we'll go into the specifics, shedding light on why local beekeepers might be your best bet—but we also consider the other options.

Local Beekeepers

Imagine having a seasoned beekeeper, someone who's navigated the ups and downs of beekeeping, right by your side. That's what you get when buying bees from a local beekeeper. They've been in your shoes and can offer you a wealth of knowledge and experience to help you avoid common pitfalls and set you on the path to success.

One of the most compelling reasons to obtain bees locally is their adaptability. These bees have weathered your local climate, survived the winter, and are genetically equipped to do it again. This resilience gives your colony a fighting chance to thrive through the seasons. But the benefits don't stop there. Engaging with local beekeepers often opens doors to local beekeeping associations.

These communities are a goldmine of information and camaraderie. You'll encounter beekeepers from all walks of life, each with their distinct insights and experiences. You might even strike up a few friendships along the way! Let's not forget the practical advantages of buying locally. When you source your bees locally, you bypass the potential stress and risks of shipping the bees. Temperature changes and unexpected delays can threaten your bees, particularly the queen. By picking up your bees in person, you completely sidestep these potential issues.

Local Distributors

Local distributors can be your best friends. These folks are the intermediaries who receive large quantities of bees and distribute them to local beekeepers like you. The process is pretty simple—you place your order online, or in person, and then wait for the magic!

One of the biggest perks of going through a local distributor is that it takes the guesswork out of the delivery process. They handle the logistics, ensuring that the bees are delivered on time, which is crucial for the health and survival of your new fuzzy buzzing friends. You'll be given a pick-up date and location, so there's no worry about leaving your bees in a hot warehouse or on your doorstep. But be prepared—you might not be the only bee enthusiast in town. Pick-up days can be busy, so you might have to wait in line, which is a small price for convenience and peace of mind.

It's important to remember that just because you're buying from a local distributor doesn't necessarily mean the bees themselves are in fact, local. They could have been raised anywhere, so don't be shy—ask where the bees came from—knowing about the bees' background, including their initial environment and conditions, is always good.

<u>Online Suppliers</u>

In our 21st century, digitally connected world, it's no surprise that you can order almost anything online—including bees! While it's not my top recommendation due to the potential stress on the bees during shipping, online suppliers can be the answer if local options are scarce.

When you're browsing through online bee suppliers, there are a few key factors to keep in mind.

First and foremost, consider where the bees are coming from. If possible, try to find bees used to a climate similar to yours. This can help them adjust more quickly and comfortably to their new home.

Another crucial point to consider is insurance. It might seem like an unnecessary expense, but it can be a real game-changer if your bees don't survive the journey. It's a sad fact, but sometimes bees don't make it through shipping, and insurance can help protect your investment.

Shipping options are another aspect to look into. Opting for faster shipping can benefit the bees if you can afford it. The less time they spend travelling, the better.

Also, please pay attention to the time gap between when the bees are ready for shipping and when they are sent. Ideally, the bees should be shipped within a few days of being placed in the container. This reduces the time they spend confined and stressed.

Finally, ensure you're ready to receive your package as soon as it arrives. You don't want your bees sitting on your porch all day in the hot sun. Be prepared to welcome them into their new home *as soon* as they arrive.

Remember, only bee packages can be shipped. If you're interested in a nuc, you'll need to pick it up directly from the supplier due to its size and complexity.

The Perfect Timing: When Should You Order Your Bees?

One of the most common questions from new beekeepers is, "When should I order my bees?" The answer might surprise you! Believe it or not, the best time to order your bees is during the winter months. Yes, that's right—winter! While it might seem counterintuitive to think about buzzing bees and blooming flowers when there's snow on the ground, don´t worry—there's a method to the madness.

You see, bee suppliers have a finite number of bees to sell each year. Once they're gone, they're gone. So, by placing your order early, you're ensuring that you're at the top of the list when it's time for the bees to be shipped out in the spring.

But there's another advantage to ordering your bees early. You have plenty of time to get ready for their arrival! Setting up a hive isn't something you want to rush. By ordering your bees in the winter, you'll have oodles of time to get your hive ready, so when your bees arrive, their new home will be waiting for them.

Welcoming Your New Buzzing Buddies

The day you've been waiting for has finally arrived—your bees are here! It's a day filled with anticipation and a dash of nervous energy. However, it's worth noting that the exact arrival date of your bees can be a bit of a moving target. Bee suppliers usually provide an estimated shipping week, which can shift due to weather conditions. Both temperature and rainfall can influence the safest shipping times, so patience goes a long way.

If your bees are journeying via the postal service, it's wise to give your local post office a heads-up about a week before the anticipated arrival. Make sure the shipper has your contact details so you can be notified as soon as your bees land. Most post offices will prefer you to collect your bees directly, and it's crucial to instruct them to keep the package in a cool, dark spot until you can swing by.

It's very important to remember that the arrival of your bees is not the time to start assembling your equipment! *Everything should be ready to greet your new inhabitants!* They will need to settle in and rest.

Once your bees have landed, here are a few steps to follow:

1. **Package Inspection:** Take a good look at your bees. Check that they are alive and well. It's normal to see a few casualties at the bottom of the package, but contact your vendor if you see an inch or more of deceased bees. They should replace your bees if the majority, or all, have not survived the journey.

2. **Homeward Bound:** Get your bees home as soon as possible. Avoid stashing them in a hot, stuffy car trunk. They will likely be warm, weary, and thirsty after their journey.

3. **Hydration Station:** Once home, give your bees a good spray with room-temperature water using a clean mister or spray bottle.

4. **Rest:** Find a cool spot, like your basement or garage, and let your bees rest for an hour.

5. **Feeding Time:** After their rest, it's time to feed your bees. Spray the package with sugar syrup.

Once your bees are inside the hive (and on the next page we will cover this!), it's critical to have a feeding system in place. A top-notch hive-top feeder, a feeding pail, or a baggie feeder can all do the job.

Feeding your bees sugar syrup twice a year, in spring and fall, is recommended.

This stimulates hive activity and provides a handy way to administer medications or nutritional supplements.

Preparing Sugar Syrup for Your Package Bees

As you anticipate the arrival of your package bees, prepare for their welcome by making your sugar syrup. This simple concoction is a vital food source for your new bees, helping them adjust to their new home in your hives.

You must combine sugar and water in a one-to-one ratio to prepare sugar syrup for your bees. This can be measured either by weight or by volume. This well-balanced mixture gives your bees the energy they need to foster brood-raising and start laying out foundations, which are essential in building a successful colony.

For each package of bees, it's recommended to prepare one gallon of sugar syrup. To make this, measure 10 ⅔ cups of sugar and 10 ⅔ cups of water. Combine these in a large pot and stir until the sugar is completely dissolved. Once prepared, this sugar syrup can be stored in a clean, airtight container until your bees arrive.

The Art of Hiving Your Bees

The moment has arrived! Your bees are here, and it's time to introduce them to their new home. This process, known as "hiving," is a crucial step in your beekeeping journey. Let's walk through the steps together.

The ideal time to hive your bees is on a clear, mild day with little to no wind, preferably in the late afternoon. If the weather is not cooperating, it's okay to wait a day or two, but remember to spray your bees with sugar syrup a few times a day while they're waiting. The sooner you can hive them, the better.

Let's now explore how to hive your bees, step by step:

1. **Preparing the Hive:** Start by donning your beekeeping suit and lighting your smoker. Approach the hive calmly and puff a little smoke at the entrance, which will calm the bees. Carefully remove the outer cover of the hive, followed by the inner cover. To create space for your new arrivals, remove three or four frames from the

center of the hive. This will provide ample room for the bees to enter their new home.

2. **Spraying the Bees:** Prepare a light sugar syrup and gently spray it over the bees in the package. This serves two purposes: it provides an immediate food source and dampens their wings, reducing their ability to fly and potentially causing chaos during hiving!

3. **Shaking the Package:** It's time to dislodge the bees from the syrup can and the queen cage. To do this, give the package a firm shake. A sharp bump on the ground or against the hive should be enough to dislodge most bees.

4. **Removing the Syrup Can:** Use your hive tool to pry off the lid on the syrup can. Keep this lid handy; you'll need it to cover the opening when you remove the can.

5. **Inspecting the Queen:** The queen cage is usually suspended from the top of the box. Carefully remove the cage and inspect the queen to ensure she is alive and well. If there's sugar candy in the cage, create a small opening to give the bees a headstart in freeing the queen.

6. **Attaching the Queen Cage:** Now, attach the queen cage to the middle of a frame with the screen facing outward. This allows the worker bees to interact with the queen and start eating through the candy to release her. Put one or two rubber bands on the cage to hold it in place.

7. **Adding Pollen Patties:** Place some pollen patties on the top bar of the frames. These will provide a supplemental food source for the bees as they establish their new colony.

8. **Shaking the Bees into the Hive:** Give the bee box a good shake to move the bees away from the opening. Place the opening above the hive where the frames were removed, and shake the bees inside.

9. **Replacing the Frames:** Carefully replace the frames once the bees are in the hive. Be gentle to avoid squashing any bees.

10. **Setting Up the Feeder:** Now, set up your feeder over the opening of the inner cover. To enclose the feeder, place an additional hive body over it. Then, add the outer cover on top.

11. **Letting the Bees Settle:** Finally, give the bees outside the hive some time to enter. Put on the entry reducer by placing the small opening facing the bees after most have entered. This helps protect the new colony from potential predators.

Hiving the Bees/Credit: Lindsay Snow(www.shutterstock.com)

The Journey Continues: Post-Hiving Care

So, you've successfully hived your bees! Congratulations! But what comes next? Well, as a beekeeper, it's just the beginning of an exciting adventure.

First things first, let's give our buzzing friends some breathing room. It might sound counterintuitive, but the best thing you can do for your bees is to leave them alone. For about 7 to 10 days, resist the urge to peek inside the hive. The only exception to this hands-off approach is when you must refill the feeder or provide a pollen patty.

During these initial days, your bees will be hard at work, crafting wax comb for the queen to lay her eggs. Providing food to support this labor-intensive process is crucial.

After roughly a week, it's time to conduct your first hive inspection. This is where your beekeeping gear, smoker, and hive tool come into play.

Home Sweet Home!

As we close the curtain on this chapter, you've now gained insights into the diverse types of bees, understood the various methods of procuring them, and mastered the steps to establish them in their new abode. This has set the stage for your ongoing beekeeping adventure, and you're well on your way to becoming a proficient beekeeper!

Now that your bees have settled into their new hive, it's time to turn our attention to the next critical aspect of beekeeping: hive inspections.

In the next chapter, we'll cover the intricacies of conducting hive inspections. We'll explore the essential tools you'll need, the key indicators to look out for, and the best practices for handling your bees during these necessary inspections.

Queen Cage/Credit: EdBockStock(<u>www.shutterstock.com</u>)

CHAPTER 7
Inspecting your hive

Consider the hive inspection a wellness check on your fuzzy, humming residents, keeping tabs on their progress from when they are installed to the subsequent months and years.

Hive inspection isn't about bothering your bees but ensuring they're in good health and prospering. It's an integral practice in beekeeping, and I will guide you through the requisite steps. We'll cover the necessary tools, the optimal time for inspection, signs of a well-maintained hive, and potential issues to be aware of.

Instill positive practices from the get-go by following proven guidelines, and be sure to adopt our checklist for hive inspections (in the hive inspection chapter). Beekeeping does not need to be an intimidating activity—it's a journey of continual learning and considerable joy!

For most newbees, something about that inaugural hive inspection accelerates your pulse. It's a mixed bag of feelings—a hint of apprehension, a spark of anticipation, and a hearty dose of inquisitiveness. There you stand, poised in front of your own beehive, the hum of industrious workers permeating the surrounding space. It's as if you're on the brink of a novel universe, ready to take that initial leap—it's okay to feel a little anxious!

On your initial hive inspection you might feel like you are conducting a very delicate procedure, and perhaps as the first bee buzzes close to you, you feel scared and twitch! That's perfectly normal—we've all experienced it. Rest assured that this apprehension will gradually disappear. You'll soon find yourself eagerly looking forward to these serene encounters with your buzzing companions.

Believe me when I tell you, you'll look forward to your inspections as they are such an incredibly peaceful time of bee exploration. Initially, it's all about the bustling activity and that sweet fragrance of honey. But eventually, inspections become more deeply introspective. They become peaceful, like witnessing a sunset or the soothing sound of waves hitting the shoreline. Every inspection peels off a layer, exposing more about the intricate and vital world of bees.

And despite discovering this new cosmos, inspections are vital to safeguard the bees' health and ensure their safety. It's like a routine health check-up. Your role is to identify early signs of illness, monitor the queen bee, and keep the hive in excellent condition.

You'll begin by understanding their daily routines, studying their behavior, and eventually, you'll feel the rhythm of their miniature world. The more acquainted you get with your bees and their routines, the better you'll identify anything unusual.

I cannot stress enough the importance of adopting a systematic and consistent approach to inspecting your beehive. It's true, you may uncover some tactics that work better for you over time, but in your first year of beekeeping, try to be methodical and precise.

Consider it to be a bit like understanding the "foundations of math" that teachers always talk about. In the early stages, it's not just about what's effective. It's about mastering the fundamentals and reducing risk. Keep in mind, we're dealing with a *multitude* of minute creatures, not just *one*. A minor error can escalate into a major issue. Hence, implementing the correct measures during your hive inspections is crucial for your and your bees' safety.

The habits you cultivate initially will likely stay with you, so make sure you start off on the right foot!

Hours to visit the hive

Every novice beekeeper ponders the same question—what's the best time to look in on your beehive? To comprehend this, let's look into the world of bees. Intriguingly, bees share some habits with us – they experience peak traffic, enjoy downtime, and even have a bedtime!

As we humans don't like unanticipated visits at ungodly hours, bees aren't too keen on getting interrupted during their peaceful times either!

So, the first rule of thumb: steer clear of checking your hive too early in the day or late at night. Bees are all tucked in at these hours, and an unexpected inspection might lead to a hive full of grumpy yellow and black fuzzy dwellers.

The Golden Period

The best time for hive inspection lies between mid-morning and early afternoon. Why? A significant chunk of worker bees are out gathering food during this time, resulting in fewer bees in the hive and, in turn, a lesser chance of upsetting them en masse.

Plus, the gentle warmth of the day seems to put bees in a more receptive, if I may say, friendly mood! Yes, friendy bees!

Another convincing reason to opt for these hours is that the queen bee will likely be active. Seeing the queen during an inspection is a comforting indication that the hive is in good shape.

When Not to Inspect

Avoid checking your hive during inclement or excessively windy weather. Bees, like us, don't enjoy harsh weather, which can make them more protective.

To sum it up, approach hive inspection like a cordial visit. You wouldn't want to pop in when everyone's asleep, irritable, or busy dealing with rough weather, would you?

Instead, you'd choose a time when they're at ease, perhaps basking in a lovely sunny day, and are open to a brief greeting.

Creating an Inspection Timeline

As you'd pencil in a recurrent chat over coffee with a buddy, making a routine check-in schedule with your beehive is essential. Consider it as a congenial check-in. You're interested in their well-being, their health, and their activities. Similar to our human friendships, regular rendezvous are crucial to fostering robust connections.

Through frequent check-ups, you can monitor your colony's health, spot any illnesses swiftly, and ensure your queen bee is performing her egg-laying duties efficiently.

But remember, inspections aren't just about the bees. They provide an opportunity for you to understand bee behavior, observe their response to varying weather patterns, how they hoard honey, and their method of constructing their comb.

How Often You Should Visit the Hive…

So, here comes the big question: How *often* should you inspect your bees? The answer isn't straightforward since it depends on various factors.

If you're a novice, a good guideline is to examine your hive once a week during their bustling spring and summer periods. These regular checks are to see what's normal and what's not. It's about getting used to the inspection procedures, like handling the frames.

However, the scenario changes in the winter, as bees are in hibernation then and aren't fond of disturbances. It's best to let them be in peace during the chillier months unless you think there's an issue.

During your First Year

In your inaugural year, it's recommended that you conduct a check-up about once every week, complemented by a more comprehensive examination every fortnight. It's crucial to bear in mind that these inspections can cause stress for your bees. So, while it's vital to maintain a regular inspection routine, especially within your first year, it's equally important not to push it too far. The key is to strike a balance.

During the Next Years

Once you've passed the initial year, it's advisable to carry out a quick check every fortnight and a thorough one every month or when the seasons change. It's all about reaching the right equilibrium in your inspection routine. While it's understandable that you'd want to closely observe your fuzzy companions, remember that every time you open the hive and use smoke on the bees, it disrupts them. They need a day or two to recover and resume their regular duties.

However, this doesn't hold true for the first year of beekeeping, when figuring out what you should be on the lookout for is crucial.

When You Have Gained Experience

Over time, as you acquire more experience in assessing a hive and knowing what to watch for, the need for frequent and in-depth inspections tends to decrease. You'll probably find yourself making an initial visit in the early spring, followed by a couple of checks in the summer, and then wrapping it up with a final visit at the season's end.

Preparing for the Inspection

The sun is shining brightly over the weekend, and your enthusiasm to visit and observe your bees is at its peak! However, despite your excitement, you can't just dash out, whip off the cover and have a quick look—a clear plan is essential.

First ascertain that you know what to look for and the actions you'll take. Diving in with no plan could provoke bewilderment and might distress your bees.

How to Manage Personal Hygiene

Getting ready for a beehive check-up requires a touch of self-preparation. It's wise to steer clear of strong fragrances on the day of the inspection, such as colognes or scented soaps, since these might upset the bees.

Don't swing by your bees for the first time in stinky, sweaty clothes after your morning workout, but refrain from smelling like a bouquet of roses! The bees can't pollinate you or gather nectar from you!

Leather and wool

Your bees won't appreciate you wearing any leather or wool attire. Bees can mistake the scent in these materials for their predators (bears, racoons, skunks)—a misunderstanding you want to avoid. Choose garments in light hues and smooth textures, which are less prone to set off the bees' protective instincts. Plus, leather tends to hold onto body odor.

Getting Dressed

So it's time to gear up for your safety during your hive inspections. Let's be real—getting a sting or two is just part of the beekeeping gig, so perhaps consider it as a mark of pride instead of worrying overly about it!

Being a newbee in the world of beekeeping, it's advisable to sport a long-sleeved shirt, considering the preference for light hues and natural materials we've discussed earlier.

If you're not equipped with a professional beekeeping suit, just secure the cuffs of your pants and sleeves with Velcro straps or rubber bands to make your clothing as bee-proof as possible.

Jewellery

I recommend you remove any accessories you might be wearing. It's not that your bees dislike them, but if you end up getting stung and your finger swells, it's better not to have any rings on.

Veil

Remember to put on your veil every time you check on your hive. This will keep the bees from getting too close to your face and stop them from getting stuck in your hair. Finding and removing a bee trapped under your veil is incredibly distracting.

If it happens, stay calm. The bee is just trying to escape, so the calmer you are, the less likely it is to sting you. Step away from the hive and gently remove your veil to make things easier. It's as simple as that.

Avoid abruptly removing your veil while still at the hive, as it might result in more bees swarming around your face.

Gloves

We looked at gloves in Chapter 4, but another word on this here. At the start, you might feel the inclination to use gloves for extra protection. However, it's best to avoid them. From the get-go, try to avoid using gloves as they can be chunky and inconvenient when handling your bees. Invest in gloves, as they are of course useful during harsh weather or harvest, but avoid using them during inspections.

Lighting the smoker

Smoker Preparation/ Credit: www.shutterstock.com(www.shutterstock.com)

Now, it's time to fire up the smoker. We aren't discussing a barbecue! Just a small whiff of smoke to soothe the bees.

Smokers are utilized to project smoke into and around the hive, providing you with somewhat undisturbed access to the hive. The challenging aspect of a smoker, despite it being a fantastic ally in beekeeping, is maintaining its flame.

Therefore, it's crucial to light the smoker properly to ensure it remains lit during your inspection.

We looked at smokers in Chapter 4, the electric and charcoal varieties. Here is more on this crucial tool!

What to Put into the Smoker

To begin with, you'll require some starter fuel for your bee smoker. Ideally, you need a material that ignites swiftly to start the fire, followed by something more solid that burns slowly, ensuring the flame lasts for the duration. You could opt for paper egg trays, a cluster of newspaper, or a ball of dry lint, roughly the size of a tennis ball.

Whatever you choose as your starter fuel should be a *natural* source to ensure the scent is bee-friendly and the smoke is clean. Organic materials that burn slowly without generating too much heat are the perfect fuel for your bee smoker.

Here are some of our top picks:

- **Pine needles** are an excellent choice, thanks to their resin and oil content that smolder superbly, and the smoke emitted is not harsh.
- **Dried herbs** have an aromatic smoke that is harmless to bees.
- **Dried citrus peels** smolder well in a bee smoker due to their natural oils.
- **Dried grass**, including lawn trimmings and hay and straw, make great fuel.
- **100% cotton fabric**, such as old cotton t-shirts or jeans, when rolled up, serves as a good smoker fuel.
- **Untreated burlap**, or hessian is an excellent natural fuel for a bee smoker.
- **Dry horse manure** is an excellent choice as fuel. It smokes well, produces little heat, and is completely natural.
- **Commercial smoker pellets** are another option that can be bought and are designed to be safe for both you and your bees.

How to Light the Smoker

It's crucial to master the proper use of a smoker, and getting some trial runs under your belt is highly recommended before the inspection. The smoke's quantity, placement, and temperature can greatly harm the bees, even killing them or causing the hive to swarm.

So, it's necessary to proceed with CARE.

1. Settle it at the smoker's bottom after igniting your chosen fuel or newspaper. A few pumps on the bellows will confirm that the paper is igniting with a small flame.

2. The next step involves adding kindling to maintain the flame and pumping the bellows throughout to ensure it lights.

3. Fill the smoker to about three-quarters full.

4. Once you've got a decent kindling, you can gradually increase the fuel's size.

5. The largest size shouldn't be thicker than your thumb.

6. Always keep pumping the bellows until everything is well-lit and burning properly.

Even if you don't need any smoke, aim to pump your smoker every 10 minutes to prevent the fire from going out. If the smoke begins to subside, check if more kindling is needed.

What to Avoid Putting into the Smoker

You should always avoid using certain items as fuel in your bee smoker due to their impracticality or the harmful smoke they produce for both bees and honey.

For example, lighting wood in a bee smoker can be challenging and time-consuming. Avoid using twigs and small sticks in a bee smoker, as these tiny items burn quickly, produce excessive heat, and generate minimal smoke. If you settle on this fuel type, you'll need to frequently replenish the smoker.

It may sound like a no-brainer but never introduce toxic materials like plastic or rubber to your smoker. Also, be aware of the kind of wood you're burning, as some trees aren't suitable. For instance, burning the Brazilian Pepper tree is harmful. Pine shavings are favored by many beekeepers.

What Smoke Does to Bees

Contrary to popular belief, bees don't get "drowsy" from smoke. In reality, the smoke conceals their distress signals. When bees sense smoke, they assume their hive is on fire and prepare to evacuate. They start gorging on honey, thinking they'll need the energy to seek a new home.

Being full of honey, their bellies become too bloated to sting efficiently. If the smoke isn't too hot, it's harmless to bees. Just make sure the smoke is cool by testing it on your arm.

To understand what they experience, think about trying to chat with your friends while loud music is playing. That's similar to what a bee colony experiences when a beekeeper introduces smoke into the hive. The smoke interrupts the bees' ability to smell, which they rely on for communication.

Opening a Langstroth Hive

Opening the Hive/Credit: Addictive Creative(www.shutterstock.com)

When your smoker is all set, it's time to tackle the beehive. Ensure you come at it from the rear to avoid running into the bees buzzing in and out. The art of beehive inspection involves methodically using smoke and taking off each box until you get to the lowest layer. Then, you carefully inspect the frames inside those boxes and make mental or physical notes of your observations before you put the hive back together.

How to Open Your Langstroth Hive

1. Position yourself at the side, keeping your smoker about 2 or 3 feet from the hive's entry, and release several puffs of dense, cool smoke towards it. Four substantial puffs should be enough. Use your

discretion and avoid overdoing it. You're not aiming to suffocate the bees but to signal your presence to the guard bees.

2. Push smoke towards the hive's entrance to disorient the guard bees.

3. Slightly lift the outer cover and direct a few smoke puffs beneath it.

4. Gently lower the cover and hold on for a minute, allowing the smoke to work its magic.

5. It's time to set your smoker aside, remove the hive's outer cover, and carefully place it upside down on the ground.

6. Feeders and the edge of the hive body may often stick together, so use the flat side of the hive tool to carefully separate them.

7. Your following move depends on whether you're currently feeding your bees during the inspection.

8. If you are, you'll need to take off the hive-top feeder next.

9. Use your smoker to send some smoke into the hive via the screened opening. Avoid frightening the bees by doing this carefully.

10. Use one hand to gently apply pressure on the feeder while using your hive tool in your other hand to pry the feeder loose. This balancing act of pressure decreases the chance of the two parts unexpectedly snapping apart with a loud "snap."

11. Loosen one side of the feeder before moving around to the back — not the front — to loosen the other side.

12. As you pull the feeder off, let out a few puffs of smoke into the space you made with your hive tool.

13. Wait half a minute before removing the hive-top feeder. And make sure not to let any syrup drip.

14. Place the feeder gently on the outer cover laid on the ground.

15. Align the feeder perpendicularly to the cover as you put it down, this will limit the contact points to just two and reduce the chances of squashing any bees that may be under the feeder.

16. If there's leftover syrup in the feeder, completely wrap it with a towel. You could use a small piece of plywood or a leftover piece of carpet. Leaving syrup out in the open is like a massive invitation to bees! You certainly don't want to ignite a robbing situation, where bees go into a chaotic frenzy upon discovering free sweets.

Uncovered containers of syrup (or honey, for that matter) can also lure bees from other colonies. All these indulging bees get whipped up into such a state that they start stealing honey from your own hive. This can trigger a war, and the invading tribe may kill hundreds or even thousands of bees.

17. Once the top feeder is off the hive, it's time to open the inner cover. Blow some smoke into the hive via the oval opening.

18. With the flat side of your hive tool, gently separate the inner cover from the hive body.

19. Loosen one edge, walk around to the back of the hive, and loosen the other edge. Be slow and careful when prying it open to avoid a loud "snap."

20. Lastly, when you raise the inner cover, blow a few puffs of smoke into the space you made with the hive tool.

21. Wait half a minute before removing the inner cover.

22. Place it on the cover currently on the ground, or just prop it against a corner of your hive so it won't disturb your inspection. Avoid squashing any bees that might still be on the inner lid.

23. Swiftly check just in case the queen bee is on the inner lid.

24. If you spot her, gently encourage her to move between the box's frames.

With your hive officially open, it's time to start your inspection!

What to do During a Hive Inspection

With the hive open, it's the perfect moment to kick things off and begin your first hive inspection. You've managed to open the hive, and as much as it was a nerve-wracking experience, you've made it through. Much like opening your hive, without having a plan and understanding what needs to happen during an inspection, it will only annoy your bees as you will no doubt keep the hive open longer than necessary.

Hive Inspection Steps

If you're just getting started, you may be curious about why hive inspections are such a frequent topic of discussion. Think of these inspections as routine health check-ups for your bees. They allow you to glimpse their world and ensure everything is as it should be.

Knowing when and what to inspect separates a mere "bee-haver" from a true "beekeeper." Sure, anyone can simply house a hive of bees, but your aim as a beekeeper is to support these beautiful small beings by comprehending their requirements and predicting their issues.

In this procedure, your hive tool will be essential.

You'll have to use it to separate the elements of the hive and evaluate the state of the comb, the queen's condition, and the pattern of the brood.

Understand the Needs of Your Bees

When you're examining your beehive, essentially, you're doing three things:

- Gauging the queen bee's effectiveness,
- Checking the colony's overall health,
- And seeing the rate of honey production.

Think of yourself as the bee's physician, confirming that the queen bee is accurately laying eggs and the worker bees are fulfilling their duties.

The benefit of regular hive scrutiny is that it allows you to identify any budding issues before they escalate. You may encounter pests, illnesses, or tension within your bee community. Spotting these early means you can intervene before they become severe crises.

Consider your hive inspections as keeping a constant check on the heartbeat of your vibrant bee community. It's an integral part of beekeeping that guarantees your honey-making venture flourishes.

Follow a Detailed Procedure

Have a detailed plan before you inspect your hive, which should include the following factors:

- Ensure they have a honey storage comb before the nectar begins to flow.

- Provide them with food when supplies are dwindling.

- Ensure they maintain good health with the right nutrition.

- Care for them and nurse them back to health when they fall ill.

- Help them prepare if the seasons are changing.

There are certain procedures you always adhere to and things you always check when examining your hive. After some time, these routines become like second nature, letting you focus on the amazing discoveries ahead.

I will share tips for making each hive inspection a breeze in this section.

Step 1: Smoke the Hive

Smoking the Hive/Credit: Addictive Creative(www.shutterstock.com)

Before you kick-start the evaluation, it's time to use the smoker again from the rear side of the hive. Gently puff some smoke in-between the frames and directly into the hive.

Remember, the puffs should be slow and drawn out, not short and swift.

How Long Should the Inspection Last?

The goal is to avoid keeping the hive exposed for more than half an hour, so swift yet effective action is necessary. Don't let overthinking hamper your initial attempts, as it could lead to errors. However, remember that you'll need to improve this over time.

When You Should Give More Smoke

If you notice heightened activity during your bee colony check-up, you may have to use more smoke to calm the bees. Increased agitation can be identified if the bees start moving wildly, buzzing around chaotically, or begin to sting.

No matter the type of hive you're examining, a couple of minutes in, you might spot the bees all aligned between the top bars, like sprinters ready at the starting line. Their tiny heads are neatly arranged between the frames, keeping an eye on you.

That's a great cue to give the bees a few more smoke puffs to scatter them before you carry on with your investigation.

And if a bee stings you, use smoke again. After a bee stings, it's almost guaranteed that others will become agitated and start stinging. This is when smoke comes to the rescue.

Step 2: Removing the First Frame of the Hive

Frame Removal/Credit: Addictive Creative(www.shutterstock.com)

It's scary, but it's time to extract that initial frame from your beehive. Don't worry; it's less intimidating than it appears. First and foremost, never forget that safety is key—for both you and the bees.

Think of the beehive frames as the individual suites for the bees, a space where they can store their honey and nurture their offspring. To take out the first frame, this is when your hive tool becomes indispensable.

1. Place the curved part of your hive tool between the first and second frames.

2. Then, gently and slowly twist the tool to part them.

3. Once they're loosened, cautiously lift the first frame straight up. Remember, it's not a race, so be gentle and steady.

4. Avoid tilting the frame to prevent harm to the bees or their young ones. Make a point to never place your fingers on a frame without first checking the bees' positions, as you neither want to harm any

bee nor get stung. It's quite simple to safely guide the bees away with a little smoke or delicately and slowly push them aside with your fingers.

5. Then, carefully position the frame on your frame rest. If you don't have one, then prop it up vertically against the hive on the side opposite where you're standing.

6. If bees are still on it, that's all right.

7. Removing the first frame provides ample space in the hive, making it easier to handle the rest of the frames without hurting any bees.

And there you have it! You've triumphantly removed your first frame.

Step 3: Remove the Remaining Frames of the Hive

Start by using your hive tool to gently loosen the second frame, following the same method as the first.

1. After moving it to the vacant spot where the first frame was, you'll have sufficient space to safely handle and lift this second frame without endangering or squashing any bees.

2. Return this frame to its position in the hive when you finish studying it, ensuring it is near but not touching the wall.

3. Your task is to follow this routine for all the frames, shifting the next frame for inspection into the empty slot.

4. After reviewing it, always place a frame back securely against the one you previously inspected.

5. Keep an eye on the progress as you gently maneuver the frames closer together.

6. Be cautious not to squeeze bees while pushing the frames together— you might be pressing the queen!

7. Always check between the frames to ensure the path is clear before merging them.

8. If some bees are at risk of being squished on the end bars, use the flat side of your hive tool to gently guide them away. A single puff of smoke can also help get them out of the way.

Take your time removing each frame, as their weights could vary. Observing the weight differences among frames with empty cells, those filled with honey, pollen reserves, and those with brood is intriguing.

Lift each frame in a smooth, continuous movement to prevent squashing bees on the sides or causing them to roll over the bees on the adjacent frame, which might irritate them.

With time and experience, you'll realize you don't have to scrutinize every frame. Your understanding of what to look for will improve, and you'll be able to assess your hive by inspecting fewer frames.

Step 4: Holding up the Frames for Inspection

Frame Inspection: 24K-Production(www.shutterstock.com)

Properly handling and examining each frame is essential. Position yourself so the sun is at your back, casting light over your shoulder onto the frame. This will highlight the intricate details within the cells, making spotting eggs and tiny larvae easier.

1. Once you've gently removed the frame, bring it to your eyes for a closer look.

2. Refrain from tilting the frame on its side, as there's a chance of losing nectar and unsealed brood.

3. Instead, hold the frame as you would a book right in front of you, and start scanning the pattern.

4. If you need to turn the frame sideways, just ensure it's directly above the hive. This way, anything that falls off the frame will end up back in the hive.

When you look at a frame, you'll notice that it has six cell groups. In each frame, learn to recognize them so you can not only distinguish one from the other but also implement necessary steps if something is missing.

Sealed Honey Reserves

Ideally, you'll find a stockpile of capped honey crowning the frame, often extending to the corners. If it's missing, the bees are critically low on food reserves, and you'll need to step in and feed them. This scenario could occur any time in the year, including summer if bad weather has kept the bees grounded for a week.

Nectar

Beneath the capped honey, you should notice cells filled with nectar. Think of it as the bees' version of having a snack bowl on a desk—something they can munch on while working. The bees consume the nectar and also offer it to the larvae.

Pollen

Pollen might not stand out as much as nectar, but cells should be brimming with it. The pollen, varying from bright orange and red to almost black, is a vital protein source for the bees. A lack of it could indicate a long stretch of bad weather.

Brood

A healthy brood area typically forms a circle, densely populated with cells housing eggs, larvae, or sealed brood, depending on the queen's recent activity on that frame.

Queen Cells

Finding a queen cell necessitates a decision on your part: leave it be or remove it. A colony with a robust queen, ample space, and a secure home will be less likely to entertain thoughts of swarming.

Empty Cells

During the day, many bees are out collecting food, but they all huddle in the hive at night. If no empty cells are at the bottom of the frames, the bees might feel it's time to find a new home, putting the colony at risk of swarming.

As the colony grows, the number of active frames in the hive increases from spring to summer. However, the composition of each frame remains constant.

Be Careful of Your Movements While Inspecting

When examining frames, moving with purpose but at a leisurely pace is crucial. Try to limit how often you adjust your hand placement. It's smarter to glide your fingers along the frames when adjusting your grip rather than picking them up and placing them down again, as you might accidentally touch a bee.

Be careful when rotating the frame; steer clear from any abrupt or needless spinning motion that could unsettle the bees or wreck the comb.

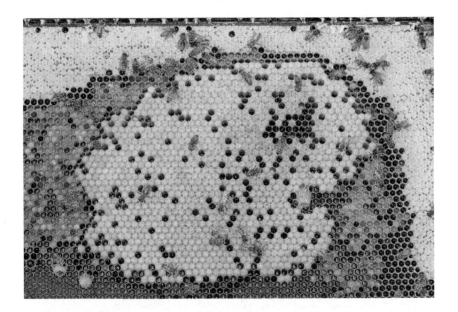

Capped Brood Cells/Credit: Chris Moody(www.shutterstock.com)

Step 5: Replacing the Frame into the Hive

With a thorough check on the first frame, you should now be in the position where all the frames are still inside the hive with the first frame leaning against the hive or resting on the frame stand.

Here's how to put that first frame back in its place.

1. First, gently move the hive frames as one group towards the other side of the hive. This is to return them to their original positions prior to your inspection. Moving them as a whole ensures they stay tightly packed and helps prevent squishing any bees. Make sure your gaze is focused on the spot where the frames meet as you push them together. This should leave you with the open space where you first removed a frame.

2. Next, give the bees a final smoke to encourage them back down into the hive.

3. Now, turn your attention to the frame left outside the hive.

4. Check to see if there are still bees on it.

5. If there are, give one corner of the frame a firm, downward flick over the bottom board at the hive's entrance.

6. Any bees knocked off will start making their way back into the hive.

7. With fewer bees left on the frame, you can return it to the hive without worrying about hurting them. Carefully slide the first frame back into its empty slot. And remember, take it slow! Ensure all frames fit tightly together and use your hive tool like a wedge to adjust the position of the multi-frame unit, ensuring the gap between the frames and both outer walls is even.

Step 6: Closing the Hive

Beehive equipment is designed considering the bees' instinct to construct comb in any available space. This is evident in the design of Langstroth hives, which are created in two styles to accommodate either eight or ten frames. If you don't use the full capacity of frames, bees will create unwanted comb in the excess space.

Moreover, if a super is added without frames, it can result in a disarray of cross comb attached to the hive's roof—a complicated situation to resolve.

Therefore, properly closing the hive is crucial!

1. If you're utilizing a hive-top feeder on a Langstroth hive, it's essential to replace it on the hive body promptly after usage.

2. Refill with more sugar syrup if the supply is running low.

3. If a hive-top feeder isn't part of your setup, the next step is to replace the inner cover.

4. Ensure to clear any bees from the inner cover. This can be done by sharply striking one corner of the cover against the bottom board at the hive's entrance—a single robust tap should suffice.

5. Carefully reposition the inner cover from the rear of the hive to avoid harming any bees. When you gradually slide it into position, any bees on top or around the edges of the hive will be gently pushed aside.

6. Ensure the ventilation hole notch is upwards and towards the front of the hive. This opening enables air circulation and provides bees with an upper-level entrance to the hive. While not all bee

equipment manufacturers include this opening, opting for one with this beneficial feature is recommended. The final step is to replace the outer cover.

7. Ensure it's devoid of bees by tapping it on the ground. Using the "bulldozer technique", slide it along the inner cover from the rear, gently moving any bees. Make sure there is a clear ventilation notch on the outer cover, and position it to be stable and level on the inside cover. Move the outer cover towards the front of the hive from the rear, opening the inner cover's notched hole, providing airflow and an alternate entrance for the bees.

An exception to the rule is that some beekeepers may use one less frame in their boxes (nine rather than ten) to allow more space while inspecting hives.

However, this is a decision that should be made once you have more experience.

What to Look for During Inspection

When you stop by your bee colony, be mindful of certain aspects you should always check. One optional inspection tool that comes in handy is a beekeeper magnifying glass; it makes spotting eggs a lot easier! Another benefit is that they are hands-free tools so you can conduct an inspection and at the same time, search for the queen and eggs.

Almost all checks are done to assess the well-being and output of the hive. The specific things you're keeping an eye out for may change slightly with each season, but there are general guidelines that apply to every hive visit.

When you scrutinize your hive, pay close attention to the happenings in the cells, as this can help you evaluate your bees' health and efficiency.

Ask yourself: Is there a good amount of pollen and nectar? Are there plenty of eggs and larvae? Do the wax caps covering the larvae look as they should, or are they perforated and recessed?

Check for Your Queen Bee

Looking over a beehive, it's always good to ensure the queen bee looks healthy. But, this is not a walk in the park—especially when dealing with a robust colony of more than 40,000 bees!

If the queen plays hide and seek, don't spend too much time trying to find her. Instead, look for eggs. Despite their small size, spotting eggs is easier than finding a queen among tens of thousands of bees.

Look for eggs when the sun is shining brightly.

Tilt the comb slightly with sunlight falling over your shoulder. This allows light to reach into the deep corners of the cells. The eggs will appear as tiny, translucent white specks, similar to tiny rice grains.

Check if There is Enough Food (Pollen and Nectar)

At times, there are instances when your bees require some extra support. While you already know what the pollen and nectar cells look like in a frame, it's important to understand key times when you may need to add food for your bees.

Here are some instances when they will need extra sustenance:

- At the onset and conclusion of each season.
- When there is a lengthy spell of bad weather which hampers their foraging.
- When a new colony is introduced.
- After harvesting honey from the hive.

Check the Brood Pattern

These are cells that the bees have sealed with a tan wax. The tan covers are breathable, allowing the growing larvae to breathe air. It permits the larvae to spin cocoons inside and transform into pupae.

Healthy Brood Pattern

Looking at the brood pattern is a crucial aspect of your hive checks. An orderly, dense brood pattern with most cells of the same age grouped suggests a strong, healthy queen.

The covers should also appear sleek and slightly bulging (plump).

Unhealthy Brood Pattern

On the flip side, a disordered brood pattern (numerous vacant cells with dispersed, varying-age cells of eggs, larvae, or covered brood) signals that your queen may be aged or ill and could require replacement.

Depressed (concave), oily, or holey covers suggest an issue.

The cell covers should be level for female bees and elevated for male (drone) bees. If the covers are depressed, there might be an issue.

Recognize the Materials Your Bees Are Collecting

Get familiar with recognizing the various substances your bees gather and store in their cells. You'll find that some cells are filled with pollen, which can be any number of colors like orange, yellow, brown, gray, blue, and more.

Upon further examination of the cells, you might spot some that are not sealed and seem to contain a "liquid" substance. This could be nectar or even water. Bees tend to use substantial amounts of water to keep the hive cool during high temperatures.

Check for Built-Up Propolis

Propolis can be likened to a thick, adhesive resin that bees utilize, similar to concrete. On warmer days, propolis sticks to your fingers during hive inspections and can also cover your hive tool. But in colder weather, it becomes as hard as cement! Bees typically use this propolis to mend any openings within the hive.

Be watchful for any excessive propolis or wax and use your hive tool to scrape it off gently. Remember to avoid harming any bees in the process.

Avoid letting it accumulate, because dealing with it can become a monumental task if it does. Make it a point to spend a few minutes on every inspection to keep things neat and tidy. Regularly tidying up will save you a great deal of effort.

Your New Colony's First Two Months

When setting up a fresh colony, additional duties need to be done, which are crucial for the initial phase months that your bees are in the hive. Actions we have already discussed such as smoking, opening and closing the hive, remain the same during any and all inspections.

However, with a new colony, some extra steps need to be implemented, and I have broken this down weekly for those first crucial two months.

Activities From Week 1 to Week 8

Week 1

Verifying the Queen was Released

Once you've settled your bee bundle into the hive, it's natural to be eager to peek inside and check their progress. However, you must resist this urge and allow a full week to pass before you open the hive.

This initial week without interruption is vital for the colony to get used to their new queen. If you disturb the hive too early, the colony could reject the queen, and they might even eliminate her, misinterpreting the disruption as her doing. So, it's best to err on the side of caution and leave the hive untouched for one week. During this period, the worker bees will chew through the candy barrier and free the queen from her confined space, effectively accepting her as their ruler.

Removing any Burr Comb

Hardworking bees have probably constructed an abundance of burr comb, also known as natural, wild, or brace comb, in the space made by the queen cage. You might even observe this comb adorning the queen cage itself. Despite its aesthetic appeal and impressive craftsmanship, it's crucial to eliminate this brilliantly white, perfectly ordered honeycomb.

This untamed comb close to and on the cage will likely house eggs—it's the queen's preferred spot for laying. Identifying these eggs verifies the presence of an egg-laying queen in your hive and offers you a firsthand glimpse of what the eggs look like!

Carefully inspect the comb to ascertain the queen isn't there. If she is, you must return her to the hive. You can position the comb she's on next to a frame, hoping she'll move from the burr comb to a frame. Alternatively, you might have to delicately detach her from the burr comb and reintroduce her to the hive.

Queens are fairly easy to handle, and even though they possess a stinger, they're not prone to using it. Hold her by her wings gently by dampening your thumb and index finger. She's nimble, so it might take a few attempts. Handle her carefully, like she's as fragile as an eggshell.

Novice beekeepers should remove all bees from the burr comb—the queen might be among them. A couple of firm shakes should knock the bees off the burr comb. Perfecting the technique of shaking bees free will prove useful frequently in the future. Shaking involves a swift downward movement, stopping abruptly just above the hive.

Preserve the natural burr comb to examine at your convenience back home. Watch for eggs, as the queen often begins laying on this comb. Ensure you save your burr comb, as the beeswax it contains can be repurposed to create interesting things, like candles.

Look for Eggs

Have you looked at the frames near the queen's dwelling? Notice any pollen or nectar? Fantastic! What about eggs? These are the key items to check during your initial inspection. If you spot eggs, it's a good sign that the queen is already busy. That's the only information you need from this first check. After that, you can wrap things up and give the bees a week of peace. Be content knowing everything is in order.

Replace Missing Frames

Remember the frame you initially took out when setting up your hive package? That's the one that gave space for the queen cage. It's important to put it back in the hive now. This frame should sit at the outermost spot, becoming your wall frame. Avoid placing it in the center. It's best to keep all the frames the bees work on closely packed.

Week 1 Checkpoints

- Ensure you take out the queen cage within 7 days post-hiving to prevent the growth of the comb amidst the frames. If the queen cage overstays its welcome, the bees might construct an extra comb between the frames where the queen cage is suspended which can be a real hassle to clean up. It's not what you need in your first week of beekeeping!

- Open up the hive, extract the queen cage, and close the frames back up.

- Avoid any other actions at this time.

- Scan the comb fragment for the queen and remove any bees from the burr comb.

- Depending on several elements like the weather, feed quantity, genetic factors, equipment quality, and robbing, they may have 1–2 partially drawn frames.

- Don't feel daunted by potential issues! You will work through any of these challenges as your experience grows.

- Such problems could include a deceased queen, death due to cold, absconding, or assuming the hive is without a queen simply because you can't find any brood.

Week 2 and 3

Look for Larvae

By the time the second week rolls around, it's quite simple to spot larvae at different growth phases. They ought to be a vibrant white, curved like the letter C, and shimmering like fresh white shrimp! If you pay close attention, you might even catch a larva squirming in its cell or perhaps see a worker bee nourishing one.

Evaluate Your Queen

Try to gauge the number of eggs the queen bee is producing. You can tell she's doing an exceptional job if you spot one or two frames where both sides are filled to about 75% with eggs and larvae.

In cases where only one side of one or two combs is filled, she's performing decently. If you notice any less than this, her performance is subpar and you might need to think about getting a replacement queen.

A high-quality queen will deposit eggs in almost every cell, only skipping a few here and there. This results in a dense layout of eggs, larvae, and capped brood that extends across most of the comb.

Hunt for Capped Brood

By week three, you'll start observing the final stage of bee metamorphosis, known as capped brood. They are easy to spot with their light tan color. However, remember that older comb brood cappings might be a deeper tan or dark brown.

The six-sided cell of the capping stands out, unlike the less distinguishable capped honey cells. You'll find these capped broods on the comb nearest to the hive's center, with egg and larvae cells on the neighboring comb.

You'll also spot a semi-circle of pollen-filled cells surrounding the brood area. Further up and towards the frame's top corners, you'll see cells brimming with nectar or capped honey. This is an ideal scenario.

However, if the brood pattern seems irregular and scattered, it could indicate a problem such as a lackluster queen. If you notice sunken brood cappings or holes, it could be a sign of brood disease, necessitating immediate identification of the cause and action to address it.

Look for Supersedure Cells

In the third week, it's important to start scouting for what are known as supersedure cells or queen cells. This is a natural process where a bee colony decides to substitute an old or sickly queen with a fresh one. A new queen will emerge from this supersedure cell and "supersede" the old queen. Most bee colonies will produce many of these which will enhance their odds of having a healthy queen and in many cases, the first one to emerge takes that role.

If the bees' sense that their queen isn't performing well or is somehow injured, they create these supersedure cells. These structures, resembling peanuts, signify that the colony might be considering replacing their queen. You can identify potential supersedure cells, usually one or two, on the upper sections of the comb.

However, suppose you notice queen cells on the lower third of the comb, particularly along the borders of a brood area. In that case, these are likely not supersedure cells, especially if they're numerous. These are known as swarm cells.

Bees create swarm cells to foster a new queen as a precursor to swarming, which typically occurs when the hive becomes overpopulated. The colony decides to split in two, with half of the bees swarming away from the hive with the old queen and the other half staying behind to wait for a new queen. We will discuss the development of swarm cells in a later chapter.

Getting a new queen is advisable if you come across supersedure cells, particularly in the early stages of your new colony's development. It's generally better to provide the bees with a new queen rather than having them generate one themselves.

Swarm Cells/Credit: Mr. Markus Wegmann(www.shutterstock.com)

Provide More Syrup

Make sure to look at your hive's feeder each week to confirm if there's sufficient sugar syrup. Top it up as required by pouring it into the feeder.

Week 2 & 3 Checkpoints:

Your job during this stage is mainly to provide food while leaving the bees to their own devices. Weekly check-ins are conducted to ensure everything is as it should be.

- Feeding
- Around 4–6 frames should be drawn. If this isn't the case, the quality of the package or queen might be questioned.
- If plastic foundation is being used, it's normal for growth to be slower than with natural wax.

What can you expect to observe?

- A large number of bees.
- Don't anticipate seeing full frames of capped larvae.
- The process of frames being drawn out.
- Open cells filled with nectar or syrup.
- Pollen.
- Various stages of brood—eggs, open larvae.
- Be on the lookout for queen cells.
- Dead bees, which is normal to an extent. Bees have a life cycle—they die and are replaced every day. However, heaps of dead bees aren't a positive sign.

Possible issues:

- No queen is present. This is evidenced by no eggs or brood, and frames aren't being drawn easily.
- Inefficient queen. Indicated by scarce eggs/brood and a poor pattern. Also, frames aren't being drawn easily.
- Queen replacement (often done by swarms. Remember, a package is like an artificial swarm)
- Death due to cold (this is rare)

Week 4

Add a Second Deep-Hive Body to Your Langstroth Hive

Assuming everything is going according to plan, you should start noticing significant growth in your bee colony by the completion of the fourth week. Most of the foundation will have been transformed into a comb by the bees.

They accomplish this by adding wax from their own wax glands to the foundation, forming hexagonal cells where they store pollen, honey, and brood. If you observe that 70 percent of the frames have been converted into a comb, it's time to introduce your second deep-hive body.

Simply put, this means adding the second body when 6 out of 8 frames are drawn into a comb in an 8-frame hive, or 7 out of 10 in a 10-frame hive.

It's crucial to anticipate when this addition will be necessary, as timing plays a key role. If you delay, the colony may expand too rapidly, with as many as 1,000 new bees emerging daily!

This could lead to overcrowding and, eventually, a swarm. Conversely, if you add the second deep-hive body too soon, the colony underneath could lose heat, which could chill and kill the brood.

When it's time to incorporate a second deep-hive body, here's the process you should follow:

1. Start by smoking your hive, just as you usually would.

2. Take off the outer cover and the top feeder of the hive (or the inner cover, if that's what you're using).

3. Set the second deep-hive body right over the existing hive body.

4. Prepare the new upper level by filling it with frames and foundations.

5. Position the top feeder of the hive right above the newly added upper deep but keep it under the outer cover.

6. Don't forget to refill the sugar syrup if required.

7. Finally, put the outer cover back on.

You'll find that the new upper deep-hive body is utilized for brood rearing in the early summer months. However, as fall approaches, it transforms into a food storage area, housing honey and pollen for the bees to consume during the winter.

Week 4 Checkpoints:

At this stage, you can slightly widen the entrance and keep the screened base shut.

- Continue with the feeding.
- Keep up with this until 8 frames are completely drawn, then decide whether to maintain the feed supply.
- There should be between 4 and 8 drawn frames, usually around 4 or 5, though 8 is outstanding!

You should notice:

- Exposed nectar, sealed honey.
- Pollen.
- Brood, eggs, open larvae, and closed pupae.
- Assess the brood pattern.
- Is there a need for an additional box? It's a maybe, depending on the amount drawn and their strength.
- The kind of box to introduce is up to you. The bees will occupy any space you provide.

Potential issues (don't let this scare you!)

- Inadequate queen. Replace if needed. This can be identified by a weak brood pattern and the bees' reluctance to draw comb.
- Supersedure. Stay alert for queen cells.

Week 5

By week five, the hives are teeming with eggs, young bees in different stages of growth, pollen, and honey. Take a close look at the fully developed larvae. You might just spot a marvel in action. Keep your eyes peeled for any movement beneath the sealed cells. A fresh new bee is on the brink of making its debut!

She will gnaw her way out of the cell and crawl out. Initially, her movements may seem unsteady, but she will quickly learn to navigate with her legs. She stands out with her lighter hue and is adorned with soft, moist hairs compared to her siblings. Witnessing this is truly a delight.

Provide More Ventilation

Around the fifth or sixth week, it's time to enhance the ventilation in your hive by making the entrance larger. Adjust the entrance reducer so the bigger one of its two slots is in the right place. This bigger opening is roughly about 4 inches in width.

Over time, this reducer will be entirely taken out. Your bee colony has grown strong enough to shield itself, and the weather has become more temperate. You can fully remove the entrance reducer by the eighth week after your bees have moved in.

Week 5 Checkpoints:

- Add additional boxes when needed, adjust combs, and ensure the screen remains shut.

- Continuous feeding is vital until 8 frames are filled. Once you've achieved this, you can decide whether or not to continue providing feed.

- As the colony's population grows, they will start to thrive more on nectar rather than sugar syrup.

- Keep the screened bottom shut. Screens are designed for controlling varroa mites, not for ventilation.

- They can still manage varroa mites effectively even when the slide is closed.

- Remember that a bee's ideal "room temperature" is 92 degrees, not 72 like ours. We're mammals, they're not; they're insects and we need to respect their unique needs. When we feel hot, they feel cool. Avoid attempting to ventilate their hives.

- They're better at managing their temperature compared to us. Keep that screen closed.

- You should notice 5–9 frames being filled out, with 3–4 being brood. If this isn't the case, you might be dealing with a weak queen.

- Expect the first new bees to hatch this week. Therefore, the population will begin to rise quickly. This means their work capacity will also increase. From this point forward, growth should be steady. Each day, the population will increase by approximately 1000–1500 bees!

- By now, you should have identified and addressed any major issues.

- When adding a second box, place two filled frames in its middle. Replace the relocated frames with foundation frames. This will encourage them to quickly move into the new box and fill out more foundation.

Week 6

Watching for Swarm Cells

Keep a sharp eye out for queen cells from the sixth to the eighth week, particularly a high concentration in the bottom third of the frames. These are what you'd call swarm cells, a telltale sign that the hive is gearing up to swarm.

If you're in your first season, don't sweat it too much if you come across a random swarm cell here and there. It's not common for a fledgling colony to swarm.

However, if you stumble upon eight or more swarm cells, it clearly indicates that the colony has swarming in mind.

When a colony swarms, half of its bees fly away with the old queen in pursuit of a roomier dwelling. Before this occurs, the bees make preparations to birth a new queen, marked by the appearance of swarm cells.

But with half your workforce gone and a few weeks squandered while the newly minted virgin queen gets her bearings, you're left with significantly fewer bees to gather honey. You will happily avoid this regrettable scenario by foreseeing the bees' requirement for larger living quarters and proper ventilation.

Week 6 checkpoints:

- Adjust the hive entrance based on the growth of the colony.
- If the bees are utilizing all the space, they're adding more boxes.
- Essentially, your role is to ensure they have ample space.

Week 7

Rearrangement of the Frames

Around week seven or eight, you'll want to rearrange the frames in your Langstroth hive to coax the bees into expanding more foundation into comb cells. This can be achieved by situating any undrawn foundation frames between frames of the new comb.

Remember, take care not to drop these frames directly in the center of the brood nest. This won't help your cause because it separates the nest, making it hard for the bees to manage the climate for their temperature-sensitive offspring.

Week 7 Checkpoints:

Take into consideration the action of your bees.

- The hive population can multiply by two given the rate at which new bees emerge.
- They're working relentlessly.
- This period is their most hectic time of the year!
- They know they need to gather and stockpile everything for the year before the nectar supply ceases in July.

They have the challenging task of amassing a year's worth of provisions quickly.

Week 8

Honey is Coming!

As we near the end of the eighth week, you might observe that the bees have not only filled out seven or more frames in the bottom box but also potentially seven out of the ten frames in your Langstroth hive's upper section.

Once this occurs, it's time to remove the top feeder of the hive (assuming you're still using one), incorporate a queen excluder, and install a shallow honey super complete with frames. Your little fuzzy workers are now set to commence the honey collection for you! Adding shallow honey supers to a colony is commonly referred to as "supering".

Multilevel Inspection

With two hive bodies now attached to your Langstroth hive (honey supers will come later), your inspection duties have expanded beyond just one box. In your inaugural season, it's crucial to examine the entire colony for the sake of experience—including the upper and lower deeps.

The inspection procedure stays the same, but you must meticulously remove all honey supers and the upper deep to access the lower deep. This is where your detailed, frame-by-frame inspection kicks off. However, as you get more seasoned, it's not necessary to scrutinize every single frame. You can then assess your colony's health by checking a few selected frames.

Remember, you're always looking for signs of the queen—a solid laying pattern, and a thriving brood. After checking all frames in the lower deep, put back the upper deep and initiate a similar frame-by-frame scrutiny.

Week 8 Checkpoints:

By this stage, your bee population will be growing immensely and their primary focus will remain on the hectic gathering of nectar and pollen and nurturing new bees.

- With the nectar flow gradually lessening, the pace of comb construction will also reduce. This is why it's important to rearrange the frames to ensure maximum comb drawing before they likely cease comb building around mid-June.

- The bees should now seal the fresh honey, possibly even producing a surplus!

- Your actions should mimic the previous week (week 7)—managing space, adding boxes when needed, and repositioning frames.

- Feeding isn't required unless the hive was underperforming previously. By this stage, the bees should be self-reliant.

- Reposition frames to encourage foundation drawing.

Inspections After the First 8 Weeks

As we move further into the season, you'll notice that the bees will start to utilize the upper deep for honey storage, meaning you'll no longer spot the queen, eggs, or brood there. The real hive action is in the lower deep, especially as summer continues. This should be the primary focus of your checks.

- Remember to complete all the previously mentioned activities.

- Think about adjusting your inspection frequency based on previous discussions regarding setting an inspection schedule.

- Consider keeping a journal to document your progress and observations.

- As a bonus, I will provide you with a handy checklist to keep track of your inspections.

As you observe your bees, you'll learn about the timing of new bees' orientation flights, when the housekeeping bees start their cleaning duties, and when the drones return for the day. Any significant deviation from these regular patterns should serve as a warning sign, indicating that something might be off, and a hive inspection is due.

Despite the importance of hive inspections, remember that disturbing the hive can stress the bees, so avoid doing it excessively.

When bees are under stress, they might:

- Depart – Abandon their hive in search of a safer or more appealing location.

- Eliminate the queen.

- Replace the queen

Beekeeping Throughout the Four Seasons

No matter where they're found, bees feel the shift in the seasons. The USA is a massive nation with a wide range of weather conditions. Whether traveling from the northern regions to the southern ones or from the west coast to the east, you can experience everything from intense cold to exhausting heat.

The US isn't confined to one specific climate zone, hence it's impossible to pin it down to just one unique landscape. The vast plains experience a desert-like climate, while California enjoys a mild and pleasant Mediterranean climate. And let's not forget the folks in frosty Alaska who have the privilege of witnessing the northern lights on their doorstep.

These varying climates result in different timelines and tasks for the hive and the beekeeper. Understanding the significant actions happening within the hive and what's expected of you during these periods is beneficial. For an effective beekeeper, foresight is the secret to success.

The following section provides an advisory timeline of seasonal tasks for the beekeeper.

However, it's important to understand that factors like geography, weather, climate, neighborhood, and even bee species can affect the timing of these activities. This book is written from the perspective of a beekeeper who experiences noticeable shifts in seasons and climate.

What Happens Inside the Hive During Each Season?

Summer

The nectar flow typically hits its zenith in the summer months, coinciding with the time when the bee colony is at its largest. At such times, your bee colonies can fend for themselves, brimming with worker bees who are constantly busy gathering pollen, collecting nectar to turn into honey, and constructing beeswax combs for storage.

However, it's worth mentioning that the queen bee's egg-laying pace does slow during late summer. On sweltering and muggy nights, you might spot a large cluster of bees clinging to the outside of the hive. No need for concern; they're not leaving. They're merely taking a breather on the hive's exterior, a phenomenon known as "bearding".

As summer draws to a close, the colony's growth starts to slow down. The drones remain, but the outside hustle and bustle cool down as the nectar flow lessens. The bees' restlessness is noticeable, and they tend to guard their honey more during this time.

Just to set the record straight, honey harvesting is not a requirement—it's a beekeeping perk. Thus, if your only aim in beekeeping is pollination, and you have no interest in honey collection, you can simply leave the bees to collect honey for their consumption during periods when there's a lack of flowers and nectar to gather.

Bearding/Credit: Michael LaMonica(www.shutterstock.com)

Autumn

As the autumn days start to shorten and the chill sets in, the availability of nectar and pollen tends to dwindle. As a result, the hustle and bustle within your beehive start to slow down. The queen bee cuts back significantly on her egg-laying, the male bees—drones—begin dwindling, and the hive's population decreases.

Your bees start gathering propolis to seal any cracks in the hive that might let in the frigid winter winds. The colony is battening down the hatches for the winter, and it's your job to assist your bees in preparing for it.

Winter

The beehive has quite a bit of activity during the frosty winter months. Thousands of worker bees huddle around their queen, providing warmth as part of the winter cluster. This cluster forms in the brood chamber when the temperature drops to around 50 to 60 degrees Fahrenheit.

This cluster, which organizes itself between the two hive bodies when the cold sets in, covers the top bars of the frames in the lower chamber and extends toward and beyond the bottom bars of the frames in the food chamber.

Despite the freezing temperatures outside, the heart of this winter cluster maintains a cozy temperature of 90 to 93 degrees Fahrenheit thanks to the heat generated by the bees as they "shiver" their wing muscles.

The hive is devoid of drones during winter, but worker broods gradually emerge as winter nears its end. All this while, the bees munch through approximately 50 to 60 pounds of honey stored in the hive over the winter. When the temperature climbs over 40 to 45 degrees Fahrenheit, they all move together as they feed within the cluster. They can transition to a fresh honey area only when the weather is warm enough for them to disperse from the cluster.

Interestingly, bees do not defecate inside their hive. They hold out for a pleasant, mild day when the temperature climbs to 45 to 50 degrees Fahrenheit at which point they venture out of the hive for cleansing flights.

Spring

Spring is literally a hive of activity for both bees and their keepers—a time of renewal and revival. As the days gradually lengthen and warm up, existing bee colonies bustle back to life.

The queen bee gets busier, laying eggs at an unprecedented rate. Drone bees start to make their presence known, and the hive becomes a bustling hub. Nectar and pollen flood in, creating a buzz in the hive. The hive is simply humming with life and activity during this time.

Your Time Commitment During Each Season

Summer

Throughout summer, you're not that busy, as most of the work is done by your bees, leading up to the honey harvest at summer's end. You can expect to dedicate eight to ten hours over the summer to your bees. The majority of this time is spent on collecting and packing the honey.

Autumn

Plan on dedicating around three to five hours to ensure your bees are nourished and ready for the upcoming winter season.

Winter

In this season, the bees are huddled up for warmth in their winter cluster, cozily tucked inside their hive. Anticipate allocating about two to three hours for the mending of preserved equipment. If you make any additional crafts from your honey or wax, winter is the time to do it!

Spring

Spring happens to be the most hectic season for those who keep bees. You can expect to devote anywhere from eight to 12 hours caring for your bees.

Hive Activities During Each Season

Summer

In between your beach escapades and sizzling barbecues, here's a rundown of tasks you'll need to slot in:

- Regularly check your bee colony every couple of weeks. Make sure all is well and the queen bee is in her place as expected.

- Stay alert and vigilant to any budding pest issues.

- Add more honey supers as required.

- Take care of swarm control throughout the summer. Swarming is less likely to happen as the summer progresses.

- Keep an eye out for honey-thieving wasps or bees from other hives. A hive under a full-blown attack is a terrible scene.

- Ensure your bees have ample access to water. They'll need it to keep the hive cool during those hot summer days.

- At the end of the nectar flow, it's time to collect your honey.

- But remember to leave sufficient capped honey for the bees to feed on during winter.

Autumn

In preparing your bees for the oncoming challenges of winter, you must check on them, peering inside the hive to confirm the queen's presence.

- Make sure you're looking for eggs and not larvae. Seeing eggs indicates that the queen has been around for the past three days. Conversely, larvae could be three to eight days old, so finding them isn't a foolproof sign of a recently productive queen.

- If you delay your inspection until late fall, you might find a scarcity of eggs and larvae. In such a scenario, spotting the queen herself is the most reliable method.

- Take your time and observe cautiously.

- Assess if the bees have sufficient honey.

- Ensure that the upper deep-hive body is filled with honey or close to being filled. Honey is a vital energy source for your bees, fueling their survival.

- Even if there's plenty of honey, you can always provide a backup food source by adding sugar "fondant" on top of the upper deep frames that serve as emergency carbohydrates for the bees. As a rule of thumb, estimate 60 pounds of honey if you live in northern United States and have longer, colder winters. If you live in the South, you can estimate around half that amount.

- You can also place a high-quality pollen patty atop these frames, functioning as their emergency protein.

- One must not undervalue the significance of providing the best nutrition for your bees. A robust, healthy hive is the best natural protection for bees against diseases and parasites.

Winter

You've already set up your hive to withstand the typical weather conditions in your area. Now, your tasks include the following:

- Keep an eye on the hive entrance, delicately removing any dead bees or snow hindering it.

- You want to avoid disturbing the bees inside.

- Ensure the bees have sufficient food! Late winter and early spring are the most dangerous times, as colonies can starve to death.

- When winter is almost over, and you have a calm, mild day with bees buzzing around, quickly glance into your hive. It's best not to move any frames. Simply lift the cover and check for bees. They should still be grouped in a cluster in the upper deep.

- You might have to initiate emergency syrup feeding if you don't spot any sealed honey in the top frames. But keep in mind that once you start feeding, you can't stop until the bees collect their pollen and nectar.

- Clean, fix, and store your beekeeping gear for the winter.

- If necessary, order package bees and equipment from a trusted source.

Spring

Spring brings a slew of tasks for beekeepers as they assess the condition of their hives and prepare their bees for the summer season. These tasks can include:

- Embarking on an initial inspection.

- As soon as spring arrives, it's crucial to do a swift check on the colonies.

- The precise timing will hinge on your geographical location—the warmer the climate, the earlier the inspection can occur, and vice versa.

- You need not wait for bees to buzz around daily or for clear spring indicators like budding flowers to start your initial spring check. Choose a sunny, calm day with temperatures around 50 degrees for your first inspection.

- If it's chilly enough to warrant a bulky coat, it's too cold to check on the bees.

- Verify if your bees survived the winter season.

- The cluster should ideally be situated high in the upper part of the deep-hive body. If it's not visible, can you hear it? Try tapping the hive's side, listen closely, and you should hear a faint buzz or hum.

- If it seems your bees did not survive, dismantle the hive, remove any dead bees, rebuild it, and order new bees as soon as possible. Don't lose hope, as bee loss happens to everyone at some point.

- Ensure that you have a queen in your hive.

- If your hive is inhabited, glance between some frames. Do you see any brood? That's a positive sign indicating the queen's presence. You might need to cautiously remove a frame from the top middle for a better view.

- You need to conduct this inspection promptly as exposure to cold air could harm the frame.

- If you don't spot any brood or eggs, your hive might be queen-less and you need to order a new queen immediately, provided the hive population is large enough to incubate the brood when the new queen arrives.

- A sufficient population means a cluster of bees at least the size of a large grapefruit, hopefully even larger. If you have fewer bees, consider ordering a new package of bees and a queen.

- Make sure your bees have food. Look between the frames to see if you can find honey, which is sealed with white cappings. If you spot honey, that's fantastic.

- If not, you must initiate an emergency feeding plan for your bees.

- Start feeding the colony. Start feeding your bees a few weeks before the start of the bloom season, regardless of whether they still have honey.

- Feed them sugar syrup. This stimulates the queen to lay eggs at an accelerated pace and activates the worker bees' wax glands. Continue the feeding until the bees start bringing in their food. When you see them walking around with pollen on their legs, you'll know.

- Provide your colony with a pollen substitute, which fortifies your hive and encourages the queen to lay eggs.

- Plan for your colony's expansion. Don't wait until your hive is overflowing with bees.

You are now furnished with an extensive checklist of tasks for beekeepers, which will differ according to your geographical position and the resilience zone you occupy within the United States. The matching dates and duties may fluctuate based on real weather situations, altitude, among other factors.

CHAPTER 8
Harvesting Honey

What Exactly is Honey?

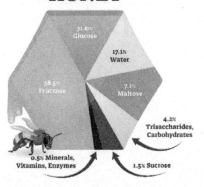

Credit: VectorMine(www.shutterstock.com)

The simple answer is: sugar. That's by far the most significant part. But it's not quite *that* straightforward because there are several different kinds of sugar. Fructose is the main one at 40%, followed by glucose at 30%. These, making up 70% of the composition of honey, are the simple sugars, sometimes called levulose and dextrose, respectively. Then we have the complex sugars, up to 22 in small amounts, including sucrose (the main ingredient of nectar) and maltose. The other 20 complex sugars are usually called the "sugar dextrin."

Honey is around 17% water. Then, throw in a few vitamins, minerals, and antioxidants and you have the complete ensemble. The key thing to note is that it's mainly sugar.

Now, we get to the interesting bit. I will state the obvious—honey is made by honey bees! But there's a bit more to it than that. The bees do two key things. First, they collect pollen and nectar, returning it to the hive. Then, they release enzymes that gradually turn the nectar into honey.

Most of the sugars aren't in the nectar, other than the sucrose. The enzymes create most of it, breaking down the sucrose into fructose and glucose.

There's another significant difference between nectar and honey; bees also play a key role in that. Nectar is 80% water, yet when bees transform nectar into honey, they flap their wings energetically, causing evaporation of a large portion of the water. The result leaves honey thicker than nectar with only about 17% water.

This honey is food for the bees but, luckily, most hives have a tendency to over-production, meaning there's some left for us humans. On average, there's an excess of around 30 to 60lbs a year from each hive.

Types of Honey

- **Comb Honey:** this is honey still in its honeycomb. Coming straight from the hive, untouched by human hands (not exactly correct, as somebody has to take it from the hive!) Comb honey is just as the bees made it, in the hexagonal beeswax cells they created. It used to be the main way we would eat honey but that's changed with growing technology. Comb honey remains a popular way to eat a natural product in its natural form.

- **Extracted Honey:** this is the most common honey these days. It refers to comb honey that's been extracted from the beeswax cells. The adoption of the Langstroth vertical hive in the mid-19th century prompted the use of a centrifugal extractor to separate the honey from the honeycomb; centrifugal extractors work effectively with Langstroth frames, which can then be reused. Most honey we buy today is extracted honey.

- **Chunk Honey**: Chunk honey is a chunk of honeycomb in a jar of extracted honey. It's a halfway house between comb honey and extracted honey, a bit of both in a jar. There's not an awful lot more to say about chunk honey. It's better to think of what it's not; it's not pure comb, although it contains a "chunk" of comb, and it's not a jar of extracted honey because it's "contaminated" by the chunky bit.

- **Whipped Honey:** Other names are aerated or spun honey. The clues are in the names. The process of aerating, usually through modern agitating machinery, gives it a fluffy and lighter texture, almost like whipped cream. It makes it more spreadable and, hence, is popular for eating with bread. It shouldn't be confused with creamed honey, which shares much of whipped honey's characteristics, but is made during the crystallization process rather than by inserting air.

- **Honeydew Honey:** Otherwise referred to as "forest honey," this is honey made from the honeydew the bees take from trees and other sap-producing plants. It's made by the bees in the same way but has a tendency to be darker than regular honey and actually has a higher amount of certain nutrients than floral honey.

Serious Honey Facts

Here are a few general facts to take on board, as you indulge in this delicious and nutritious foodstuff:

- Don't ever think about storing your honey in a refrigerator. Honey will last longer at cold temperatures but it will increase the rate of crystallization, causing the honey to become thick and sludge-like. You've made a lot of effort to set up hives and let the bees get on with what they do best. Don't ruin it all at the last minute by popping it in the refrigerator! It will last perfectly long enough at room temperature.

- Crystallization is the process by which sugar crystals grow in the honey. The first thing to bear in mind is that it's a completely natural phenomenon. The precise rate at which crystallization occurs depends on the interaction between two factors: the ratio between fructose and glucose (F/G) and the ratio between glucose and water (G/W). A high F/G combined with a low G/W is what you're aiming for as it will keep crystallization at a moderate pace (remember, there's nothing you can do to stop it completely). As the glucose increases (moving towards a low F/G) so the glucose will tend to crystallize. This will look like the honey has thickened up considerably, becoming awkward to spread. It's a natural process, but one you can and should avoid as it makes the honey look less desirable. If you're not careful, you'll end up with a shelf full of honey jars that nobody wants to buy.

- If you do notice crystallization, all is not lost. You can warm your honey jar gently by putting it in hot water on the stove. However, this shouldn't be done frequently because it can wreck the taste while reducing the microbial stability. Do it as a last resort but, remember, honey doesn't have nine lives—best to keep it out of the refrigerator and eat it up before it crystallizes.

- This last point is a serious health warning. **Don't ever give honey to a baby.** The point at which you can introduce honey is generally held to be at the one-year mark; after that, it should be safe because the digestive system quickly matures to become capable of managing the bacteria found in honey. Before this age, there is a distinct possibility of the baby developing infant botulism, something you definitely don't want on your conscience. It's a serious disease with symptoms that include muscle weakness and constipation.

Honey's Healing Properties

Enough of the downside. Remember, honey is good for you, it's official. Yes, it's got a lot of sugar in it, but balance that against the other attributes it offers. First amongst these must be the antioxidants in honey. These take the form of phenolic acids and flavonoids as well as a host of other antioxidants. They work to counter the damaging effect of oxidants on the human body that contribute to cancer, diabetes, inflammatory and thrombotic diseases, cardiovascular problems, and allergies.

While the exact way the antioxidants in honey work remains uncertain, they are known to utilize free radicals, hydrogen donation, and flavonoid substrate action; as more research into these particular healing properties of honey is done, the precise causes and mechanisms will become clearer.

Suffice it to say that honey works as an excellent source of antioxidants.

Regarding diabetes, honey has been used back into the depths of history, but its capability was based on the casual observation of the benefits of diabetic patients consuming honey over other sugars. A study completed in 2018 indicated that the high level of fructose in honey, and the antioxidants, may make it a viable and effective source of sweetener, compared to sugar. It is now thought that the pancreas (the source of both insulin and glucagon, two important glucose-regulating hormones) benefits directly from the antioxidant features of honey.

Honey also contributes to antibacterial activity including fighting antibacterial resistance. Manuka honey, containing methylglyoxal, has been shown to be particularly effective in this regard. The theory is that the high sugar content of honey acts with the low PH value to slow down the growth of microbes. Manuka honey is made by bees that gather nectar and pollen exclusively from the manuka tree.

Not only do the component parts of the honey fight against oxidants and bacteria in humans but it has been shown to be effective in countering viruses such as the common cold and flu while simultaneously boosting the immune system to prevent a reoccurrence of the virus.

Honey Variations

The crucial thing to get here is that honey is a natural product. You might feel that *you've* made it after all the effort you've put into setting up and monitoring your hives—but you've got to face the reality that *bees,* not humans, make honey. They race around collecting pollen and nectar, take it back to their hives, and—hey presto—turn it into honey.

They collect nectar; that's the second crucial fact. They will buzz around their local area to find as much of the stuff as they can. That means the flowers growing in that region will, undoubtedly, affect the taste of honey, its consistency, and nutritional value. The "terroir" is the area over which bees will travel to collect nectar. Bear in mind, a bee can travel as far as five miles from its hive on collection duty, although a mile is more common; that makes for a big terroir with potentially a lot of variety in plant life.

No two terroirs are the same, and no two honeybees are the same for that matter (hence different enzymes from different bees will have a bearing on the resulting honey). And bees don't set out to collect from a particular flower on a Monday or another on a Tuesday; they mix their nectar together, not caring too much about where it comes from.

All this affects the flavor of honey, its color, consistency, and nutritional value. It's also part of the beauty of the variation; wouldn't it be boring if all honey was made to be identical?

One variation that *can* be controlled to a certain extent is honey made from wildflowers, simply by having wildflower meadows predominant in the hive's terroir. Wildflower honey varies by its very nature—who is to say if one wildflower species has a better year than another? Generally, however, it is darker than regular floral honey and tastes stronger. It also carries a little more antioxidants, making it marginally healthier to eat.

Wildflower is essentially one type of honey, made from the pollen and nectar of wildflowers and sometimes used as a generic description when the plants used are unclear or unknown. Many other types of honey are uni-floral and each has a unique taste, color, and composition.

<u>Chief amongst these are the following:</u>

- *Clover*—sweet and aromatic, pale in color.

- *Orange*—distinctive orange taste, amber in color, (as one would expect).

- *Buckwheat*—varies by region but is generally darker and strong-tasting, often with an aftertaste of malt and molasses.

- *Blueberry* is surprisingly quite delicate in flavor with a buttery complexion, although there are no surprises as to its fruity taste.

- *Alfalfa*—mild and light, almost white in color.

- *Avocado*—smooth, almost velvet in texture with a rich and strong taste.

Raw Honey

Then there's raw honey as compared to processed. Raw honey is just as it comes, straight from the hive. Making it processed means pasteurizing the raw honey and sometimes adding extra sugar. There's no doubt that raw honey is more beneficial for your health, although people disagree about the extent to which the pasteurization process removes the antioxidants and enzymes.

Organic Honey

Let's move on to organic honey. Two aspects make organic honey stand out. The first is that it's made from the pollen and nectar of organic plants—plants grown without synthetic fertilization, genetic engineering, chemically based pesticides or irradiation. The second is that the bees themselves have not had any form of chemical treatment so they can be truly classified as organic.

And given that long process, it is easy to see how proving the source of the pollen and nectar is chemical free is difficult. After all, the only way to manage this is to monitor the surrounding area carefully, bearing in mind that bees, while they normally stay within about a mile of the hive, can wander off up to five miles! That means there is an awful lot of wild flora to watch over. Of course, not applying chemicals to the bees is much easier to manage.

There are no other restrictions concerning organic honey. It can still be pasteurized, therefore you can get both raw and processed honey that's organic. If you're in the market for organic honey, it's best to look for an organic certificate—they are not handed out lightly.

Strained & Filtered Honey

Next, we have the difference between strained and filtered honey. They sound similar, but they are not at all. Strained is the simplest, and it means what the word says: the honey has been strained to remove large particles but it leaves behind the smaller stuff, such as the pollen.

Filtering involves heating the honey, then rapidly cooling it, and then straining it. This has the effect of reducing all particles. The benefit of this is that it delays crystallization and, hence, increases shelf life. The disadvantage is that some of those added bits are patently good for you.

It's swings and roundabouts with regard to filtering and every hive owner needs to make his or her own decision in this regard. You could try both and see what you and your customers prefer.

Infusions

Now we get on to another fun bit—infusing your honey with other flavors. These can be anything from spices, herbs, nuts, fruit and vegetables (the latter two once dried).

There's a lot of trial and error with infusing flavors. That's mainly because there are a lot of variables. The strength of the chosen flavour, for instance. The quantity of honey is another. Then there's whether you want a hint, or a mouthful, of lemon or pepper.

It's best to start small with your chosen infusions and keep checking by tasting every other day; that way, you stop when you've reached your target and are pleased with the result. By checking every couple of days, you can stir the honey and add more infusing ingredients if needed. Finally, when you're happy with the flavor you've achieved, filter it, bottle it, and you're ready to go.

You can try any flavor you like for your honey; that's the beauty of it, you can create your own combination of tastes to add to the honey your bees have worked hard on. The result is going to be unique and created by your bees and you!

Harvest Time

This book concentrates on extracted honey because this is a beginners' guide and producing extracted honey is the easiest way to start.

Now, you've judged it's time to collect some honey from your hive—this is how you go about it.

Rule Number One: don't expect too much; chances are you'll have *something*, but you won't be breaking records or winning prizes the first time around! Treat it as a learning experience.

The Equipment

- **Honey Extractors:** these look like trash cans on legs or old-fashioned stoves. They're mechanical devices working on centrifugal force. You place the honeycomb in the basket and put the basket in the drum. As the basket inside the drum spins around, the honey is literally flung out through the holes in the basket into the drum. The beauty of this is that you don't destroy the honeycomb when extracting the honey. These extractors are often hand-turned with a wheel on the top, giving the centrifugal force required through gearing. It typically takes about five minutes to extract all the honey. The empty honeycombs can then be returned to the hive, ready to start again.

Honey Extractor/Credit: Matchou(<u>*www.shutterstock.com*</u>*)*

- **Uncapping Knife:** this is a serrated knife used to cut the cappings from the frame before placing them in the extractor. They can be manual or electric.

Uncapping Knife/Credit: FotoHelin(www.shutterstock.com)

- **Honey Strainer:** a honey strainer is no more than a plastic or stainless steel holed container used to strain the honey coming from the extractor into the bucket. Strainers come in different grades, governed by the size of the holes, usually measured in microns (a micron is a thousandth of a millimetre so we're talking incredibly small). The strainer can be placed in the top of the bucket so that it sits there and the honey can flow directly from the extractor placed above. Sometimes, the flow of honey is too great for the straining process and there's a risk of overflow. If this looks likely, take away the strainer and let the honey flow directly into the bucket unstrained. Leave the bucket for a day or so, and then there's the option of doing it all again to get the level of straining you need.

Honey Strainer/Credit: Vikentiy Elizarov(www.shutterstock.com)

- **Uncapping Tank:** this device removes wax from the honey frame and allows the honey to fall to the bottom. It comes in two halves and is usually made from plastic but with a stainless steel holed bottom to the top half. A bar across the top allows you to rest the frame on the top as you use your uncapping knife to scrape the wax into the top half, from which the honey then drains through the stainless steel bottom into the lower half of the tank.

Uncapping Tank/Credit: lantapix(www.shutterstock.com)

- **Uncapping Fork or Roller:** an uncapping fork looks like a nit comb with many fine metal teeth on a handle. You can use it to edge off the wax from the frame without damaging the frame or disturbing the honey beneath the wax. An uncapping roller looks like a small paint roller but has many small pins on it. As you roll across the frame, the pins make tiny piercings into each cell of the frame. This allows the honey to flow out during extraction but leaves much of the wax in place. You can put the frame back in the hive like this; the bees will clean it up for you before starting again on making honey.

Uncapping Fork/Credit: Yuri A(www.shutterstock.com)

- **Bottling Bucket:** this is a plastic bucket, often five gallon capacity, that takes the filtered honey following extraction. It has a tap at the bottom to allow easy pouring into the jars you store your honey in.

Bottling Bucket/Credit: Pavlo Lys(www.shutterstock.com)

- **Solar Wax Melter:** think cold frames and the warming effect of glass. A solar wax melter is a tilted box with a glass lid. You can put all your wax cuttings in there and face the lid towards the sun which then does all the work. The wax melts and drips into a collection pan.

- **Honey Containers:** whatever you do, don't forget something to put the finished honey in, ready for your pantry or for sale.

Honey Harvest Set Up

Honey Harvest Setup

First, you need to find a place for honey prep where your fuzzy friends, the bees, aren't going to bother you. If you have an outhouse, so much the better. Close the doors, set up your equipment, and get ready.

Second, you need a water source. Hot *and* cold is best but, failing that, a large basin of warm water is fine. This isn't for the process at all, but honey is a very sticky foodstuff and it's best to have some way of rinsing your hands, (which you'll need to do frequently).

Third, think ahead to clean up time. Place a large cloth or multiple sheets of newspaper on the floor; you'll be grateful for this when clearing up afterward.

Think about the particular equipment you're planning to use. Are you using a manual extractor? In which case it might be easier to sit as you turn the handle. If electric, or using anything electric (such as an electric uncapping knife), then you'll need a power source. Ensure you've got extension cables in place before starting the extraction; you don't want to be distracted during this crucial stage.

It's best to run through the flow, not just in your mind—but acting out the process. You'll start by bringing in some frames. Where are you going to place them? How will you get the cappings off so you can extract the honey? What size bucket are you using? Is that going to be big enough? Going too big will be awkward to handle, of course. Where are you going to put the tools when not using them? The one thing you *won't* need on extraction day is the jars or bottles you plan on placing the honey in, because it's best to let the honey settle in the bucket for a while. There is plenty of time to get the jars out later rather than risk knocking them over now!

After you've run through the process a couple of times, making any adjustments to the setup you deem appropriate, you've finished with the dress rehearsals and are on to the opening night.

Big breath everyone, first time harvests are fun, provided you've prepared well for them!

Honey Harvest: You've made it!

Capped Frame/Credit: Megan Kobe(www.shutterstock.com)

The first question has to be, how on earth do you know it's time to harvest? Is it something to do with ancient gods and the cycle of the moon?

Not at all. There's a lot more common sense to it than that. First, there's the rule of thumb with three principal nectar flows (in the northern hemisphere) as follows:

1. Mid-April to end of May: this will be pollen and nectar from fruit trees and bushes, oil seed rape, sycamore, and hawthorn—the main spring providers of pollen and nectar.

2. Mid-June to the first week of August: clover, willow herb, blackberry, etc., basically the summer producers of pollen and nectar.

3. August and September: for heather, the late summer flowers.

Whichever broad category you fit into, setting the harvest day towards the end of the nectar flow period is best. That's because you want the bees to have maximum time to produce honey.

But, we're still not asking you to take a blind leap of faith in selecting your harvest day! Weather varies, and so does the bee population. These dates are just rough guides. You need to start harvesting when at least 75% of the frames are capped with the honey beneath. It might easily take a week or even two weeks after the end of the nectar flow to get to this point. You can buy a refractometer to check that the honey is dry enough. (The best percentage of naturally occurring water in honey is between 15.5% and 18.6%). Or you can check periodically; if you can shake loose some nectar from any uncapped cells within the selected frame, it's not quite ready yet.

So, you definitely can't put a honey harvest date in your diary on New Year's Day; best to stay flexible and watchful and start when you judge there's enough capping to cover most of the frames that you want to use.

The main problem with a delay is that there's a risk that the honey will become crystallized, and this will make it very hard to extract it. If this happens once, I can guarantee you won't make the same mistake again!

Another consideration before harvest starts is how much honey you're going to take and how much you should leave as bee food for the winter. A rough rule of thumb as to what the bees need is 20–30lbs in a warmer climate and 60–70lbs of honey in colder areas. To estimate what you're likely to get, each long frame in a Langstroth hive gives about 6 lbs of honey. A medium frame comes in about 4 lbs while the smaller one does only 3 lbs. Do the calculations and work out what you need to leave to feed the bees in winter; the rest is yours.

Getting the Bees out of the Supers

This is always Stage One on harvest day. You need to remove the bees from the honeycomb—and you aren't going to get too far unless you succeed in this preparatory stage! There are several ways to do this and we will look at each one:

Shake them out

This is the simplest way to get the bees off the frame but it gets tricky with multiple frames so best to do this with small-scale honey production only. That's because the bees will cotton on to what's happening and get more aggressive. Make sure you're well-protected before following this method.

Choose a frame and shake it above the hive, a good sharp shake should do the trick. Repeat if necessary, the bees should fall off into the open hive. If any remain, you can brush them off with short sweeps rather than long brushes. When the frame is pretty clear, take it to your collection box and secure it inside, doing up the box. Go back for the second frame and start again. When you have all the frames you intend harvesting, take the collection box further away, open it again, and gently remove the few remaining bees. Project complete.

Blow them out

This can be a simple leaf blower, with no need for specialized equipment. It's best to do this away from the hive rather than shake the bees back into the hive. The big advantage is that you don't have to go frame by frame (as with shaking), you can do a box at a time. A few bees will inevitably perish, but no more than with most other methods of separating them.

A bee escape board

Escape Board

This is a thin platform inserted between boxes containing frames within the hive. The platform has a hole in the bottom, underneath which is constructed essentially a one-way system using wood pieces and cage wire; the bees drop down through the hole and work their way through the one-way system which leads to the box below. They can't find a way to go against the flow and re-enter the higher frame. The advantage of this technique is that no bees are hurt but the disadvantage is that it takes a few days for all the bees to drop through the system; it's a good way of getting the bees away from the super if you've got the patience to wait.;

Fume and bee repellent method

A fume box is a wooden open box on which you spray a repellent chemical with a strong, nasty smell.

The steps to complete this technique are:

1. Locate the fume box and repellent spray close to the hive.
2. Prepare the fume box by spraying a liberal amount of repellent spray on the inside lid of the fume box.
3. Remove the lid of the hive and place the fume box on the top of the hive.
4. Leave for 20 minutes or so.
5. Remove the fume box. You should notice very few bees on the frames as you pull them out to extract the honey.
6. Take care—the bees dislike the spray's smell, moving away from the source, further down into the hive. However, they do get much more agitated as a result.

Using a fume box is an effective way to rid the bees from the frames you want to extract honey from but it involves annoying the bees and is also not compliant with making organic honey.

The Process of Extracting Honey

You're ready for it now, all prepared, so dive in. Here's the step-by-step process:

1. Open the hive—remove the top cover and inner cover.
2. Separate the bees from the first frame selected using one of the methods detailed above.
3. Take the cappings off the honey cells—use one of the methods detailed previously (uncapping knife, uncapping roller, uncapping fork).
4. Remove the frame to the collection box, away from the hive.
5. Go back to select the next frame and continue the procedure until all selected frames are secure in the collection box.
6. Remove the collection box further from the hive and open it to ensure no more bees remain. Any remaining should be brushed off.
7. Take frames to the honey extractor and place the first frames in the basket. Ensure they are balanced in the extractor to prevent unnecessary vibration when running.

8. Turn the handle or apply electricity to the extractor. After a few minutes, you will have extracted all the honey.

9. Next, strain the honey by opening the tap at the bottom of the extractor after placing a honey strainer below the tap, and a bottling bucket below the strainer.

10. Take care that the flow of honey doesn't overflow the honey strainer. If there's a risk of this happening, remove the honey strainer and let the honey flow freely into the bottling bucket. You will need to leave it a day or so and then strain again.

11. Finally, bottling time. You can position the bottling bucket on a table and hold a jar under the tap at the bottom. Turn the tap on and the strained honey will fill the jar, ready to eat. Continue with new jars until the honey has all been bottled in this way.

Harvesting Beeswax

1. Beeswax is an important by-product of honey production. While its used commonly in candles, it has many other uses, such as making wraps to store food, as furniture polish, waterproofing your shoes, rust prevention in tools, homemade cosmetics, lip balm, and so much more!

2. Here's how to get the most from your endeavors by also harvesting the wax from your hive:

3. Open the hive and remove the first selected frame as detailed above for the extraction procedure.

4. Use an uncapping knife to separate the cappings from the frame. Place the cappings in a bucket so that the honey contained within will naturally fall to the bottom.

5. Assuming you're not collecting honey at the present time, place the frame back in the hive and start again with the next frame. Repeat until you've got the quantity of cappings you need.

6. Pick up the cappings after about half an hour and prepare them for rendering by placing them in a small bowl after holding them over the bucket for a moment to allow as much honey as possible to drain into the bucket.

7. To render the beeswax, use at least two pieces of cheesecloth, wrapping the beeswax in successive cheesecloths, tying with a piece of string, a clip, or a twist tie.

8. Place the bundle in a large pot of water so that the cheesecloths containing the beeswax are completely covered in water. Place on a stove and heat. As the water warms up, the beeswax will melt away from the cappings and come through the cloths into the water.

9. Squeeze the bundle to ensure that as much beeswax as possible has passed through the cheesecloth wrappings. You can use tongs to squeeze.

10. When you have seeped the maximum beeswax through, lift the cheesecloth bundle completely and discard it.

11. The next stage is to turn off the heat and let the pot cool. This will probably take up to four hours.

12. Finally, tip the remaining water out of the pot, holding the solid beeswax in place so it remains in the pot. This resulting beeswax can be melted down and used for candles, or your next cosmetic line!

CHAPTER 9

Anticipating and Preventing Potential Problems

This chapter concentrates on some of the more common but non-health-related bee conditions, describing the effect, the signs, how to anticipate and avoid them, and what to do when they happen anyway!

Swarming

Swarming is when about half your bees decide to move somewhere else. It has several implications for your beekeeping activities and the bees' ability to produce surplus honey. There are four main indicators that your bees might be getting ready to swarm:

1. A population explosion—the winter population of 10,000 bees could quickly increase six-fold over the summer, risking overcrowding. Another sign is an increase in idle population numbers, or in drone bees. An increase in bee numbers is to be expected and doesn't mean a swarm is imminent, but it should be taken as an early warning.

2. Increase in honey and nectar stored—another sign of the population growth. There's less room to store the honey so it gets put in the brood cells.

3. Changes to the queen—she will lose weight (preparing to fly off to new pastures) and lay fewer eggs.

4. Increased queen cups and swarm cells– these are a relatively certain indication of swarming about to take place. The queen will leave with the swarm, which requires a new queen. Swarm cells are produced before a swarm, usually around the bottom of the comb. It's preparation time for a swarm that will happen pretty soon.

The queen comes into contact with worker bees who wash and feed her and take care of her waste. As they touch the queen, she secretes tiny amounts of pheromone onto them. Pheromone is a chemical signal passed from one body to another through physical contact. The nurse bees move off, come into contact with other bees in the hive, pass pheromone on, and so on. Studies have shown that the resulting pheromone spread is quite dramatic. This is vital for the self-regulation of any hive. Pheromone changes with the queen's condition and is used to provide reassurance to the many bees who may seldom, if ever, come into contact with the queen. Correspondingly, when the pheromone levels drop, confidence amongst the bee population also reduces.

It is generally held that a reduction in pheromone levels is a precursor to a swarm. You can't see it but you will see the resultant signs, as listed above.

Regular inspection of your hive is vital. In time, you will do many of these checks naturally, but you will need to make a conscious effort at first.

Swarming isn't something you want to happen; nor is it good for the bees, with only one in six swarms succeeding.

The main reason to avoid swarming is that it is uncontrolled. Remember, swarming is an entirely natural process and the successful beekeeper will just want to add an element of control. There's a significant risk that the swarmed bees will settle off your land. Then, you face the risk that the old colony doesn't create a new queen—or that the new queen is young and inexperienced, and it's later on in the year, therefore she has less time to learn the right way to do things.

At the end of the day, having a hive is only good when there's an element of control.

Swarms are all about population. What does one do when the human population rises dramatically? You build new houses to accommodate the increase! That's the first step with beekeeping, add boxes so the bees have more space; stack them up, like building an extra few stories on your high-rise apartment complex!

There's another simple method to try and prevent swarming with a Langstroth hive. If you notice a lot higher density in the higher-up boxes—switch them around. The displaced bees will move up again to the less-crowded box you've just placed at the top of the hive.

Another option is around preemption. If you think there's a chance of swarming, prevent it by splitting the hive—essentially, this is swarming—but with you in control. You choose the time and place and monitor each stage of the process.

Another smart way to cut down on swarming is called *the 70% rule.* It's another measure of population growth but with an added action that can make a massive difference in the struggle against swarming. First termed by David Avvisato, it states that the right time to add a super is when 70% of the existing frames have been covered. This gives periodic expansion of the hive—a much better option than swarming.

The time of the year is important. Swarms occurring early in the year have a better chance of becoming established and surviving the winter than those involved in a swarm in the late summer. Perhaps you've heard the old rhyme that goes:

A swarm in May is worth a cart of hay

A swarm in June is worth a silver spoon

But a swarm in July, isn't worth a fly.

The earlier the swarm starts, the better the chance of generating enough honey and nectar to see them through the pending winter.

It's interesting that the odds are far more stacked against the swarm than the original colony. The swarming bees have to find a new home and build everything from scratch. Estimates run from one in five to one in six actually surviving. In contrast, all the original hive has to manage is producing a new queen; this is an entirely natural and instinctive process that only takes a few weeks. There are risks associated with a young queen, but this still leaves about four out of five original hives surviving after a swarm.

If you still get a swarm happening despite all the precautions you take, all is not lost. There's still every chance you can recapture the swarmed bees and re-hive them. A swarm usually leaves the original hive and then hangs off a nearby branch. You can recapture them usually in one of three ways.

The easiest way is to cut the branch they're hanging off and gently lower them into the brood box. If the branch is out of easy reach, you might be able to shake them loose. This might sound far-fetched but one good shake and the swarm should fall into the brood box—provided you've positioned it correctly. The disadvantage over lowering is that some bees will, through confusion, fly in different directions and may never find their way into the brood box.

If you have the swarm happening lower down, say at ground level, lowering or shaking isn't possible. Take a deep breath and hand scoop them into the brood box in these instances. Most will then follow suit and relocate but it's important to keep scooping until most of them make the move.

Typical equipment you may need, other than the brood box—and protective equipment—is a ladder and a pair of clippers.

Once captured, keep the brood box near the original swarm site—you're trying to make it as easy as possible for returning bees to find their new home. Let them settle for a week and start building up their new hive.

<u>There are two more important points for consideration:</u>

1. Make sure you have the queen in your brood box. The best way to be sure about this is to check activity levels. If the bees seem excited and move into the box and through it, it's a good sign that you have the queen. Correspondingly, if they show such signs of activity at another location, the chances are that the queen is there and you may have some more collection activity to get her into your box.

2. You can increase your hives under management by collecting the swarms that other people find in their yards. This is a free gift as many people are just glad to get rid of them, and you are well on your way to expanding your hives.

Absconding

This is much more serious than swarming as it involves losing almost everything. The entire colony of bees just ups and goes, leaving very little, if anything, behind.

The exact reasons behind this mass desertion aren't fully known but can be divided into two clear categories:

1. Environmental

This covers everything from excessive heat to a lack of flora for forage. If life is unbearably hot with the full force of the summer's sun, the bees will want to move somewhere cooler. Equally, if there's nothing much around to eat, what choice do you have but to migrate, following the food source. This also applies to water sources; bees need water, (as do most lifeforms).

2. Disturbance

Disturbance comes in two forms, predators and beekeepers, the latter mean no harm but sometimes act in ignorance, forcing the bees on to somewhere else. Predators can be ants, moths, beetles and other insects alongside racoons, skunks and bears. A thoughtful beekeeper can attempt to manage other predators with wire caging or placing the hives in hard-to-get-to places, but predators are tenacious. They may eventually drive a collective decision for the entire hive to move on.

The process of absconding takes a couple of weeks and is thorough. First, brood-rearing goes right down. When the major part of the worker brood has emerged, the queen stops laying altogether. A day later, everything is gone.

How do they know where to go? Scout bees go out, just like with swarming. Having found a good location, they go into the waggle dance routine, a vital form of communication as to direction and distance.

There are plenty of stories in the beekeeping world about losing your entire investment as the bees happily disappear into the distance. You can take a few actions that seem to make a difference. Putting a queen excluder under the brood box is one way to trap the queen, thus preventing her from buzzing off. Likewise, adding a frame of open board is thought to help, certainly it will give the bees something to work on, taking their minds off depressing thoughts, like survival.

Neither solution is satisfactory. Forcing the queen to remain in one place is no guarantee that the other bees won't abscond without their queen.

The best solution is a bait hive—an empty hive, ready for the bees to move into. You set it up and hope that the scouts find and recommend it, when they go back for the rest of their fuzzy companions.

Queenless Hive

Queenless hives, otherwise known as droney hives (a lot of drones and few worker bees) are relatively frequent occurrences, usually happening through a procedure known as supersedure. Drones use up vital resources while not contributing to the hive, so it's not a good situation.

Supersedure is a process whereby the bees kill the old queen. It's quite natural, typically happening every couple of years. It seems even queens aren't immune to mob rule. The biggest threat to a reigning queen happens when the first nectar flow draws towards its end, late May and into June. The threat can be because the queen is older or because it has just been introduced and the other bees sense something is not right. This comes back to the pheromone that the queen bee secretes on those around it.

In determining whether supersedure is likely to happen in your hive, consider the population's age. If it's evenly spread, the chances are that the queen is healthy and doing a good job. A disparity across age indicates the queen isn't laying eggs consistently. You can be sure that the bees know all about these problems.

A queenless hive will eventually die out as no new fresh bees are being born into the colony. In most cases this will happen in under two months. This is serious for you but even more serious for the bee colony.

That's why the worker bees will quickly start a process that should lead to a new queen emerging. They will select a larvae and alter the royal jelly they give it as feed very slightly. Those selected for worker bee status have a radically changed diet from the third day after the larvae hatches, with substantial amounts of pollen introduced. Therefore, larvae must be selected early on, before they go too far down the worker bee road.

In the case of a queenless hive, worker cells will be modified to become queen cells. Several such queens will develop. They will fight until one emerges supreme, the new queen.

However, it's better to introduce a new queen rather than waiting for the bees to develop their own. It reduces the risks of failure quite considerably.

The first thing is to decide whether to introduce a virgin queen or a mated one. A virgin queen bee has not yet reached full maturity, meaning her reproductive system is not yet fully formed and she is smaller. She moves throughout the hive, taking on mating flights. Mated queens can be harder to source but are recommended because they are much more likely to be accepted by the hive.

<u>Here are the steps to follow when introducing a new queen after she has been delivered:</u>

1. Check her condition—healthy-looking? Moving around? Not too cold?

2. You need to plan the move as soon as possible because the hive will start the replacement process and might reject your new queen. If the old queen has just disappeared, allow up to 24 hours for her pheromone to dispel. Note, if the bees are particularly aggressive, it's best to wait longer for the bees to come to terms with the fact that they need a new queen; this will make them more receptive when the queen is introduced.

3. It is strongly recommended to use the time-release cage option (as opposed to quick-release) because it allows the bees time to get used to the pheromone of the new queen. A time-release cage uses bee candy which the bees will eat through to get to the new queen. This typically takes between two and four days.

4. With the new queen in the cage, place it near the center frames of the brood. This puts the queen in the area where most bees are nurturing the brood.

5. Once in, leave the hive alone for two weeks, only take a quick look around day four, to check that the queen has been well received. If the queen is out of her cage, all's well. If she has not yet emerged and the candy block is intact, place a small stick through the candy to

make a hole. This shouldn't let bees through the hole but will reduce the amount of candy eating necessary.

6.   Check again in three days. If the queen still has not escaped, opening up the quick-release exit will be necessary. This exit is sealed by a cork and by removing it, she can escape quickly.

Chilled Brood

This is a weather-related condition where a cold spring can play havoc with the natural expansion plans of a hive. The queen expands the brood area as the weather starts to warm with the end of winter. This creates vulnerability because there aren't enough bees to cover and keep it warm. When you get a subsequent cold snap, the bees have little choice but to pull back in and keep the main part of the brood warm. The outer edges of the recently expanded brood thus become chilled.

You cannot hope to control the weather, but you can inspect your hive regularly and look out for symptoms of a chilled brood. The chief symptom is discolored larvae. You might also notice a dead brood near the entrance; a few are normal every year, but more should tell you there's a problem inside. There can also be a nasty smell, another good warning sign.

The best way to prevent chilled brood is through ventilation plus changing your inspection habits; keep the inspections short when the temperature drops and never do them on windy days, wait for more settled conditions.

Robbing

Robbing is when one set of bees attack another hive to steal honey. Once inside, they tear open the capped hives and eat the honey to carry it away in their stomachs. The home bees put up a fight and the result is a gruesome battle with many lives lost. By recognizing the signs of robber bees, you can try to head them off.

Put yourself in the bee's mind for a moment. You're a compulsive hoarder, the type they make reality TV shows about. You're bored because, despite your busy-bee ethic, there's no nectar to collect. Someone rushes back to the hive where you're kicking tires with a few thousand buddies, signaling that they've discovered another hive, sniffed around a bit and think it's weak. In true Viking-style, you launch your longboats and make off for some plunder. Every bee is a potential honey thief, it's just built into their DNA to get as much honey as possible, whether you make it or steal it.

You need to keep a sharp lookout for the following:

1. Bees fighting, either in the air or on the landing board.
2. Dead bees lying beneath the area of fighting or in front of the hive.
3. Bees swaying from side to side while looking for a way in to your hive, around the back often.
4. Wasps—they love the honey but also like eating dead bees.
5. A pickup in activity around a dull, lethargic hive. You might be delighted but come back a day later and the place is deserted. You've been robbed.
6. Bees looking shiny because they lose their hairs during battle.
7. Wax comb lying on the landing board—from the robber bees ripping open capped cells in order to get to the honey.
8. Louder than normal bees—it goes with the martial outlook on life.
9. Overburdened bees trying to get off the ground and fly away.

It's clearly too late to do something after the attack, like closing the stable door after the horse has bolted. This is where you need to be on the lookout for the signs above and act accordingly:

1. Make entrances smaller when the nectar flow falters (usually hot and dry weather). A drawbridge mentality gives your defending bees a greater chance of holding out.
2. Keep a strong queen because weak queens seem to trigger an invasion.
3. Avoid using entrance feeders during peak plunder season (hot and dry weather).
4. Of course, the obvious. Weak hives are more vulnerable. The scout bees will pick up on this and then they will pounce. So, combine weak hives to ensure they have the best chance of survival.
5. Consider buying a robbing screen. These unique devices allow your bees to enter and leave but make it hard for robber bees to do so.

If, despite these precautions, you end up with an attack taking place, all is not lost. Use smoke and close as much of the entrance as possible. Consider closing it completely. You're trying to make it as hard as possible for the bees to get into the hive. Some people use smelly compounds such as vapor rubs, while others put wet towels down over the hive. Another technique is to open up all other hives in the vicinity; sometimes, this can prevent the attack by sending the attacking bees back to defend their own hive. If you do this, just watch out for attacking wasps.

Laying Worker Phenomenon

The phenomenon known as "laying workers" serves as a desperate attempt by bee colonies to ensure their survival, representing the final effort to avoid the inevitable demise of a doomed hive. This behavior is a manifestation of the bees' deeply ingrained instinct for self-preservation, which has been passed down through generations over thousands of years. This encoded instinct governs and shapes their highly organized social interactions.

Laying workers in a beehive are essentially worker bees that take on the role of egg-laying. However, unlike the queen bee who goes on a mating flight and produces fertilized eggs, these worker bees have not mated and can only lay unfertilized eggs. In a bee colony, unfertilized eggs develop into drones or male bees, while fertilized eggs become female bees—either queens or workers.

This situation poses a challenge for the hive because drones' sole purpose is to mate with another queen. While this strategy helps spread their genetic material to other hives, it is detrimental to the survival of the colony as drones do not contribute any work. Consequently, without new workers being raised, the worker bee population will decline over time.

Without intervention or assistance from beekeepers, a laying worker colony will almost always perish. This underscores the importance of proper management and care to maintain healthy colonies and ensure their longevity.

In a hive with laying workers, there are not just one but potentially hundreds of them. The presence of the brood pheromone is responsible for suppressing the laying workers' natural inclination to lay eggs. However, once the brood is absent, these laying workers spring into action and start depositing eggs in various locations within the hive.

To rectify a laying worker colony, the most effective approach is merging it with a robust hive with a queen. Avoid combining it with a feeble colony, as this may result in the death of their queen and further expansion of the laying worker population.

Another effective method is to provide them with a frame containing an open brood once every week for three weeks. This process continues until they show signs of attempting to raise their own queen. By the end of the three weeks, the laying workers should have successfully produced their own queen or become more receptive to accepting a new one. The presence of the open brood pheromone inhibits laying workers from continuing their egg-laying activities. Implementing this strategy over an extended duration allows the laying workers sufficient time to adapt and adjust.

It's important to consider the severity and duration of the laying worker problem before taking action. Colonies that have been dealing with this issue for several weeks and have experienced a significant decrease in population may not be worth salvaging at all. It is not advisable to bolster these colonies by diverting resources from other colonies since it only weakens stronger ones, potentially exacerbating laying worker bee production.

In such cases, it may be best to disperse or remove the bees, gather the equipment, and move on from that hive situation altogether.

Pesticide Poisoning

Poisoning is a growing problem that can cause devastation within a hive. Unfortunately, the main symptoms occur when it is actually happening— dead bees or a decline in worker bees going out for nectar and pollen.

There are actions you and your neighbors can take to reduce the risk. Speak to your neighbors and ask them to check if the pesticide they are using is harmful to bees, or ask them to spray only in the evenings, given bees are less active then. You could also find out how the pesticide is applied. The worst application is aerial spraying which affords the least control over the direction of the pesticide. Likewise, spraying on a windy day is not advised.

The only sensible option is to locate your hives away from crop-spraying areas. Ideally, four miles away, which is a tall order for anyone beekeeping in their backyard. You can use screens and dampen the hives with wet towels, but you must recognize that you're trying to cope with a very threatening situation for the bees.

Once pesticide poisoning gets into your hive, the colony should recover naturally, if the bee deaths stop naturally and there's honey in the hive. If bees continue dying, you'll need to wash everything thoroughly, leaving it to soak for a day. You'll then need to support the newly washed hive with syrup, pollen and water as you nurse it back to health. Consider, also, combining two weakened hives into one.

Africanized Honeybees (AHB)

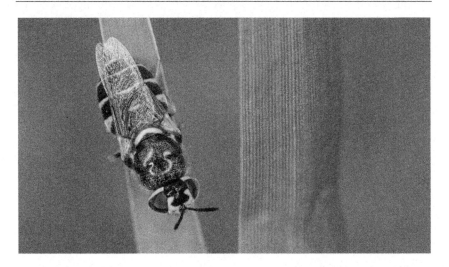

Africanized Honeybee/Credit: aeiddam0853578919(www.shutterstock.com)

Africanized honey bees (AHB) make honey just like any other honey bee; they are the bee of choice across much of Africa, and Central and South America. To give you an idea of their honey production capability, a normal hive may produce 7 to 12 pounds a year of honey, while one colonized by African honey bees can manage 20 or 30 times that amount.

Undoubtedly more aggressive and invasive than other honeybees, they often attack humans. Bear in mind that the Western (originally European) honey bee has been bred for centuries to increase its tolerance of humans, hence its less aggressive.

Suppose you reside in a region where Africanized honey bees have been sighted. In that case, it is crucial to refrain from capturing swarms or introducing bees into your hive that do not come from a reliable supplier.

Otherwise—you may be dealing with a highly aggressive and difficult-to-manage hive. In areas where the AHB has already infiltrated, vigilant beekeepers serve as the community's primary defense against its further spread.

By regularly inspecting their hives and identifying their marked queen, beekeepers can ensure the purity of their colony. The introduction of an unfamiliar queen, potentially an AHB, poses a significant risk to the genetic integrity of the colony. Henceforth, beekeepers play an even more essential role in preventing the AHB from becoming a nuisance within any given community.

Colony Collapse Disorder

Colony collapse disorder (CCD) refers to the sudden reduction of most worker bees with the queen and a number of nurse bees remaining. It's not the same thing as a queenless hive; the queen is still there but has been abandoned by most of her subjects. You will notice fewer bees but few dead bodies; the bees have left, not died.

The causes of CCD aren't known precisely but investigations center on the varroa mite, diseases (e.g. Israeli Acute Paralysis), pesticides, relocation stress, inadequate foraging area or a change to that area and immune-suppressing stress caused by these factors. The US Department of Agriculture has set up a CCD Steering Committee who have created an action plan to concentrate on causes of CCD. The Environmental Protection Agency is also involved regarding the impact of pesticides. The rise of cellphones with the associated proliferation of cell towers was thought to be a cause but this has been ruled out following an extensive study.

The concept of CCD is recent, as unexplained hive collapse has accelerated over the last 30 years. There has been a strong response in the USA and worldwide to this phenomenon because of bees' vital role in pollination, which is of infinitely greater value than simply looking at honey production alone.

New protein-rich diets have been developed to help colonies survive more vulnerable times such as winter and drought.

The actions the beekeeper can take on finding CCD has occurred are as follows:

- Resist the temptation to combine the hive with healthy hives.

- Do not reuse suspect hives or associated equipment—new bees may move in and quickly regret that decision.

- Replace with new combs every few years to ensure limited exposure to chemicals.

- Follow best practices to maximize the health of hives (ventilation and feeding, for instance, also minimize the use of pesticides), including managing Varroa through an integrated pest management system. All to lessen the incidence of stress in your colonies.

- Start new hives and encourage others to become beekeepers, bringing new and varied bee life into your area.

CHAPTER 10

Understanding and Managing Bee Diseases

A s a beekeeper, your role extends beyond simply installing and regularly inspecting the bees. You're also responsible for their ongoing survival and productivity. This brings us to the next exciting chapter of this guide—bee health and hive management.

This chapter discusses why good nutrition is essential for your bees to prevent potential diseases, and we consider the pros and cons of using a medicated approach. We'll also provide a thorough overview of the primary diseases affecting your hive, how to spot them, understand their symptoms, and how to prevent and treat them.

The Cornerstone of Bee Health: Understanding Nutrition

The health and vitality of your bee colony are intrinsically tied to its nutritional status. With the increasing challenges bees face today, such as declining natural forage, pesticide exposure, and many parasites and pathogens, ensuring your bees are well-nourished has never been more critical.

The Bee's Menu: What's on the Plate?

Just like us, bees need a balanced diet to thrive. This includes water, proteins, fats, carbohydrates, vitamins, and minerals. Bees can be picky about their water sources, often favoring certain ones, possibly due to taste differences.

Proteins are a crucial part of a bee's diet, primarily from pollens. Once ingested, these proteins are broken down into amino acids and reassembled into specific proteins and enzymes that the bees need for various bodily functions. The protein content in pollens can vary significantly, hence the need for bees to gather pollens from a diverse range of plant sources to meet their protein needs.

Fats, or lipids, are also sourced from pollens and, to a lesser extent, nectars. These lipids are broken down into fatty acids, used for energy and incorporated into the bee's cell walls. The bee even uses some fatty acids to produce pheromones and reproductive hormones.

Carbohydrates, derived from sugars and starches, provide the energy bees need for flight and in-hive activities. They also play a role in the production of honey and bee bread. Bees cannot digest raw starches, such as those found in raw grains, but can better digest cooked starches.

While the roles of most vitamins and minerals in bees have not been demonstrated in scientific research, it is safe to assume that they play the same fundamental biochemical roles in bees as in other species.

Natural Products

The world of beekeeping has been abuzz (couldn´t resist that word!) with a growing fascination for natural products. This surge of interest is hardly surprising, given the wealth of research pointing to the effectiveness of these natural wonders in combating viruses and bacteria. From the ancient wisdom of traditional Chinese medicine to the meticulously curated European pharmacopeia, natural products have long been the bedrock of numerous medicinal practices. They're the secret sauce in many everyday remedies, whether aspirin for easing pain and inflammation, quinine for battling malaria, or penicillin, the antibiotic powerhouse.

Beekeepers, many of whom are nature enthusiasts at heart, find the prospect of using natural products in their hives quite appealing. The idea of harnessing naturally made and sourced compounds, like propolis, resonates with the community's deep-rooted naturalistic ethos.

However, while the allure of natural products is undeniable, it's crucial to approach their use with a balanced perspective. These products, as promising as they may be, are not a magic bullet. Their effectiveness can vary significantly and should not be considered a standalone solution. Instead, they should be integrated into a broader, more comprehensive strategy prioritizing good hive management and proactive disease prevention.

Moreover, it's essential to remember that not all natural products are created equal. While some are safe for human consumption, others may need additional screening and testing to ensure their safety. Consider this point carefully, especially if you plan to harvest honey.

The Importance of a Healthy Gut

The bee gut hosts a variety of beneficial bacteria (microflora) that break down the complex proteins, lipids, and sugars of the bees' diet into their simplest forms. Only then can the bees' food be converted to energy that allows them to carry out their activities. Good gut health keeps your bees strong, healthy, and active. Several natural food supplement products are now on the market to enhance bee gut health.

Proactive Steps for Bee Nutrition

Based on recent studies, ensuring your bees are well-fed is an effective strategy for preventing the damage caused by multiple diseases that can afflict your colony.

Feeding bees sugar syrup and pollen substitutes in spring and autumn is important. But there is more you can do. These days, many natural food supplements are on the market to further help bees' nutrition through essential oils, vitamins, minerals, probiotics, proteins, and amino acids. These nutritional food supplements have been developed to keep bees healthy, vigorous, and productive.

In the next part of this chapter, while we present the most common diseases that might affect your hive, I will also provide recommendations of the supplements you might consider for preventing or curing each disease.

A well-nourished bee is more resilient to diseases and better equipped to perform its duties within the hive. On the other hand, malnutrition can weaken the bees' immune system, making them more susceptible to diseases and pests.

American Foulbrood (AFB)

The American Foulbrood (AFB), brought on by the bacterium *Paenibacillus larvae*, is a menace to honey bee larvae. This silent destroyer can decimate a colony in weeks if not treated promptly. The disease is transmitted through spores, which are incredibly resilient and can lie dormant in beehives or used equipment for up to seven decades! The spores spring into action when nurse bees unknowingly feed larvae with food tainted by these spores. Once inside the larvae, the spores transform into a vegetative state, multiplying within the larval tissue and leading to their untimely death. The term "foulbrood" is derived from the unpleasant smell of the larvae killed by the bacteria.

The larvae usually succumb to the disease after their cell is capped, during the transition from the larval to the pupal stage. The death of the larvae triggers the formation of new spores. As these spores dry, they form a scale that sticks to the cell, a telltale sign of AFB. Unfortunately, AFB is incurable, and immediate action is required upon detection.

So, how can you spot AFB? Look out for an irregular brood pattern that appears spotty. The cell cappings might seem hollow, dark, and greasy, with perforations. The pupal mass beneath the cappings turns brown and develops a stringy texture. In the advanced stages, you might find dark, hard scales that are impossible to remove. These scales can house up to 100 million spores. Other signs include a pupal tongue protruding from the remains and a foul smell in the later stages.

Diagnosing AFB involves several tests.

Ropiness Test

You can perform this quick and easy test right at your hive. Here's how it works:

- Find a suspicious-looking cell. It might be darker than usual or even appear slightly sunken.

- Gently insert a small stick or toothpick into the cell, stirring it.

- As you withdraw the stick, watch closely. If the cell is infected with AFB, the contents will stretch string-like, like melted cheese. This is the "ropiness" that gives the test its name and is a telltale sign of AFB.

Holst Milk Test

This test requires a bit more preparation, but it's still something you can do yourself. Here's how:

- Prepare a weak milk solution. Add a dash of milk to water until you get a slightly cloudy liquid.

- Stir in a sample of the suspicious larval remains from your hive.

- Watch the color. If it turns a clear brown, you may have AFB. The AFB bacteria contain an enzyme that breaks down the milk proteins, causing this color change.

Diagnostic Test

You can purchase this commercial product through beekeeping suppliers. It's a bit more high-tech, but it's also very reliable. Here's how it works:

- The kit includes a special bottle and a test device. Add a sample of the suspicious larval remains to the bottle and shake it well.

- Then, add a few drops of the solution to the test device. It works like a pregnancy test with lines indicating the result.

- If you see lines under "C" and "T," it's a positive result for AFB. If only the "C" line appears, it's negative. If there are no lines or only the "T" line, the test didn't work correctly, and you should try again.

There are benefits and drawbacks to each of these exams. The Ropiness Test and Holst Milk Test are quick and cheap but might not be as accurate as the Diagnostic Test Kit. The Diagnostic Test Kit is more reliable but also more expensive. But remember, the most important thing is to catch AFB *early*. With early detection and proper management, you can protect your bees and keep your hive healthy.

Preventing and Controlling AFB

As you can see, American Foulbrood (AFB) is a formidable adversary in beekeeping. But don't worry; you can keep this foe at bay with the right strategies. The key lies in a comprehensive approach that combines prevention and control. This is where an integrated pest management (IPM) strategy comes into play. This strategy is all about using a mix of cultural, mechanical, and physical tactics before resorting to chemical control. However, it's worth noting that there's currently no chemical solution that can tackle AFB spores. Therefore, the most secure method of managing the disease is to kill the bees and destroy the equipment.

So, how can you prevent AFB from invading your hives?

Well, there are several steps you can take. For starters, you can prevent drifting and robbing between colonies. This can be achieved by arranging your hives in a horseshoe, serpentine, or a random pattern rather than a straight line. Additionally, when colonies are young or weak, keeping entrances small and employing a robbing screen can be helpful.

Another preventative measure is to avoid sharing equipment between colonies. If you must transfer frames between colonies, inspect them thoroughly. Also, clean your hive tools with isopropyl alcohol between colonies and apiaries. And remember, leather gloves can harbor spores. So, it's best to use disposable nitrile gloves or, as we recommended earlier in this book, no gloves at all. A hand sanitizer with alcohol in it may be used to disinfect nitrile gloves and hands.

You can also consider comb culling, which involves removing old combs on a 3-year cycle. Every year, you should replace the 3–4 oldest frames in each box. It is a good idea to label new frames with the date they are added to the colonies.

When it comes to equipment, new is always better. If you're considering used equipment, request the seller's inspection records. Avoid buying equipment from a beekeeper who has had AFB. If you buy used equipment, ensure it's irradiated before use.

Irradiation is a sterilization process that uses gamma radiation powered by Cobalt-60 to kill microorganisms on equipment. The radiation enters cells and damages their DNA. This technology is safe, leaves no residual radiation, and doesn't use chemicals. Contact your state or local beekeeping club for more information on the cost and scheduling of hive equipment irradiation. If you want to irradiate equipment you know is AFB-infected, keep it away from bees to stop the disease from spreading.

Your Course of Action When AFB Infects Your Colony

Discovering that your bee colony has been afflicted with American Foulbrood (AFB) can feel like a punch to the gut. However, it's not the end of the world. You can take measures to manage this predicament and prevent the disease from wreaking further havoc.

Shook Swarm Control

The shook swarm technique is all about giving your bees a fresh start. You'll need to prepare new equipment, such as old boxes that have been meticulously cleaned and sterilized using a blowtorch or irradiation, or literally brand new equipment. The goal is to create a clean, disease-free environment for your bees.

Let's break down the shook swarm technique into steps:

- First, you'll need to get your hands on new equipment. If you have old hive boxes, they can be reused, but only after a thorough cleaning and sterilization process. You can achieve this by using a blowtorch or through irradiation. The aim is to create a clean, spore-free environment for your bees.

- Next, add a healthy, empty, drawn comb frame to the new equipment. This is an inviting beacon for your bees, signalling them to settle into their new abode.

- Now comes the critical part—moving the bees from the infected colony to the new hive. During this process, handle the queen with the utmost care. She is the lifeblood of your colony, and her well-being is crucial.

- Once the bees have been transferred, it's time to provide fresh sugar syrup. This will give them the much-needed energy to start building new comb.

- Shake the bees off the drawn comb after 24 hours, then take it out and swap it out for a new frame. This step is vital as it helps to remove any residual disease spores.

- Lastly, remember to treat all equipment from the infected colony. This includes the frames removed from the new hive after the bees were shaken off. They should be destroyed or sterilized to prevent the disease from spreading.

Remember that all equipment from the infected colony should be treated per the guidelines provided. The shook swarm method is a calculated risk, as it may not eliminate the spread of the spores. However, it's a risk worth taking to save your bees.

The Last Resort: Total Incineration in the Face of AFB

In the battle against American Foulbrood (AFB), there are times when the only path to victory is the most severe one: the complete incineration of the entire bee colony and all related equipment. This measure, while harsh, is the only guaranteed method to eradicate the disease. In some regions, this action is not just a choice but a legal requirement when dealing with colonies infected with antibiotic-resistant AFB.

The decision to proceed with incineration should be made swiftly upon the detection of AFB. It's vital to resist the temptation to salvage any honey from these colonies, as it will likely teem with spores that could contaminate your extraction equipment.

While it's possible to disinfect and reuse hive bodies, supers, and covers, there's always a risk that the disease could come back. Therefore, you might opt to burn everything. However, remember that burning plastic hive components can pose an environmental hazard. These components can be double-bagged and taken to a waste facility for burial or stored in a bee-free area until they can be irradiated.

Euthanizing the colony should be done in the evening after all foraging activities have ended. By closing all hive entrances and drenching the bees with diesel fuel at a rate of 1 cup per hive body, the bees should become immobile after about 10 minutes.

Before you ignite the fire, check if you need a burn permit. If one is required, make sure to obtain it. To be prepared for the burning, create a sloped pit at least 18 inches deep and large enough to fit all the equipment. Have a fire extinguisher or water nearby, and start a fire in the pit using kindling.

Place your unopened hive next to the fire and pour combs and dead bees into the fire. Never leave a fire unattended; the process should take 2-3 hours. Be highly cautious during this step to avoid flares from fuel residue.

Cover the ashes with earth once everything has been properly burnt and the space is clear of any last bits of comb or bees.

Chemical Control

There are chemical tools at your disposal that can help you manage this destructive disease. However, it's important to remember that these are not cure-alls. They should be used as part of a well-rounded strategy to manage AFB.

Among the chemical controls available, you'll find Terramycin (oxytetracycline), Tylan (tylosin tartrate), and Lincomix soluble powder (lincomycin hydrochloride). These antibiotics don't eliminate the *Paenibaccillus* larvae spores, the culprits behind AFB, but they can inhibit their growth when present in the food that worker bees feed susceptible larvae. This can help the larvae survive but doesn't eradicate the virulent spores lurking in the contaminated equipment. As a result, the disease often reemerges once the antibiotic feeding ceases.

It's critical to remember that beginning on January 1st, 2017, these medicines may only be acquired in the United States with a prescription from a veterinarian. Additionally, there have been increasing reports of AFB-infected colonies resistant to the antibiotic Terramycin. Therefore, treatment methods like burning or irradiation are often recommended, and can be more cost-effective.

European Foulbrood (EFB)

This disease has made its presence known on every continent where *Apis mellifera* is kept, making it a universal concern for beekeepers. Interestingly, EFB often gets mistaken for its more destructive cousin, American Foulbrood (AFB). The two diseases share similar life cycles and can cause similar symptoms in affected colonies. However, EFB is less severe, thanks to its causative bacteria, *Melissococcus plutonius*, which doesn't form spores, unlike *Paenibacillus* larvae, the bacteria behind AFB. This crucial difference means EFB can be treated, while AFB remains untreatable. Beekeepers must differentiate between these two diseases to manage their colonies effectively and prevent the spread of both diseases.

Now, let's take a closer look at the life cycle of EFB. The journey of EFB begins when a larva, not more than 24 hours old, consumes food contaminated with the bacteria, usually provided by nurse bees. Once inside the larval gut, the EFB bacteria multiply and compete with the larva for nutrition. This competition triggers an increase in the larva's appetite. Nurse bees can identify and remove these ravenous larvae in strong colonies, eliminating the disease from the nest. This means that EFB doesn't pose a significant threat to colonies that are robust and capable of timely removal of dead and infected larvae.

However, the story doesn't end there. The bacteria can linger in the brood cells or infected larvae's faeces—even after the adult bees have removed the larvae. This means that nurse bees can inadvertently pick up and transfer the disease from infected larvae to healthy ones during feeding and cleaning activities. Therefore, while strong colonies can control EFB, the risk of transmission within the colony remains. This highlights the importance of vigilant monitoring and management practices in maintaining the health of a bee colony.

Symptoms

In a healthy hive, you'll notice that the larvae are plump and exhibit a pristine white color. They nestle in their cells, forming a distinctive "C" shape. However, when EFB strikes, the larvae undergo a drastic transformation. They might appear to melt with a shrunken, rubbery, or dehydrated look. Their color may shift from the usual white to shades of yellow or brown, and you might even see their tracheal systems through their outer layer. In some instances, the affected larvae might twist or curl upwards within their uncapped cell.

You might notice a patchy pattern when you examine the brood comb of an EFB-infected hive. This pattern, characterized by a mix of capped and empty cells scattered throughout the comb, arises because some larvae survive the infection and get capped. In contrast, others fall victim to EFB and are removed by their adult sisters. While this spotty brood pattern isn't exclusive to EFB, it can serve as an additional sign of infection when observed alongside other symptoms.

To differentiate between EFB and its more destructive counterpart, American Foulbrood (AFB), beekeepers often employ the "ropiness test" previously described. This involves inserting a small twig or matchstick into a brood cell containing a diseased larva or pupa. After stirring the cell's contents, the twig is slowly withdrawn. If the contents "rope" or stretch out, it indicates AFB. If they don't, it's likely EFB. The contents are considered "ropey" if they stretch to 1 inch or more. While this test is helpful for field diagnostics, it should be used with other signs of disease for accurate results.

Consider using a diagnostic test kit for a more definitive diagnosis, similar to AFB. These kits are designed to detect EFB and AFB quickly and accurately in the field. Remember, these kits are specific to EFB or AFB, so ensure you purchase and use the correct kit for the disease you suspect.

Measures Against European Foulbrood

Sanitation is your first line of defense. Keeping your beekeeping tools and equipment clean is crucial in preventing the spread of EFB. This includes everything from your hive tools and smokers to the frames. Start by thoroughly cleaning them with soapy water. Follow this up with a disinfecting soak in a bleach solution, mixed at a ratio of one part bleach to five parts water. This step is essential because EFB can easily hitch a ride from one colony to another via contaminated equipment.

Starting with fresh, unused equipment and tools is a good idea for setting up a new colony. This way, you're not inadvertently introducing EFB into your new setup. Inspect all the combs for any signs of diseased brood when purchasing nucs or entire colonies. It's always better to err on the side of caution, so avoid any colonies that raise your suspicions.

Another effective strategy is to opt for hygienic bee stocks. While no bee breeds are entirely immune to EFB, hygienic queens produce worker bees proficiently removing diseased larvae from the hive. This behavior can help keep EFB in check. As a bonus, hygienic bees are also good at controlling other pests and diseases, such as the Varroa mite, sacbrood virus, and chalkbrood. (I will cover these diseases very soon).

Lastly, consider the use of antibiotics as a preventive measure. However, per the AFB case, you'll need a licensed vet's prescription or a Veterinary Feed Directive for the correct antibiotic treatments. Once you have the necessary paperwork, you can purchase the antibiotic from a beekeeping equipment supplier, a pharmacy, or a vet clinic. Remember to follow the label instructions when using the prescribed antibiotic.

Taking Action: Post-Diagnosis Treatment for European Foulbrood

When faced with a confirmed European Foulbrood (EFB) case, it's time to roll up your sleeves and get to work. The treatment options at your disposal range from chemical to non-chemical, and your choice will depend on the infection's severity and your personal preferences as a beekeeper.

Antibiotics, specifically oxytetracycline (Terramycin), are a standard first line of defense against EFB. This antibiotic doesn't wipe out the bacteria but suppresses their growth when present in the food that worker bees feed to susceptible larvae. While this permits individual larvae to survive, the dangerous spores in the contaminated equipment are unaffected. As a result, the disease often reemerges once the antibiotic feeding ceases. It's worth noting that there are no documented cases of EFB developing resistance to Terramycin, but the possibility is a concern.

Non-chemical treatments also offer practical solutions for managing EFB. One of these methods involves adding extra frames with young and mature brood from a colony that isn't infected to the afflicted one. This action increases competition between healthy and sick brood. Consequently, sick brood receive less food, die off, and are removed from the hive, reducing the EFB presence.

Another non-chemical approach mimics a nectar flow by feeding bees a 1:1 sugar syrup. This stimulates the production of new brood in the colony, increasing available workers for foraging. The influx of brood results in less individual care for larvae, allowing healthy larvae to outcompete the sick ones.

Finally, the shook swarm method previously presented can disrupt the EFB cycle.

Chalkbrood

Chalkbrood, known in scientific circles as *Ascosphaera apis,* is a fungal menace that targets the brood of a bee colony. This disease is infamous for its swift invasion and the substantial damage it can inflict on the larvae within a hive. Initially, chalkbrood manifests as a chalky-white substance. However, if not addressed promptly, it can lead to the mummification of sealed larvae, causing a significant decrease in the brood population. This can have a domino effect, disrupting the hive's operations and reducing honey production. Moreover, chalkbrood can leave the hive vulnerable, making it an easy target for other diseases and infestations.

Spotting Chalkbrood

Identifying chalkbrood can be challenging, as its symptoms resemble other hive conditions or infections. However, there are sure signs that beekeepers can keep an eye out for:

- **Chalky-White Appearance:** In the early stages of chalkbrood, the larvae are enveloped in a cotton-like, chalky-white substance. This can be seen either evenly distributed or scattered across the larvae.

- **Color Shift to Gray or Black:** As the disease progresses, the chalky-white coloration gradually darkens to grey or even black. This color change is a clear indication of the disease's advancement.

- **Mummification of Larvae:** The final stage of the disease results in the larvae hardening into a mummified state. These mummified larvae can often be found at the hive entrance, in pollen traps, or within the brood nest.

Understanding Chalkbrood Transmission

The initial encounter with chalkbrood fungal spores typically occurs when honeybees collect pollen. These spores are then introduced into the colony and its food supply, which is subsequently consumed by the larvae. In the latter stages of the sickness, the fungus then grows inside the larvae's intestines, producing noticeable symptoms.

In the early stages of infection, the larvae do not exhibit any external symptoms. However, the larvae typically succumb to the disease within two days of being sealed in their pupae. It's important to remember that the disease only spreads via the larvae; there is no proof that adult bees are still susceptible to it today.

Decoding the Signs

Recognizing chalkbrood in your hive is the first step towards tackling it. This process, while straightforward, requires a vigilant eye.

Begin by scanning for petrified or mummified larvae around the hive entrance. These lifeless larvae, a classic hallmark of chalkbrood, often appear as if they've been frozen in time. If you come across these, it's time to delve deeper.

Next, scrutinize the brood for a chalky white, grey, or black growth. This is the fungus at work, and its presence confirms chalkbrood. Remember, the infection typically starts along the edges of the brood, so that's an excellent place to commence your inspection. However, as the disease advances, it can permeate the entire brood area.

Don't overlook the pollen traps. Dead and mummified larvae often end up here, providing another piece of the chalkbrood puzzle.

Overcoming Chalkbrood

Once chalkbrood has been identified, it's time to roll up your sleeves and take action. The secret to defeating chalkbrood lies in maintaining a robust and thriving colony. A healthy, populous hive is more resilient to fungal infections than weak or sparse ones. The optimal scenario is to keep a colony robust to combat potential infection.

In severe cases, you might need to replace the comb frames to eradicate the disease completely. Many beekeepers advocate burning infected wooden frames and replacing them with new ones. While this might seem extreme, it's a surefire way to obliterate the fungus.

If the fungus has already wreaked significant havoc, requeening with a more substantial brood and stock may be the way to go. Many mummified larvae indicate that the worker bees aren't adequately cleaning the hive. When this occurs, you should get rid of the dried-up larvae, clean the afflicted areas, and requeen the colony to make it more resistant.

Remember, chalkbrood is a formidable adversary, but with careful observation and decisive action, you can safeguard your hive and ensure its continued productivity.

Proactive Measures Against Chalkbrood

The best strategy against chalkbrood is not just reacting to an infection but preventing it from taking hold in the first place.

First and foremost, maintaining a clean and controlled beekeeping environment is critical. It's not uncommon for beekeepers to unintentionally facilitate the spread of chalkbrood across their hives. By being mindful of cleanliness, sanitation, and the potential for cross-contamination, you can help keep the infection from spreading.

Always be conscious of the condition of your beekeeping tools and equipment, especially if there's a suspicion or confirmed presence of chalkbrood. Regular sanitation procedures and responsible beekeeping practices are your best defense against this fungal disease.

Another crucial aspect of chalkbrood prevention is the physical environment of your hives. Chalkbrood is more likely to spread in cooler, damp conditions. By ensuring your hives are in warm, dry, and well-ventilated areas, you can help stave off potential infection. This is particularly important during cooler seasons when it's advisable to position hives in sunlit locations.

In regions with cooler climates and high humidity, keeping bees in a temperature-controlled environment may be beneficial. This is usually only necessary in areas where chalkbrood infections persist despite other preventative measures.

By taking these proactive steps, you're not just *reacting* to chalkbrood but actively working to keep your colonies healthy and productive.

Sacbrood

Sacbrood, known as *Morator Aetatulas* or Sacbrood virus (SBV), is a viral infection primarily targeting honey bee larvae, worldwide. This virus infiltrates the larvae, hindering their successful transformation into pupae, eventually leading to their demise. The aftermath of this infection leaves a unique sac-like appearance in the affected brood. The onset of this infection is typically during the colony's growth phase, often coinciding with spring.

While Sacbrood may initially appear as a minor concern, it can wreak significant havoc within a colony already under stress or weakened. The infection can lead to extensive areas of the affected comb where the queen bee abstains from laying more eggs. Adult bees infected with the virus also tend to have a reduced lifespan. Consequently, the overall vitality and productivity of the colony are compromised.

Spotting Sacbrood

The initial sign of a potential Sacbrood infection is the presence of dead or visibly dying larvae. These larvae meet their end after their cells have been capped but before they can fully metamorphose into pupae. Beekeepers can spot these expired larvae in both capped and uncapped cells. A common sign of the disease is a tiny hole the size of a pin on the top of afflicted cells.

In the early stages of the infection, the affected brood first appears with a grayish hue. As the Sacbrood infection intensifies, the larvae change to a yellow color with a darker head. Over a few days, this yellow color transitions into a darker brown to black.

It's worth noting that Sacbrood can often be confused with other infections, such as the Black Queen Cell Virus (BQCV) or the more severe Foulbrood. However, the unique color changes associated with Sacbrood can help you distinguish it from these other conditions.

Spread of Sacbrood

Research suggests that the contraction of SBV primarily occurs through contaminated nectar, pollen, and water. Worker bees may encounter the virus during their routine collection procedures and then return the infection to the colony. Subsequently, nurse bees feed the larvae the contaminated food, leading to the contraction of the virus.

The spread of the virus within the larvae is often swift, leading to their inevitable death. Although just a few colonies in an apiary are usually affected, beekeepers may accidentally help the virus spread to new hives during transportation and honey harvest.

Taking Action Against Sacbrood

Once you've identified Sacbrood in your hive, it's time to spring into action. Here's what you need to do:

- **Larvae Extraction:** Begin by removing the dead or dying larvae from the hive

- **Color Watch:** Keep a vigilant eye out for the characteristic color changes in the larvae.

- **Hive Surveillance:** Maintain a close watch on your hive, especially during the colony growth phase, often when Sacbrood strikes. If you notice large areas of the affected comb where the queen refuses to lay more eggs, or if the adult bees seem to have a shorter lifespan, these could be signs of a Sacbrood infection.

Prevention and Eradication Strategies

A proactive approach is your best bet when managing Sacbrood virus (SBV). As a beekeeper, you create a clean, hygienic environment that minimizes the risk of SBV and other diseases. This involves a commitment to regular cleaning and sanitizing of your beekeeping tools and equipment. Remember, you could be the one spreading the virus across your hives.

Water sources within your apiary can act as potential hotspots for SBV contamination. Therefore, it's crucial to refresh the water and sanitize the containers regularly. This becomes even more important if you detect SBV in any part of your brood.

The health and vitality of your hive are your strongest allies in the fight against SBV. A thriving, well-fed hive is more capable of fending off diseases and other threats. You can drastically lower the danger of SBV spreading throughout your colonies by regularly controlling your hives and ensuring they are strong.

It's encouraging to learn that, in many instances, the hive itself can withstand and erase the presence of the disease without any further assistance in eradication. However, in extreme circumstances, you may need to take more drastic action, including requeening the hive or moving the whole colony to a location that isn't infested.

Nosema

Nosema is a formidable adversary targeting adult honey bees, including the all-important queen bees. This microscopic menace is caused by a spore-forming microsporidian named *Nosema apis*. To see these spores, you'd need the aid of a light microscope. Interestingly, (but sadly) a new variant of Nosema, known as *Nosema ceranae*, is a culprit in the infection of honey bees in various parts of the globe.

Life Cycle

Picture this: a bee ingests the spores of *Nosema apis*. Within half an hour, these spores spring to life within the bee's stomach. They then infiltrate the cells lining the stomach, where they grow and multiply at an alarming rate, feasting on the cell's contents. Within 6 to 10 days, many spores are produced within the host cell. The parasite doesn't stop there, though. It can invade and infect neighboring healthy cells, spreading the infection further.

Healthy stomach lining cells are shed into the stomach as part of the bee's regular digestion. These cells burst open, releasing digestive enzymes. However, when infected cells are shed, they release Nosema spores instead of digestive enzymes. These spores can then infect other healthy cells in the stomach lining. Many of these spores pass through the intestines and end up in the bee's feces. This cycle continues, allowing the disease to propagate within the bee population.

Spread

This disease affects adult bees, including the queen, and is not typically passed directly from generation to generation. Instead, it's the unsuspecting young bees that become infected when they ingest spores while performing their cleaning duties on the contaminated combs.

During the sunny summer months, it's not uncommon for a few infected bees to be present in most colonies. However, these few bees don't seem to cause any noticeable harm to the colony. The spores, though, can linger on the combs, and when the weather takes a turn in autumn, these dormant spores can trigger a Nosema outbreak. This can lead to a significant loss of bees during this period.

The winter season can also see heavy losses. When inclement weather confines infected bees within their hives, they may defecate inside the hive, contaminating the combs and the hive's interior with excreta and spores. This may result in an infection outbreak in the spring when combined with the spores created in the previous fall.

Spring outbreaks usually kick off when temperatures rise. These outbreaks can last until late spring or early summer. However, with the arrival of warm weather, the disease begins to wane due to improved flight conditions. The bees can now defecate outside the hive, which helps reduce the contamination of the combs.

Thankfully, severe Nosema outbreaks are not an annual occurrence. Research indicates that certain conditions seem to be associated with serious autumn outbreaks and Nosema epidemics. These include heavy summer rainfall and an early break in fine weather. In these epidemics, even strong colonies can be seriously weakened before winter, shrinking to the size of a nucleus colony within days. Infected colonies that make it through the winter may need additional time to recover before the number of adult bees returns to normal levels.

Nosema Impact on Bees

The young nurse bees are usually busy caring for the brood and are forced to grow up too soon. They swap their nurturing duties for the roles of guards and foragers, tasks typically reserved for their older siblings. It's as if they've been robbed of their childhood, all because of this pesky invader.

But that's not all. The royal jelly, the bee version of a superfood for their brood, takes a hit too. The nurse bees—the royal jelly chefs of the hive—lose their ability to whip up this vital nourishment. This leads to a domino effect where many eggs the queen lays fail to hatch into mature larvae. It's a tough blow to the colony's growth and survival.

Now, let's talk about the lifespan of our buzzing friends. In the presence of Nosema, their lives are cut short, especially during the spring and summer. Seeing them live only half as long as they would in a Nosema-free world is heartbreaking. The queens, the heart of the hive, are hit the hardest. They stop laying eggs, and they're gone within a few weeks. And while Nosema isn't the main culprit behind bee dysentery, it contributes to an uptick in cases among the adult population.

Spotting Nosema

Identifying Nosema can be a bit like playing detective. The symptoms aren't always obvious, and many bees carrying the parasite may not show any signs. The most foolproof way to confirm a Nosema infection is to look closely. A microscopic examination can reveal the presence of Nosema spores in adult bees.

However, some telltale signs can raise a red flag. For instance, a sudden drop in the adult bee population can cause concern. This rapid decline, often called "spring dwindle," can be alarming. But remember, it's important not to confuse this with the natural weakening of colonies in early spring, due to the death of over-wintered bees.

Other warning indications include dead bees lying around the ground, ill or crawling bees near the hive entrance, and dysentery symptoms on the various components of the hive. But here's the catch—these symptoms can also be caused by other diseases or abnormal conditions. So, while these signs can point towards a Nosema infection, a microscopic examination is the only way to confirm it.

Your Action Plan

First things first, let's talk about the queens. A queen with strong egg-laying potential is like the engine of a colony, driving its growth and survival. Ensuring your colonies are bustling with young bees is crucial as winter approaches. But how do you achieve this? The answer lies in the autumn season. Providing your colonies with a hearty supply of high-protein pollen during this season can help nurture a robust population of young bees.

Let's move on to honey. As you prepare your hives for winter, ensure they're well-stocked with this sweet nectar. Studies have shown that a hive filled with half or more honey tends to have lower Nosema spore counts. It's like a natural shield against the parasite.

The location of your hives can also make a world of difference. During the cooler months, find a sunny spot for your hives, preferably with good air drainage and protection from cold winds. Avoid putting them in areas that are chilly, gloomy, or wet. A well-placed hive can reduce Nosema infection levels from 85% to zero. It's like giving your bees a sunny vacation spot during the cold season!

When it comes to winter colonies, think compact and warm. Remove any supers or boxes of combs not needed by the bees. This helps keep the colony cozy and reduces the chances of Nosema infection.

Stress is a big no-no for your bees. Your bees may get stressed out and more vulnerable to Nosema if you open the hive, manipulate the combs, feed them, or move colonies too often. So, remember to handle your hives with care.

Water sources are another area to watch out for. Stagnant water can become a breeding ground for Nosema, especially if contaminated by dead bees and bee excreta. So, keep an eye on the water sources around your hives.

Lastly, don't forget to replace old, dark brood combs. While this won't eliminate Nosema, it can significantly reduce its prevalence. Each spring, many beekeepers remove two or more old combs from the brood nest and replace them with brand-new sheets of beeswax foundation.

Nosema Ceranae: A New Player in the Field

Nosema ceranae was discovered in Asian honey bees _(Apis cerana)_ in 1994, but it wasn't until 2005 in Taiwan that it came into contact with European honey bees _(Apis mellifera)_. Since then, it's been popping up in various corners of the world, including Europe and the USA.

Now, _Nosema ceranae_ is still a bit of a mystery. Researchers are working tirelessly to understand its impact on individual bees and colonies. Unlike its cousin, _Nosema apis, Nosema ceranae_ doesn't cause sudden, rapid losses of bees.

One interesting thing about _Nosema ceranae_ is its year-round presence. While _Nosema apis_ prefers the milder autumn and spring seasons, _Nosema_ *ceranae* doesn't seem to mind the calendar. It also has a broader reach within the honey bee gut, affecting more cells than *Nosema apis* at the same temperature. This might explain why bees infected with *Nosema ceranae* have a higher mortality rate.

Summer can be a tough time for colonies infected with *Nosema ceranae*. They may experience a gradual loss of adult bees, leading to reduced honey production. In some cases, the colony might not survive. While dysentery is often a sign of a *Nosema apis* outbreak, it's less common with *Nosema ceranae*.

Interestingly, *Nosema ceranae* has been found in honey and pollen. But here's a silver lining—recent research has shown that its spores lose their viability when subjected to freezing and chilling conditions.

Conclusion

Wrapping up this chapter, we've covered the intricate world of bee diseases, unravelling their mysteries and learning how to prevent or combat them. As stewards of our buzzing friends, it's our responsibility to stay alert, recognize the signs of these diseases, and spring into action when needed.

With the insights you've gained from this chapter, you're better prepared to face any challenges buzzing your way. But don't put your beekeeper's hat away just yet! Next, we're focusing on another critical aspect of hive health— the pests that might threaten your colonies. We're about to give you the knowledge you need to protect your bees from some unwelcome guests.

Let's continue this journey together for the love of our buzzing, fuzzy friends and their very vital role on our planet.

CHAPTER 11

Pests

Welcome, fellow bee enthusiasts, to a chapter about uninvited guests in the bee world—pests. We will start with a deep dive into two little troublemakers causing quite a stir recently—the varroa mite and the tracheal mite. But that's just the beginning.

As we venture further, we'll meet many other pests, from the sneaky wax moths and small hive beetles to the larger, brazen mammalian intruders like bears and raccoons. And let's not forget those pesky ants, mice, skunks, birds, and wasps. Each of these creatures has its unique way of causing havoc in our hives, and we will get to know them all!

But don't worry; we're not here to scare you. For each pest, we'll arm you with the knowledge to spot, prevent—and show them the door if needed. We're in this together, and with a little knowledge and determination, we can ensure our hives remain safe and thriving.

Varroa Mite

Varroa Mites/Credit: Kuttelvaserova Stuchelova(www.shutterstock.com)

Let's spotlight the Varroa mite, or as scientists call it, the Varroa destructor. This tiny critter, no bigger than the head of a pin, has truly earned its ominous name. These pesky ectoparasitic mites, known as Varroa mites, made their grand, unwelcome entrance to the U.S. in 1987. Initially, they were bothering the Asian honey bee, *Apis cerana*. But then, they decided to expand their horizons and hopped over to the European honey bee, *Apis mellifera*. And from there they decided to take a world tour, spreading their nuisance and damage globally.

The Intricate Life Cycle

The Varroa mite is an external parasite that doesn't discriminate between adult bees and developing larvae—it targets both. Adult mites have reddish-brown, flattened oval bodies and are about 0.06 inches wide. The life cycle of these mites is a fascinating, albeit destructive, process. It starts when a mated female mite infiltrates a bee larva's cell and lays up to six eggs.

As these mite offspring grow, they feed on the pupae. Depending on their numbers, they can kill the pupae, cause deformities—or have no visible effect. While the male mites die within the cell, the adult female mites latch onto an adult worker bee, feeding on its hemolymph, or bee "blood." The female mite can then restart this cycle by infecting the cells of other developing larvae. Interestingly, mites have a preference for drone larvae over worker bee larvae. However, if left unchecked, they will infest worker larvae, leading to the eventual demise of the colony.

But the damage caused by the mites doesn't stop at direct infestation. These mites can also carry several deadly viruses that can kill bees. The disease known as Parasitic Mite Syndrome (PMS) may result from secondary infections made easier by the mites' ability to undermine the bees' immune systems. This condition can wipe out entire colonies within months of infestation.

Detection

One of the most critical tasks is the detection of Varroa mites. Let's explore some of the most effective methods to keep these pesky parasites in check.

Sugar Shake Method

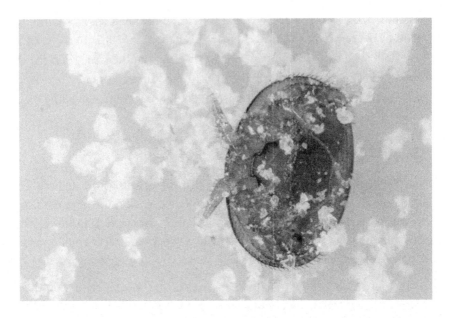

Varroa Mite in Sugar/Credit: Chris Moody(www.shutterstock.com)

This clever technique helps you estimate the percentage of adult bees in your colony playing host to these pesky mites. So, let's roll up our sleeves and dive into the step-by-step process of this bee-friendly method.

- **Step 1: Gather Your Tools:** First, you'll need a clear 1-pint jar or a similar container. The important thing is to use a cover made of ⅛-inch hardware cloth or another kind of mesh material. If a mesh lid jar isn't readily available, no worries! You can craft a mesh lid for your container.

- **Step 2: Collect Your Sample:** It's time to collect some bees. Put about 200 adult bees from a frame with developing brood into your jar with a gentle brush or shake.

- **Step 3: Sweeten the Deal:** Add two to three teaspoons of 6X powdered sugar via the mesh cover while keeping the bees in the jar secured with the mesh lid.

- **Step 4: Patience is Key:** After adding the sugar, let the jar sit for several minutes. This gives the bees and any mites a chance to get a good sugar dusting.

- **Step 5: Shake it Off:** Now for the shake part of the Sugar Shake Method! Shake the sugar (and any loose mites) firmly out of the jar and onto a spotless, flat surface. A white surface is ideal as it makes spotting the mites easier. And don't worry about your bees—they'll be sugar-coated but unharmed and can be safely returned to the colony.

- **Step 6: Count and Conclude:** If you spot 10 or more mites among your 200 bees, it's time to control the mite population. (You might find a magnifying glass helpful to see the mites.)

The Sugar Shake Method is a non-invasive, bee-friendly way to keep tabs on Varroa mites in your colonies. Regular checks can help you catch a potential infestation early, giving you the upper hand in protecting your bees.

Sticky Board Method

This method gives you a clear picture of the total mite load in your hive, helping you understand just how many of these pesky mites you're dealing with. Let's walk through the process step by step.

- **Step 1: Get Your Board Ready:** You can start this method by purchasing a commercial sticky board from a beekeeping supply company or making your own. Commercial boards come with a pre-applied adhesive and a handy sampling grid. If you're going the DIY route, you'll need a stiff sheet of white paper. Apply a thin coating of petroleum jelly or an aerosol cooking spray on the top surface (the side that will be in contact with the bees). This creates a sticky surface that will trap the mites.

- **Step 2: Cover Up:** Once your sticky board is prepared, you'll need to cover it with two 8-mesh wire covers, one on the top and one on the bottom. This ensures your bees don't end up stuck to the board.

- **Step 3: Position Your Board:** Now, it's time to place your sticky board on the bottom floor of the hive. As the bees do their business, some mites fall off, pass through the mesh screen, and stick to the board.

- **Step 4: Patience is a Virtue:** Leave the board in the hive for 24 hours. This gives enough time for mites to fall and stick to the board.

- **Step 5: Count them Up:** After 24 hours, Take the board out, then count the number of mites. If you find between 60 and 190 mites (depending on the size of your colony), it's time to take action to control the mite population.

Alcohol Wash Method

Much like the Sugar Shake Method, this method involves collecting adult bees into a clear container. Let's look step by step:

- **Step 1: Set Up Your Container:** In a transparent 1-pint jar or other clear container, add 1 to 2 inches of rubbing alcohol (isopropyl alcohol). Make sure the lid on your container is sturdy.

- **Step 2: Gather Your Bees:** It's time to collect some bees. Gently shake or brush 200 adult bees into your prepared container from a frame with newly emerging brood.

- **Step 3: Give it a Good Shake:** Give the bees in the container a vigorous shake for at least 30 seconds. This action will dislodge the mites from the bees and cause them to mix with the alcohol.

- **Step 4: Count Your Mites:** After shaking, it's time to examine the container. Look for dead mites that have sunk to the bottom. If you spot 10 or more mites among your 200 bees, it's time to take action to control the mite population.

Drone Brood Inspection

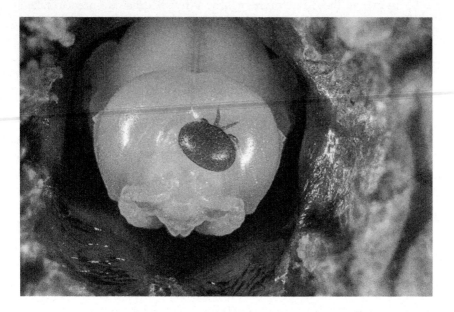

Varroa Mite on Pupa/Credit: Kuttelvaserova
Stuchelova(www.shutterstock.com)

It's important to remember that this method isn't the bee-all (pun intended!) and end-all for detecting Varroa mites. It won't always give you a perfect snapshot of the mite levels in your colony due to the natural variations in sampling. But, it's a handy tool in your beekeeping arsenal, as it can help you gauge the relative degree of Varroa infestation. So, how does it work? Let's break it down.

- **Step 1: The Hunt for Drone Brood:** Should you accept it, your mission is to find any capped drone brood within your hive. Where might you find these? They're typically hanging out on the outskirts of the brood nest.

- **Step 2: Uncapping the Cells:** Once you've located the drone brood, it's time to uncap those cells. But remember, we're dealing with living creatures here, so be gentle and careful not to harm the pupae inside.

- **Step 3: The Inspection:** After you've uncapped the cells, it's time to extract the drone pupae gently. Why? Because we need to take a closer look at them. We're on the lookout for adult Varroa mites.

- **Step 4: Making the Call:** If 10 percent or more of the drone pupae are playing host to Varroa mites, it is a clear sign that you must take steps to control the mite population in your colony.

Your Monitor Strategy

In beekeeping, it's crucial to maintain a vigilant watch over all honey bee colonies for signs of Varroa mite infestation. This isn't a task to be performed sporadically—monitor the colonies multiple times throughout the season. This consistent overview allows timely determination of when, and if, treatment is necessary.

Moreover, it's important not to rely solely on one detection method. Various sampling techniques described earlier are advised to ensure a comprehensive and accurate assessment of each hive. In this way, we can maintain a responsible and informed approach to beekeeping.

Control: From Traditional Methods to Innovative Solutions

In beekeeping, Varroa mite control has long been a significant concern. Some control solutions include the following:

- **Synthetic Chemical Treatments**: Historically, the primary control method has involved chemical pesticides, typically embedded within plastic strips and placed strategically between the wax combs of bee hives. However, the rapid development of resistance among Varroa mites to these common treatments has necessitated exploring alternative strategies.

- **Structural Modifications:** One alternative involves implementing structural or mechanical changes to the bee hives. These modifications aim to disrupt the life cycle of the mites or create an environment less conducive to their survival and proliferation.

- **Development of Mite-Tolerant Bee Stocks:** In addition to structural changes, cultivating bee stocks with increased mite tolerance is another promising approach. Through selective breeding, these bees exhibit enhanced resistance to mite infestations.

- **Bio-Pesticides:** Given the growing resistance of mites to synthetic treatments, bio-pesticides are also being explored. These naturally-derived substances can effectively control mite populations without the associated risk of resistance development, which is inherent in synthetic treatments.

Structural Modifications in More Detail:

These methods are all about shaking up our beekeeping practices, and the best part? They don't rely on chemicals, so you can use them even when your bees are busy making honey! Sure, they might take a bit more elbow grease or require some new gear, and they might not pack the same punch as other methods, but they're certainly worth considering.

- **Screened Bottom Boards:** First, let's talk about swapping that standard wooden hive bottom for a wire-mesh screen or another non-solid surface. Research has shown that this simple switch can help lower mite levels in your colonies. It is not entirely clear why this works, but it could be down to better ventilation in the hive, or mites accidentally dropping through the floor. This method alone might not be enough, so be prepared to pair it with other treatments.

- **Drone-Brood Trapping:** Next, we have drone-brood trapping. Varroa mites have a soft spot for drone brood—the developing pupae of male honey bees—because they're larger and take longer to develop, giving female mites more time to produce offspring. So why not take advantage of this? Adding special combs with drone-sized cells to your hives can lure the mites away from the rest of the brood. Then, remove these combs before the drones and mites can emerge. Depending on the season, this can be a real game-changer for controlling mite populations.

- **Inert Dusts:** Adult mites get around the hive by hitching a ride on adult bees. However, those mites may lose their hold and slip off if small dust particles, such as talcum powder or powdered sugar, are applied to all the adults in a colony.

Development of Mite-Tolerant Bee Stocks in More Detail

Here, we see some of the most exciting advancements in Varroa mite control. We're talking about breeding specific strains of honey bees that can stand up to these pesky mites. While we continue to learn about how this works, certain behaviors and physiological traits seem critical to this mite resistance. Today, a few bee strains show real promise in reducing Varroa mite numbers in their colonies.

- **Russian Strain:** First up, we have the Russian strain. These bees came from the Primorsky area in far eastern Russia and were imported by researchers at the USDA Honey Bee Research Lab in Baton Rouge, Louisiana. They've been living side by side with *Apis cerana*, the original host species of Varroa mites, for a long time. This long-term exposure seems to have given them a leg-up in resistance to the mites. They're over twice as resistant to Varroa as other commercial stocks. Plus, they seem to have a knack for fending off tracheal mites, another parasitic mite that infests honey bee colonies.

- **VSH Stock:** Next is the Varroa-Sensitive Hygiene (VSH) trait. Bees with this trait have a keen sense for detecting Varroa mites in the cells of developing pupae and booting them out before they can reproduce. To select this characteristic, USDA researchers have put much effort into employing traditional bee breeding and instrumental insemination methods. They've even crossed this stock with common commercial stocks to spread this helpful trait.

- **Hygienic Behavior:** Many queen breeders have focused on breeding for "hygienic behavior." This is all about how well a colony keeps its brood nest clean. The Minnesota Hygienic stock and other colonies that have been selectively bred to uncap and remove infected or parasitized brood have been demonstrated to have reduced levels of several diseases. While these stocks aren't immune to Varroa, they can significantly reduce the need for other control methods.

Bio-Pesticides in More Detail

These substances derived from nature—organisms or their by-products—
have been given the green light for controlling Varroa mites in honey bee
colonies. They can be as just effective as conventional chemical pesticides,
but how we use them can be slightly different.

- **Apilife VAR®:** First up is Apilife VAR®, a product that combines the
  power of essential oils like thymol, eucalyptol, and menthol. Studies
  have shown it can wipe out between 65% and 97% of varroa mites.
  You administer it by breaking up a vermiculite tablet into four
  pieces and placing them in the corners of the hive adjacent to the
  brood chambers. You'll need to wrap each piece in wire mesh to
  stop the bees from chewing it and removing it too soon. You'll need
  to replace the tablets weekly for three weeks for full effectiveness.
  But watch the thermometer—Apilife VAR® works best in
  temperatures above 60°F and below 90°F. It might cause a
  significant drop in bee brood, so it's often best used as a fall
  treatment when brood-rearing naturally declines. And remember,
  even though Apilife VAR® is considered an organic pesticide, it's a
  restricted-use chemical, so you'll need a valid N.C. Pesticide
  Applicators License to buy and use it.

- **Formic Acid:** Next, we have formic acid, a method recently
  approved by the EPA for Varroa mite control in the United States.
  For many years, beekeepers in Canada and Europe relied on it as
  their go-to insecticide, since it is the only chemical that can be used
  to still produce organic honey. There are a few ways to apply formic
  acid, like placing pads soaked with the stuff on top of the hive (sold
  under the trade name Mite-Away II®). The daily maximum
  temperature has to be between 50°F and 79°F, and you can't use it
  while there is a honey flow. To avoid a major loss of adult bees and
  brood during the first week of treatment, you must remove it from
  the hive if temperatures rise beyond 82°F. Also, the fumes can
  overwhelm small colonies (fewer than 6–20 frames of bees). And
  beekeepers, be careful—formic acid is highly corrosive and
  poisonous to humans, so take the proper precautions to avoid
  exposure.

Synthetic Chemical Treatments in More Detail

These treatments have been the go-to for many years and involve synthetic pesticides. How do we administer them? By placing plastic strips soaked with the active chemical inside the hive. These treatments have been highly influential in the past, but we're seeing an uptick in resistance to these chemicals, making them less reliable.

- **Apistan®:** This was one of the first treatments to be registered by the EPA for Varroa mite control. It uses fluvalinate, a synthetic pyrethroid, and comes as a plastic strip soaked with the pesticide. These strips are hung in a hive's frames above the brood nest. Fluvalinate is a contact pesticide and can wipe out up to 100% of varroa mites when used correctly. But here's the catch: growing studies indicate that Varroa mites are becoming resistant to this insecticide. So, it's highly recommended to rotate Apistan® with other treatments. This can help slow down the development of resistance and ensure the treatment remains effective.

- **Apivar®:** This is a newer product that uses the chemical amitraz. It works similarly to Apistan®, but the good news is that the mites haven't developed a resistance to it… yet.

- **Checkmite+®:** This was mainly developed in response to fluvalinate resistance. It's another synthetic chemical registered by the EPA as a Section 18 emergency-use pesticide for Varroa control. It uses coumaphos, another synthetic pesticide, and is sold as a plastic strip soaked with the active pesticide. Checkmite+®, when applied properly, can provide up to 100% control of the mites when they come into contact with it. But there's a downside: coumaphos is part of the organophosphate group of pesticides, and residues can build up in wax and harm bees at high levels. There have been instances of Varroa mites developing tolerance to this herbicide, much as with Apistan®. As a result, it must be taken as directed on the label and in combination with other authorized treatments.

Tracheal Mite

The tracheal mite, or *Acarapis woodi* as it's known in the scientific community, is a minuscule parasite with a significant impact. It sets up residence in the trachea of the European honey bee, causing substantial harm to these industrious insects.

Imagine this: a female mite lays her eggs on the inner walls of a bee's trachea. These eggs hatch within 10 to 15 days and grow into adult mites. They target less than two-week-old bees, piercing the tracheal walls to feed on the bee's haemolymph, a fluid equivalent to our blood. The effects on the bees are devastating. Infected bees display signs of weakness, such as an inability to fly and disjointed wings. This condition, known as acarine disease or acariosis, indicates a tracheal mite infestation. These tiny mites are more than just a nuisance. They block the oxygen flow within the bees, leading to their death. As beekeepers and lovers of nature, it's our responsibility to understand and control the spread of these mites.

Recognizing the Signs of Tracheal Mites

A peculiar change in the bees' wing alignment is one of the most distinctive signs of a tracheal mite infestation. Bees plagued by these mites often exhibit disjointed wings, sticking out almost perpendicular to their bodies. This condition, often called the "K-wing" phenomenon, is a clear red flag of a mite problem.

Beyond physical alterations, bees under siege of tracheal mites may also show signs of dysentery and an unusual inclination to swarm. The overall vitality of the hive can also take a hit, with a significant number of bees opting to stay within the hive rather than embarking on their usual foraging expeditions, even on days that are otherwise perfect for gathering resources. This lethargy can result in slower-than-normal population growth within the hive.

Interestingly, the effects of tracheal mites can fluctuate with the changing seasons. During the warmer summer and autumn, a mite-infested hive might give the illusion of strength. However, as winter sets in, the hive can rapidly deteriorate due to the shortened lifespan of the bees, a condition known as acariosis. In the depths of winter, a hive might be reduced to just a queen and a few bees, despite an abundance of honey.

It's worth noting that tracheal mites prefer young bees, particularly those that have just emerged and are less than a day old. As bees mature, their susceptibility to mite infestation rapidly diminishes.

Diffusion

These tiny creatures spread within the hive through direct bee-to-bee contact. Picture this: a female mite cleverly exits the spiracle, latching onto the tip of a bee's hair. When bees come into close contact, the mite seizes the chance to hop from an infested bee to a non-infested one.

But the mite's journey doesn't stop within a single hive. It can quickly spread from one hive to another through a process known as "bee drifting." And it's not just the bees that can inadvertently aid in the mite's spread. Even well-meaning beekeepers can contribute to the transfer of tracheal mites when they combine or divide colonies. Furthermore, the movement of colonies by migratory beekeepers and swarms from infested colonies can also facilitate the dispersal of this mite.

Prevention

Two key steps in the prevention process are cleanliness and regular hive inspections. Regularly checking your hives for infection is crucial, particularly in the summer and fall. By collecting a sample of 50–75 bees and examining them, you can determine whether or not mites infest the hive.

Another preventive measure is to avoid moving colonies and combining or dividing colonies. This can help prevent the spread of the mite, especially in cases where hives are minimally infested. Remember—an ounce of prevention is worth a pound of cure, and these steps can go a long way in keeping your hives mite-free.

Eradicating Tracheal Mites

The good news is that tracheal mites can be eliminated without causing harm to the hive's inhabitants. Various treatment options are available, many of which are entirely natural and pose no threat to the bees.

Menthol Treatment

One such method involves the use of menthol. A packet containing approximately 50–60 grams of menthol pellets is introduced into each infected hive. Depending on the temperature, the menthol packet is placed either on top of the frames (when temperatures are below 15°C or 60°F) or on the bottom board (when temperatures exceed 26°C or 79°F). As the temperature rises and the menthol is exposed to air, it vaporizes, filling the hive with fumes. The tracheal mites are eradicated as the bees inhale the vapor. It's important to note that while the vapor effectively kills adult mites, it does not affect eggs or larvae. Therefore, the menthol packets should remain in the hives for about two weeks, corresponding to the mite's development time. The recommended dosage for treating infested colonies is 2 ounces for each two-story hive.

Grease Patties

Another natural method to combat tracheal mites is the use of grease patties. These patties combine 1 part solid vegetable shortening, such as Crisco, with 2 to 3 parts granulated sugar. Some beekeepers prefer to use 1 part liquid vegetable oil mixed with 2 to 3 parts powdered or granulated sugar. Natural oil extracts, like lemongrass or spearmint, can be added to make the patties more appealing to the bees. The oil or grease in the patties serves to mask the scent that mites use to locate young bees.

The patties resemble hamburgers and are placed on wax paper in the center of the frames within the infested hives. When bees come to consume the sugar, they get oil on their bodies, which hinders the mite's ability to spread to other bees. Consequently, the mite eventually dies.

Wax Moths

Wax Moth/Credit: Ihor Hvozdetskyi(www.shutterstock.com)

When we think about the challenges faced by our fuzzy, buzzing friends, the European honey bees, wax moths might not be the first thing that comes to mind. However, these seemingly insignificant creatures, specifically the greater wax moth *(Galleria mellonella)* and the lesser wax moth *(Achroia grisella)*, can significantly threaten bee colonies' health and productivity.

In the grand scheme of nature, wax moths play a beneficial role. They are nature's clean-up crew, helping to eliminate old combs once a bee colony has abandoned a hive or succumbed to other threats. However, when these moths set their sights on *active* apiaries, they can cause considerable damage, impacting both the colonies and the hives and reducing the potential yield of honey and comb.

Wax moth infestations can occur in living colonies and combs stored for the winter. Interestingly, stored combs tend to be more susceptible to infestation. Once the moths have taken hold, they can render the comb and honey unsuitable for sale, hitting beekeepers where it hurts most.

Beeswax, especially raw beeswax, pollen, honey bee larval remnants, honey bee cocoon silk, and even the encapsulated honey bee excrement found on brood cell walls, are all favorites of the larger and lesser wax moths. They are considered pests of active hives, but they typically exploit already diseased or declining honey bee colonies, indicating other underlying problems with the colony.

These moths are particularly destructive to unattended combs in storage, especially in dark, warm, and poorly ventilated areas. This damage can lead to a decrease in the yield and saleability of honey products, affecting the overall productivity of the apiary.

Spotting Wax Moths in Your Hive

Wax moths can be a nuisance for beekeepers, but you can identify their presence in your hives with a keen eye and knowledge. Here's how:

The first step in detecting wax moths is to look inside your hive. You might be dealing with a wax moth infestation if you see larvae nestled in the comb. These little critters are known for their tunneling habits, leaving behind a trail of webbing as they move through the hive frames.

But be careful! Wax moth larvae can be mistaken for another common pest: the small hive beetle. To tell them apart, pay attention to their legs. Wax moth larvae have three sets of thoracic legs at the back end of their bodies and additional pairs of uniform legs along the rest. They also have a soft, fleshy body. On the other hand, small hive beetles only have thoracic legs and their bodies are more rigid.

Wax moth larvae are quite the little weavers. They produce a silky web spread across the hive, covering honeycombs and larval cells. This webbing and the waste left behind by the larvae can make the comb unsuitable for extraction or sale. Even worse, the webbing can trap bees in their cells, preventing them from emerging, and thus decreasing the hive's population.

Taking Action Against Wax Moths

Wax moths can be a real headache for beekeepers, but don't worry! There are several strategies you can employ to send these pests packing.

- **The Hands-On Approach.** Sometimes, the most straightforward methods are the most effective. If your hive has a minor infestation, you can roll up your sleeves and manually remove the moth larvae from the frames. Keep an eye out for signs of their presence, like webbing. This direct approach can nip the problem in the bud and prevent the infestation from spreading.

- **DIY Moth Trap:** If you're a fan of DIY solutions, you might want to try creating a moth trap. You only need a 2-liter soft drink bottle, sugar, vinegar, water, and a banana peel. Drill a small hole in the bottle, mix your ingredients inside, and let it ferment for a few days. Hang the bottle near your hive, and watch as the moths are drawn to the trap and meet their watery end.

- **Chemical Countermeasures:** If the infestation proves stubborn, it might be time to bring out the big guns. Paradichlorobenzene (PDB) is a chemical agent that can help protect your stored honeycombs from wax moths. However, remember that it's not suitable for honey or combs destined for your dinner table. Use this method as a last resort when other, more environmentally-friendly methods have failed.

- **The Scorched Earth Strategy:** In extreme cases, you might need to consider burning your hive containers to eliminate the infestation. This drastic measure might also require requeening to ensure a strong, healthy bee population can rebuild and return to producing honey.

Prevention

First things first: the health of your bee colony is paramount. Consider it your first line of protection against wax moths. A robust and bustling colony of honey bees is like a well-oiled machine, naturally spotting and kicking out any unwelcome wax moth larvae. It's like having your very own security force! So, how do you ensure a healthy colony? It's all about care, attention, and love for your bees. Keep them robust; they'll return the favor by keeping those pesky moths out.

Now, onto the second part of our strategy: cleanliness. It's not just about keeping your home tidy; it's also about keeping your bees' home tidy. Your apiary is your bees' sanctuary, and it's your responsibility to keep it clean and safe. This means being meticulous about your equipment, hives, and all the bits and pieces that come with them. Untreated wax and old combs are all potential hotspots for wax moths. Keep them clean, and you'll keep the moths away.

But remember, it's not just about preventing an infestation; it's also about stopping it from spreading. One moth can quickly become many—you'll have a full-blown infestation before you know it. So, stay vigilant and keep your apiary healthy. It's a team effort, and every little bit helps.

Small Hive Beetle

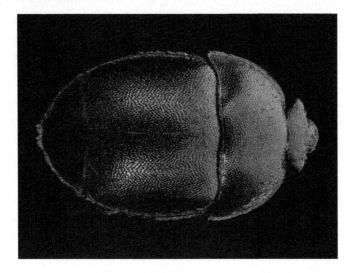

Small Hive Beetle/Credit: lego 19861111(www.shutterstock.com)

Picture this: European honey bee colonies, bustling with industrious activity, are suddenly besieged by a silent yet formidable intruder—the Small Hive Beetle (SHB). This menacing pest insect has cast its dark shadow over apiaries worldwide, posing a grave threat to the delicate balance of these essential pollinators.

Measuring a mere 5mm in length and cloaked in dark brown or black hues, the SHB is native to the vast plains of Africa. However, its ambition knows no bounds, spreading across continents at an alarming rate. In 1996, the United States was taken aback when it first encountered this relentless invader. Since then, it has made its mark in other corners of the world.

Symptoms

You know the drill—the severity of SHB presence can vary, so let's be attentive to the signs. Here's what we need to keep an eye out for:

- **Damaged/Destroyed Brood Combs:** Those mischievous SHB larvae love nothing more than chowing down on the colony's precious brood combs. They'll munch and burrow away, causing quite a mess if we don't catch them in the act. So, be on the lookout for combs with unusual, chewed-out sections—that's our cue that these little pests are up to no good.

- **Contaminated Honey Stores:** Our honey stores are a treasure trove, but the SHBs can't resist a sweet treat. They'll indulge in our golden nectar, but not without leaving their mark—contamination. Watch out for slimy honeycombs emitting a funky smell, like rotten oranges. If you catch a whiff of that, we've got SHB troubles.

- **The Nose Knows:** Ah, the unmistakable power of smell! Our sense of smell might come in handy when battling SHBs. Sometimes, these crafty invaders leave a peculiar aroma in the hive—a clear signal that they're up to mischief.

- **Hive Abandonment:** The Worst-Case Scenario: Picture the heartbreak—our hardworking bees, pushed to their limits, might make a heart-wrenching decision. If the SHB infestation gets out of hand, our bees might just up and leave, abandoning their hive in search of a safer abode. We can't let it come to that!

How it Spreads

The Small Hive Beetle (SHB) is a master of infiltration, finding its way into new colonies through various means. Beekeepers unwittingly aid its spread by transporting queen and package bees, allowing these crafty intruders to hitchhike and infest fresh hives. Not just content with bees as carriers, SHBs can lurk in beeswax, equipment, fruits—and even soil, ready to seize any opportunity to make themselves a home in new territories.

The resilience of adult SHBs adds another layer of complexity to the issue. With the ability to survive up to two weeks without sustenance, and up to 50 days with honeycomb, these invaders are well-equipped for long journeys.

Due to its toughness, the pest is difficult to contain during shipment, storage, and transportation.

Prevention

A proactive and methodical strategy is crucial to protect our valuable honey bee colonies from the Small Hive Beetle (SHB).

- **Maintaining Robust and Healthy Hives:** As dedicated beekeepers, we understand the importance of cultivating solid and thriving colonies. A professionally managed hive, filled with active and healthy bees, can naturally defend itself against potential SHB infestations. By prioritizing the well-being of our bees, we equip them to combat these invasive pests effectively.

- **Embracing Integrated Pest Management (IPM):** IPM allows us to adopt a systematic and environmentally-conscious approach to SHB control. By combining knowledge, scientific insights, and responsible practices, we can minimize the risk of infestation and protect our colonies. Understanding the SHB life cycle and identifying potential vulnerabilities within our apiaries empowers us to pursue successful beekeeping.

- **Setting Action Thresholds:** In our professional stewardship of honey bee colonies, establishing action thresholds is pivotal. By setting clear criteria for intervention, such as the presence of multiple SHBs, signs of hive damage, or evidence of slimy discharge, we can take timely and appropriate action to mitigate infestations. Responsible vigilance allows us to address potential problems before they escalate.

- **Continuous Monitoring and Observation:** Vigilance remains essential to our beekeeping practice. Regularly monitoring our hives for signs of SHB presence (and the range of diseases and pests) enables us to detect early warning signals. Through keen observation and systematic assessments, we can effectively intercept SHB invasions, minimizing their impact on our colonies.

- **Adopting Best Beekeeping Practices:** By diligently cleaning and storing hive equipment and maintaining strict quality protocols, we create an environment that discourages SHB infestations. A responsible and professional approach forms a formidable defense against these invaders.

- **Responsible Pest Control:** In the unfortunate event of a well-established SHB presence, we must proceed with caution and prudence. The use of pesticides may become necessary to control the spread of infestation. However, as responsible beekeepers, we opt for pesticide application only when *essential,* prioritizing the well-being of our bees and the environment.

Protecting Your Beehive from Ants

When inspecting your beehive, you might find some uninvited guests creeping around, trying to crash the party. Yep, we're talking about those pesky ants! They're notorious for sniffing around our hives; they can really "bug" our bees if left unchecked!

Before we get into the nitty-gritty of ant-proofing, let's address the big question: do ants harm our beehives? These tiny raiders are usually lured in by the sugar water in the feeder or the tempting honey our bees have worked so hard to produce. A few ants might not bother the bees much, but a full-scale invasion can spell big trouble, especially for smaller colonies or fresh bee packages.

Methods for Safeguarding Beehives from Ants

- **Hive Stand:** A hive stand elevates your hive off the ground, like a fortress keeping ants at bay! These stands can even have built-in moats around the legs, giving those ants no way of climbing up and crashing our bee party.

- **Say No to Tall Grass and Weeds:** Ants are crafty climbers, and those tall grass and weeds make for perfect hideouts and ant highways leading straight to your hive. So, roll up your sleeves and clear the area around your beehives.

- **Repair and Reinforce:** Those sneaky ants can sneak in through tiny cracks and holes in your bee boxes. Regular inspections and timely repairs keep those ants out in the cold where they belong. Plus, checking for ants on the comb during inspections is always a good idea.

- **Know the Ants:** Knowledge is power, beekeepers! Take some time to research the ants in your neck of the woods. Know their habits, peak seasons, and what attracts or repels them.

- **Clean Bee Yard, Happy Bee Yard:** Tossing burr comb on the ground might be tempting, but it's an open invitation to ants. So, let's be proactive—bring a bag or bucket during hive inspections to collect any debris. A tidy bee yard keeps ants away and our bees happy!

- **Diatomaceous Earth to the Rescue:** Ever heard of diatomaceous earth or cinnamon powder? These natural wonders create a barrier that ants can't cross. Sprinkle some around each hive stand leg, and watch those ants turn tail and run! But remember, watch for reapplication—the elements can be tough on our ant deterrent.

- **An Oil Barrier:** Now, here's an idea—let's make it slick for those ants! Place cans or containers filled with vegetable oil or soapy water around each hive stand leg. The slippery surface keeps ants from climbing up and bothering our lovely bees.

- **Tanglefoot the Sticky Stopper:** Tanglefoot, a gooey insect barrier used on fruit trees, can also be our secret weapon. Wrap a band around each hive stand leg, then spread Tanglefoot with a putty knife. Watch out, ants—there's no escape from the stickiness!

By implementing these savvy strategies, you can create a protective shield against ants around your beehives and ensure busy bees can do their thing in peace.

Safeguarding Your Beehive Against Bear Intrusions

Yes, you heard it right, bears! If you've ever watched Winnie the Pooh, you'll know that our furry friends have a serious sweet tooth for honey. And just like in the cartoons, they can cause quite a stir when they find a beehive. Imagine a bear, with all its might and power, tearing apart your carefully constructed beehive, all in pursuit of that sweet, golden nectar. The aftermath? A scene of devastation that would break any beekeeper's heart.

But here's the kicker—bears have an excellent memory. Once they've found your hive, they'll remember where the honey jackpot is. Rebuild in the same spot, and it's like sending them an engraved invitation for a second feast. It's a cycle that can leave you frustrated and your bees homeless.

Now, if you're living in a bear country, don't despair. There is a solution to keep your buzzing buddies safe. It's time to think like a bear and outsmart them. How, you ask? Well, with a high-voltage electric fence! It might sound extreme, but trust me; it's a game-changer. This fence is your beehive's knight in shining armor, a barrier that even the most determined bear won't dare to cross. It's practical, effective, and a small price to pay for the peace of mind it brings.

Electric Fence/Credit: dcwcreations(www.shutterstock.com)

Defending Your Beehive Against Rodent Intrusions

Let's shift gears now, and discuss another challenge you might face as a beekeeper—rodents. Those pesky mice and rats that can turn your home into a nightmare can do the same with your beehive. They're not just a nuisance; they're carriers of diseases, making them unwelcome guests in any setting.

You might wonder, "What harm can a tiny mouse or rat do to my beehive?" Well, quite a lot. These little critters love the warmth and shelter that beehives provide during the winter. And while they're in there, they can wreak havoc on the hive's structure, damaging the foundation and the combs. They might not bother the bees, but the structural damage they cause can lead to big problems down the line.

So, how do you keep these unwanted tenants out of your beehive? Here's a simple, two-step plan:

- Grab a long metal stick, and use it to delicately broom the bottom of the lowest board of the beehive. This will help to flush out any rodents that might have already set up shop. Be careful not to damage the structure, and make sure you cover all the corners—we don't want to leave any cozy hiding spots for them.

- Next, install a metal guard at the entrance of the beehive. Why metal, you ask? If you've ever had (unfortunate) contact with mice or rats, you'll know that they can chew through wood like it's butter. A metal guard will keep them out and your bees safe.

Guarding Your Beehive Against Skunks, Raccoons, and Other Small Mammals

Now, let's turn our attention to some no less cunning adversaries: skunks, raccoons, and other small mammals. You might not think of these critters as threats to your beehive, but let me tell you, they can be quite the handful.

Take skunks, for example. These little guys have a surprising appetite for bees and other insects. They're crafty, too. They'll stir up a ruckus outside your beehive at night, waking the bees. And when the bees come out to see what's going on, it's dinner time for the skunks.

Then there are raccoons. These masked marauders are known for their problem-solving skills. Give them a beehive with a secure lid, and they'll see it as a challenge, not a deterrent. They'll work at it until they find a way to remove that lid and get to the honey inside.

So, how do we outsmart these clever critters?

As previously discussed, try the old "heavy rock on the lid" trick for raccoons. It's simple but effective. A large, heavy rock can make it much harder for a raccoon to pry open the lid.

On the other hand, skunks don't like exposing their bellies. So, elevate your beehive. This forces the skunks to reach it on their hind legs, leaving their bellies vulnerable to bee stings. That's usually enough to send them packing.

And for an extra layer of defense, consider a DIY bed of nails around your beehive. Just push some nails through a piece of wood, and voila! Most predators will think twice before crossing that prickly barrier. But remember, safety first! Don't forget where you've placed that bed of nails! It would be best if *you* didn't fall victim to your clever trap.

Shielding Your Beehive from Birds

Regarding safeguarding your beehive, it's not just ground-based threats you need to consider. Birds, the aerial predators, can also pose a challenge. Several bird species have a penchant for bees, including thrushes, kingbirds, swifts, mockingbirds, and woodpeckers.

Typically, the number of bees these birds consume doesn't significantly impact the overall health of your beehive, as the bees that survive greatly outnumber those that fall prey. However, there are instances when these feathered foes may become a problem requiring a solution.

To protect your beehive from these aerial threats, consider implementing the following strategies:

- **Install feeders around the beehive**. You can divert the birds' attention from your bees by providing an alternative food source.
- **Use mock-ups of natural predators to scare off the birds.** This strategy works on the same principle as scarecrows on farms, deterring birds from approaching the beehive.
- **Surround the beehive with chicken wire.** This physical barrier can prevent birds from reaching the hive and feasting on your bees.

Defending Your Beehive Against Wasps: The Winged Rivalry

Let's talk about a rivalry as old as time: the feud between bees and wasps. If you thought the drama in your favorite TV show was intense, wait until you hear about the battles that take place right in your backyard! Wasps, you see, have a sweet tooth for honey. They'll stop at nothing to get *more* once they taste the honey in your beehive.

- So, how do we keep these winged warriors at bay? Here's a three-step plan:

- First up, **traps.** You can use a commercial trap like the NoPests® Wasp Dome Trap or make one yourself. Either way, a good trap can significantly reduce the wasp population around your beehive.

- Next, it's time for a bit of **detective work.** Look around for any wasp nests in the area and remove them. You might need to use an insecticide for this. Remember—safety comes first—always follow the instructions on the label.

- Finally, consider installing an **entrance reducer** on your beehive. This makes the entrance smaller, so your bees have less area to defend. It's like closing the gates to the castle when the enemy approaches.

CHAPTER 12

How to Start a Beekeeping Business

As you read through this chapter, you'll discover the secrets to making your beekeeping dreams profitable. We'll start by helping you estimate the potential earnings of each hive and guide you in determining how many hives you can *realistically* manage. Then, we'll navigate the intricate art of pricing your honey, just right. But remember, the world of beekeeping offers more than just honey, and we'll explore those avenues too. And, of course, we'll break down the costs to kickstart and keep your business buzzing. Lastly, we'll help you find the perfect spots to showcase your liquid gold. Let's get started!

Estimating Hive Profitability

Now, imagine your hive as a tiny, humming factory. This little powerhouse can churn out 30 to 60 pounds of sweet, golden honey in a good year. But hold on—it gets even better! If your colony is tip-top, you might be looking at a whopping 100 pounds of honey! How's that for a sweet deal?

The price tag on your honey isn't just pulled out of thin air. It's a delicate balance of quality, location, and what the market is willing to pay. You could be raking in anywhere from $5 to $15 per pound. But let's be practical here; a safe bet would be around $10 per pound.

So, let's do the math. With these figures in mind, you could pocket a cool $300 to $600 per hive yearly from selling honey. But wait, there's more! Selling additional bee products and the actual bees will increase your income.

Before you start counting your cash however, let's get real for a moment. As we have seen, running a hive isn't all sunshine and honey. There are costs involved. You have maintenance, harvesting, packaging, and marketing to consider. You'll need to subtract these expenses from your revenue to get a clear picture of your profit.

How Many Hives Can You Handle?

So, if you've got a taste of the sweet profits a hive can bring in, you're probably wondering, "How many hives can I manage?" Well, my friend, that's a great question, and the answer isn't one-size-fits-all. It's like asking how many balls you can juggle—it depends on your skill, focus, and how much *time* you can dedicate to the task.

Be prepared for a bit of a challenge. Managing many hives for honey production isn't a walk in the park. As you have seen reading this far, it can get quite involved. It's like running a mini factory—more time, equipment, and all hands-on deck.

But let's break it down a bit. Say you're a part-time beekeeper, balancing your love for bees with other life commitments. With some elbow grease, you could comfortably manage up to 25 hives.

Now, if you've got a bit more experience under your belt and your *focus* is on raising honey bees for sale, you could handle a whopping 100 to 150 hives. And the best part? You can do this while holding down a regular job!

It's all about leveraging your skills and managing your time effectively.

For those who are all in, dedicating your full time to beekeeping, you could manage between 400 to 600 colonies. But remember, with great numbers come *great* responsibilities. You'll probably need to bring in seasonal workers to help with the honey harvest.

And for the big players, those managing over 300 hives, welcome to the world of commercial beekeeping. It's a different ball game, but the profit potential is substantial.

Mastering the Art of Honey Pricing

So, you've got your jars of golden goodness ready to go. Now comes the million-dollar question: "What's the right price for my honey?" Price it too low, and you're selling yourself short. Too high, and your honey jars might gather dust. Here's a step-by-step guide to help you hit that sweet pricing spot.

- **Step 1: Scope Out the Competition:** Let's see what the other guys are doing. What's the going rate for honey similar to yours? If you're eyeing the farmer's market scene, stroll through a few local ones. Planning to go retail? Check out the prices at your local stores. Just remember to compare apples to apples—or in this case, honey to honey. Look at products similar to yours in size, variety, whether raw or pasteurized, any special infusions, and the source of the honey.

- **Step 2: Crunch Those Numbers:** It's time to get down to brass tacks—your costs. Start with the basics: the jar, the label, and other packaging materials. This gives you the base cost for each jar of honey. Then, factor in the costs of selling your honey. This could include shipping, packaging materials, delivery costs, farmer's market fees, or website hosting. If you're selling online, a good rule of thumb is to add $1–3 per product to cover these costs. Ideally, you want to make *at least double* your spending.

- **Step 3: What's Your Time Worth?** Finally, don't forget to factor in the value of your time and effort. This becomes especially important once you start pulling in more than $6,000 yearly or averaging $500+ monthly. At this point, you're running a business taking a significant chunk of your time. Estimate how much time you spend on your beekeeping activities and calculate your hourly earnings. If it turns out you're making about $2 an hour, it might be time to rethink your pricing and/or your operations!

A Few More Honey Pricing Tips

- Remember, it's easier to lower prices during a sale than to hike them up later. So, start a bit higher and offer discounts as needed.

- Deliver on your promises. There's nothing like poor customer service to turn a customer sour.

- Think about how you can add value to your honey. Infusions of creamed honey or adding a piece of comb to the jar can help you command a premium price.

- If you're selling at a pricier venue or event, don't hesitate to charge more for your products.

Making Your Honey Irresistible

The key to easy sales is finding a product that is in demand ... with little competition. If a particular type of honey is prevalent in your area but not widely available, that's your golden ticket. If your local grocery store is already brimming with local honey, consider how to make your honey stand out from the crowd.

Diversifying Your Beekeeping Revenue: More Than Just Honey

Honey might be the show's hero(ine), but it's not the only role in the story! Your buzzing buddies produce a variety of other substances that can be harvested and sold, opening up a world of opportunities.

Pollen

Bees are very diligent pollen collectors, bringing it back from flowers to feed the colony. But did you know that humans also use pollen as a health supplement? Given its limited supply, pollen can fetch a pretty penny— typically selling for $3 to $5 an ounce. You'll need to install a pollen trap at your hive entrance to harvest your own pollen. But remember, moderation is key. Harvest only a few days a week so your bees have enough pollen for *their* needs.

Propolis

Dionisvera/Credit: Dionisvera(www.shutterstock.com)

Propolis is a sticky, resin-like substance bees use to seal cracks and sanitize their hive. But its uses don't stop there. Humans value propolis for its medicinal properties, and it usually sells for $6 to $8 an ounce. Harvesting propolis involves using a propolis trap, and while the amounts harvested are small, a healthy colony can provide a steady supply.

Royal Jelly

Royal Jelly/Credit: JPC-PROD(www.shutterstock.com)

Royal jelly, or bee milk, is a protein-rich secretion from worker bees. It's the exclusive diet of queen bees and is fed to all larvae for their first three days of life. Due to its limited production and challenging harvesting process, royal jelly is a precious commodity, selling for $6 to $8 an ounce.

Beeswax

A route you also could take is selling blocks of pure beeswax to other crafters and body product makers. While it can be tough to compete with online prices, it's definitely worth a shot if you find there's a demand for it in your area.

Bee Venom

Bee Venom/Credit: Fabio Alcini(www.shutterstock.com)

Bee venom is an exciting new frontier in apitherapy, used to treat conditions like arthritis. This technique, known as bee sting therapy, involves bees stinging certain body parts. As research progresses, bee venom could open up a lucrative new market for beekeepers. However, if you're considering offering bee sting therapy, you need to consider liability issues and have a waiver in place for venom users.

Venturing into Beeswax Products and Candles

Beeswax/Credit: kosolovskyy(www.shutterstock.com)

If selling raw beeswax isn't quite your cup of tea, don't worry. Once you've rendered your wax—(beekeeper-speak for melting and cleaning the honeycomb into a solid wax block)—you've got a treasure trove of possibilities at your fingertips. Let's explore some exciting products you can create with your beeswax.

Candles: The Beeswax Classics

Candles are a fantastic option for a high return on investment. All you need, besides the wax, is a wick and a mold—both of which are pretty easy on the pocket.

Body Products: Beeswax's Beauty Secret

Beeswax isn't just for candles—it's also a star player in many body products. Lip balm is a crowd-pleaser, but why stop there? You can whip up soaps, salves, body butter, and lotions with beeswax. Plenty of recipes are available online. While the profit margin for body products might be slimmer due to the cost of labels, containers, and additional ingredients, they're a great option if you're working with a limited wax supply. Remember, any wax used in cosmetics or food-related products should be free from mite treatments. This should be the wax harvested during extraction.

Profiting from Pollination Services

Renting out your bees for pollination services can be quite a sweet deal indeed. Some beekeepers have turned this into a full-time gig, managing hundreds of hives for large farms. This venture, while profitable, demands a significant investment in equipment, a large number of hives, and a wealth of beekeeping experience.

But don't let that intimidate you. The pollination market isn't just for the big guns. Smaller farms and horticultural businesses often have more modest needs, requiring just a handful of hives. This allows smaller bee farmers and part-time beekeepers to offer services.

The price tag for renting out bees for pollination services can vary. Factors like your location and the season can influence the rates. However, it's common for farmers to shell out up to $150 for these services.

Beekeeping Education and Advisory Services

As you develop from being a novice to a seasoned beekeeper, you will amass a wealth of knowledge and experience. Why not turn this expertise into a source of income by offering training and consultation services to those new to the beekeeping world? The first year of beekeeping can be a whirlwind of learning, and having a seasoned guide to provide training and advice can be a game-changer.

Even if you're balancing a full-time job, offering classes and consultation services is feasible. Beekeeping workshops and demonstrations may be scheduled on weekends, and customers needing your advisory services should only need a few hours each month. After an initial client visit, you can provide much of your advice and assistance remotely, making this a flexible venture.

If you feel you're not quite ready to offer comprehensive classes, there's another avenue you can explore—offering bee or farm tours to the general public. These tours are fantastic because they appeal to a broader audience, not just aspiring beekeepers. Plus, they're shorter in duration, and you don't have to provide suits and veils for participants.

Bee Removal: A Win-Win Service

For experienced beekeepers, offering local bee removal services can be lucrative and beneficial to your business. Not only does it provide an additional source of income, but it also allows you to expand your hive count without incurring the cost of new bees. On average, bee removal services can fetch around $450. However, prices can range from $150 to $1500 or more, mainly if the bees have made a home within a structure and are challenging to access.

Apiary Maintenance: A Helping Hand for Farmers and Horticulturists

Another profitable avenue to explore is offering apiary maintenance services. There are numerous instances where horticulturists or farmers recognize the benefits of beehives for crop pollination but lack the necessary expertise or time to manage them effectively. These individuals are often more than willing to pay a good fee to a knowledgeable beekeeper to care for their bees and maintain their hives.

Selling Bees

Selling bees can be a "hive of opportunity" (sorry!) for beekeepers. By harnessing the potential of your existing hives, you can produce starter hives and replacement bees for other bee enthusiasts. While it may take some time to amass the necessary knowledge and bee numbers, it can be a highly profitable venture once you're up and running. Here's a look at some of the ways you can profit from selling bees:

- **Bee Packages:** A bee package is essentially a starter kit for beekeepers. It typically includes one queen and 3 pounds of bees. These packages are a hot commodity among beekeepers looking to kickstart new colonies or replenish existing ones. You can typically sell a bee package for around $175.

- **Nucleus Colonies:** A nucleus colony, or "nuc," is a mini hive in a box. It includes several honeycombs, bees, and a queen. When bees are introduced into a new hive, the existing honeycomb provides them with a headstart. A five-frame nuc with a queen can fetch a price between $200 to $250.

- **Established Beehives:** Selling established beehives can also be a profitable venture. These ready-to-go hives can be sold for between $250 and $350.

Beekeeping Starting Costs

Now that I have provided you with an overview of the profit streams of beekeeping, we'll unravel the financial intricacies for newbee beekeepers to consider. We'll dissect the various cost elements associated with starting beekeeping and discuss the myriad of choices you'll face that can significantly influence your expenses in the first year.

Protective Clothing

In the world of beekeeping, your safety is of utmost importance. Your protective ensemble will typically include a full bee suit or a bee jacket, a veil to shield your face and eyes (unless integrated into your suit), and gloves. The degree of protection you opt for and the design specifics of the products you select will directly impact your costs. While my cost estimates are primarily based on "economy" products, you can choose more premium items like vented suits and jackets. Costs can span a broad spectrum, but I project a minimum expenditure for protective gear to be in the ballpark of $90–$120 per person as a crucial part of your initial beekeeping investment.

Beekeeping Tools

As a novice beekeeper, you'll need a few indispensable tools in your arsenal. These include a bee smoker (around $30), a hive tool ($8), and a bee brush ($5). Starting, one set of tools should suffice, even if you're a team of beekeepers. However, it's always wise to have extra hive tools at your disposal as they have a knack for getting misplaced, and having spares will barely dent your initial beekeeping costs.

Investing in a Langstroth Hive

My estimates are based on a typical configuration for 10-frame boxes. This setup includes:

- A bottom board (equipped with an entrance reducer)

- Two deep boxes for brood

- Two honey supers

- Inner and outer covers

- 10 frames per box, complete with foundation

Hive components are available in various quality levels, including commercial, economy, and budget. From my experience, budget boxes from trustworthy suppliers are more than up to the task.

You can purchase boxes and frames, either assembled or unassembled. Assembled boxes may come painted or unpainted. While unassembled components are cheaper, as a beekeeping beginner, you might find fully assembled and painted kits more cost-effective and convenient.

On average, the cost of one complete beehive falls in the range of $260–$275. There might be a slight price difference between 8-frame and 10-frame components, but it doesn't significantly impact the total costs. Note that this is the cost of a *basic* Langstroth hive. As discussed in the chapter about the different types of beehives available, depending on your budget, you can also consider purchasing more expensive versions of the Langstroth hive, such as the Honeyflow hive or Apimaye hive.

Deciding on the Number of Colonies

As a novice beekeeper, you might be inclined to start with just one colony. If all goes well and no unexpected issues crop up, you might never need to buy another bee! However, it's important to remember that beekeeping can be unpredictable, and there's always a possibility of losing a colony for various reasons.

I strongly suggest starting with two colonies. This approach increases your chances of success and ensures you won't have to start from scratch in your second year if one colony fails. However, I understand that this can significantly increase your initial beekeeping costs. Therefore, it's crucial to ensure that this fits within your budget.

Cost of Bees

The cost of bees can vary based on several factors. On average, a package of bees is priced at around $175. If you're considering nucleus colonies or "nucs," you can expect to pay about $200 for spring nucs, while overwintered nucs are typically closer to $250. These prices can fluctuate based on your location and whether you pick up your bees, or opt for them to be shipped to you.

Cost of Varroa Mite Treatments and Miscellaneous Expenses

You *will* cross paths with the notorious Varroa destructor mites as a beekeeper. Various treatments are available as we have covered earlier in the book. Options such as Mite Away Quick Strips and oxalic acid are available but have an associated cost. Some treatments require additional equipment, so you should factor in this expense in your first and subsequent years.

I have estimated that the annual cost of treating Varroa (and potentially other pests like small hive beetles) is around $25 per hive. The cost of reestablishing a lost colony should be weighed against this ongoing expenditure.

If you opt for vaporized oxalic acid treatment, this cost could escalate significantly in your first year. A vaporizer can cost anywhere from around $50 to nearly $500. Moreover, safety is paramount when using a vaporizer, so you'll need a face mask to prevent inhalation.

Factoring in Miscellaneous Costs

My startup cost estimate includes an additional $75 for miscellaneous expenses. This rough estimate covers a variety of somewhat universal items, such as:

- Paint for beehives
- Sugar and pollen patties for feeding bees

Other miscellaneous costs can fluctuate significantly depending on your location and specific circumstances.

Protection from Animals

Moving on, let's discuss protecting your bees from animals. As previously discussed, small creatures like mice, skunks, and racoons can cause a lot of trouble, from harassing your bees to knocking over your hives. Elevating your hives can help deter these critters, but you might also want to consider some fencing. Ratchet and lashing straps are affordable to secure your hive, especially in areas prone to strong winds or harsh winters.

If bears are a concern in your area, you'll need a more robust solution. Bears are not just interested in your honey; they're after the bee brood too. The best line of defense? An electric fence. It provides a good psychological deterrent that keeps bears at bay after a few zaps. Yes, it's an additional expense, but when weighed against the cost of losing your bees and equipment, it's a worthy investment. A small electric fence can cost around $200–$300.

Honey Extractor

For those aspiring to harvest honey, acquiring a honey extractor will be necessary. However, it is prudent to exercise patience and refrain from harvesting in the first year of your beekeeping life. The initial year should be dedicated to nurturing your colonies and ensuring their survival through the first winter. The honey produced during this period should ideally be left for the bees' sustenance. Investing in a honey extractor is more likely to be a consideration for your second year in beekeeping. This approach is practical and responsible, as it prioritizes the health and growth of your bee colonies.

The cost of a honey extractor can vary widely, influenced by several factors. These factors include the extractor type (manual or electric), the material it's crafted from (commonly plastic or stainless steel), the capacity of frames it can accommodate, and the brand's reputation.

At the entry level, a manual plastic extractor holding two frames might set you back somewhere between $100 to $150. These are typically a good fit for hobbyist beekeepers managing a small number of hives. They're budget-friendly and practical, but be prepared for a little physical workout!

If you're overseeing more hives, or prefer convenience, a manual stainless steel extractor designed to hold four to six frames might be more up your alley. These models offer enhanced durability and are easier to clean than their plastic counterparts. However, they come with a heftier price tag, usually from $200 to $400.

An electric extractor might be the way for commercial beekeepers or those with a larger hive count. Depending on the model, these power-driven devices can accommodate six to over 60 frames. They offer the perks of speed and ease, doing the spinning for you. However, they're also the priciest option, with costs starting from $500 for a smaller model and soaring to several $1,000s for a large, commercial-grade extractor. These models are not recommended for beginners.

Though the initial cost of a honey extractor can be substantial, it's a long-term investment. A well-cared-for, quality extractor can serve you for many years, making it a valuable addition to your beekeeping arsenal. As always, weigh your specific needs, budget, and the scale of your beekeeping operation before choosing.

Managing Costs

Embarking on your beekeeping journey doesn't have to be a daunting financial commitment. There are numerous ways to keep your expenses in check while making sure you're well-equipped for your new venture.

One practical approach is to start with a "Beginner's kit." These kits often bundle the essential items you need to kickstart your beekeeping, typically at a lower cost than buying each item separately. While some of the items in these kits may not be the highest quality, they're generally adequate for beginners. However, be savvy. Some kits may only include one deep-hive box, which might seem sufficient initially, but as your colony expands, you'll need more. So, don't be fooled into thinking one box will cover all your needs.

If you're handy with tools and have a knack for woodworking, you can save money by undertaking DIY projects. For example, you could repurpose scrap wood and old mason jars to make top feeders, construct bottom boards, or even create homemade candy for winter feeding. Additionally, you could build robbing screens to protect your colonies during a nectar shortage.

Purchasing locally can also help you save on shipping costs. However, exercise caution when buying used hives. Unless they're from a reputable beekeeper with disease-free colonies, used hives can pose a risk of contamination to your colony. Even if they are from a reliable source, they should be thoroughly cleaned before use.

Beekeeping is clearly an investment, but you can make it cost-effective with intelligent choices and some DIY spirit.

Beekeeping Starting Costs: Summary

Venturing into the world of beekeeping is an exhilarating pastime filled with unique experiences and the sweet reward of honey. However, knowing that this adventure comes with its own financial commitments is obviously essential. On average, you might invest roughly $760 to navigate a new hive through its first year—but remember, this figure is merely a starting point.

Beyond the initial investment, there are ongoing costs to consider. These can encompass everything from hive maintenance to pest treatments and equipment replacement. Moreover, unexpected expenses are part and parcel of this journey. For instance, losing colonies during the winter months is (sadly) common, and the cost of replacing these bees can significantly impact your budget.

This information isn't intended to dissuade you—but to paint a realistic picture of what to expect. When I embarked on my beekeeping journey, I was aware of the additional costs but didn't fully grasp the extent of the financial commitment.

A clear understanding of these potential expenses upfront allows you to budget effectively and make informed decisions about allocating your resources. Furthermore, as you move further into the world of beekeeping and gain more experience, you'll likely find ways to cut costs without compromising the health and productivity of your apiary.

Maintenance costs

Maintenance costs, although not exorbitant, can vary annually based on weather conditions, nectar availability, and the age of your hives.

Supplemental Feed

Depending on the season, this could be a mix of syrup and protein to either boost growth or prep the bees for the chilly winter. While the market is flooded with feed options, syrup prices hover between $3.30 and $4.39 per gallon. And if you're thinking of protein supplement patties, set aside about $1.09–$1.57 per pound.

Requeening

A colony's heart and soul? The queen bee! But sometimes, she might need to be replaced. Whether she's getting a bit old, isn't performing her royal duties, or has simply just vanished, requeening is common. The price tag? Mated queens can set you back anywhere from $24–$75, while queen cells are a tad cheaper, ranging from $5–$8.

Medication and Treatments

Ah, the challenges of beekeeping! These tiny fuzzy buzzy creatures face formidable foes, from the notorious Varroa mite to diseases like American Foulbrood (AFB) and European Foulbrood (EFB). But fear not! With regular monitoring and the right treatments, these threats can be managed. While treatment costs can vary, being proactive and not skimping is essential. A rough estimate might place the annual maintenance costs for medication and treatments between $50 to $150 per hive. However, this is a ballpark figure, and actual expenses can vary based on individual circumstances and choices. It's always a good idea for beekeepers to consult with local experts or beekeeping associations to get a more accurate estimate tailored to their region and situation.

Additional Maintenance Costs—Painting and Repairing

Every couple of years, your beehive might start looking a bit weathered. Depending on where you live and the whims of Mother Nature, this could be sooner rather than later. Investing in quality paint that's bee-friendly is crucial. You're looking at between $25 to $50 for a gallon of the good stuff. But here's the silver lining: one gallon can stretch across multiple hives, so an annual touch-up might only set you back around $5 to $15 per hive.

Beehives are sturdy, but they're not invincible. Over time, you might notice a loose nail here or a chipped wood piece there. What is the cost of these minor fixes? Anywhere from $5 to $50, depending on the severity. If you're a DIY enthusiast, you've got this in the bag. But if carpentry isn't your strong suit, you might need to factor in additional costs for professional help.

Sales and Marketing Expenses

First up, packaging. Think of it as the attire your products wear to their debut ball. It's not just about holding the honey; it's about presenting it in a way that makes people say, "I need that!" And trust me; the proper packaging can make all the difference to your business.

Cost Breakdown

- For honey, glass jars (8 oz): $0.50–$1.50 each.

- Lids/Caps: $0.10–$0.30 each.

- Total for packaging (assuming an average beehive produces about 30 pounds or 60 jars of honey a year): $36–$108.

Next, let's talk branding. Those vibrant labels, the catchy taglines, and those informative leaflets? They're not just bits of paper; they're your product's ambassadors. Sure, there's a cost to getting them printed, but think of it as investing in your product's passport to fame.

- Labels: $0.10–$0.50 per label. For 60 jars: $6–$30.

- Promotional leaflets (assuming 500 brochures): $50–$150.

In this digital era, you're quite invisible if you're not online. A website is more than just a page; it's your 24/7 storefront. While setting it up might seem daunting, remember, it's like laying down the welcome mat for customers worldwide.

- Domain registration: $10–$30 annually.

- Web hosting: $50–$150 annually.

- Website design (one-time or infrequent cost, can be amortized over several years): $200–$1000. Considering this over three years, it's roughly $67–$333 annually.

Have you ever considered showcasing your products at a local farmers' market? Yes, there's the stand rental to consider, but the direct feedback and the community vibe? Priceless!

- Rental costs vary widely based on the location and popularity of the market. A typical range might be $20–$100 per day. If you attend once a month: $240–$1200 annually.

Lastly, and this is *crucial,* value your time. Every moment you invest, from nurturing your bees to strategizing your sales, is golden. It might not have a price tag, but it's the backbone of your venture.

Where should you sell your honey?

Navigating the honey-selling landscape can be a maze without understanding the potential buyers in your vicinity. Thus, it's crucial to identify local establishments with a penchant for honey and foster strong ties with them. Let's walk down some avenues that can be gold mines for local bee producers:

- **Farmers' Markets:** These local hubs are more than places to sell; they're platforms to share your honey's unique story, its varietals, and the passion behind its production. Engaging directly with your community here builds trust and lets you set a price reflecting your honey's value.

- **Online Marketplaces:** Platforms like Amazon, Etsy, and eBay are not just for crafts and gadgets. They're vast oceans where many honey producers have cast their nets and reaped bountifully. The beauty of these platforms? They break geographical barriers, allowing your local honey to be savored by someone across the globe.

- **Local Grocery Stores:** The "local produce" trend isn't just a fad; it's a real movement. Grocery stores are *looking* for local gems; your honey could be the next big thing on their shelves. Building a rapport with store managers can pave the way for a long-term partnership.

- **Restaurants and Food Establishments:** Imagine a local chef drizzling your honey over a dish, enhancing its flavor profile. Collaborating with restaurants can be a win-win, offering them quality ingredients while broadening your reach.

- **Festivals and Food Events:** These events are more than just fun; they're opportunities. They offer a platform to introduce your honey to a broader audience, many of whom might taste it for the first time. Plus, with the rising trend of honey as a favored gift, consider tapping into souvenir shops or tourist hotspots.

- **Skincare Manufacturers:** Honey isn't just a treat for the palate; it's a boon for the skin. Its natural properties make it a sought-after ingredient in skincare products. Partnering with manufacturers can open a whole new market for your produce.

- **Bakeries and Pastry Shops:** The sweet allure of honey has always been a baker's delight. Connecting with local bakeries can lead to fruitful collaborations, with your honey becoming the star ingredient in their best-selling pastries.

Crafting and Designing Your Label

Honey Jar Label/Credit: Artfriend(www.shutterstock.com)

In the honey market, it's clear that first impressions matter. Your honey might be the sweetest in town, but without the right label, it might be just another jar on the shelf. So, how do you ensure your product stands out and speaks volumes? Let's dive deep into the art and science of designing honey labels that catch the eye, and tell a compelling story.

Imagine walking through an aisle filled with honey jars. What would make yours stand out? The answer lies in crafting a label that's both original and enticing. Whether you're selling wildflower, clover, or any other type of honey, the right label really matters. It's not just about aesthetics; it's about creating a connection, a memory, and then, a loyal customer.

It's not just about design. While we all want our labels to be the talk of the town, they also need to adhere to specific standards and regulations. Don't worry; we have you covered there as well. By the end of this book, you'll have a clear understanding of how to design beautiful—and compliant—labels.

Step 1: Shape and Size Matters

First off, consider the vessel holding your golden delight. Is it a classic jar, a sleek bottle, or a user-friendly squeezable container? The container's silhouette is the canvas for your label, setting the stage for its design.

Now, while some beekeepers are venturing into avant-garde territory with honeycomb cell-shaped jars and other intricate designs, many still prefer the timeless charm of traditional containers. These innovative designs, though eye-catching, come with their own set of challenges for labeling. With unique curves and multiple facets, they need a label that complements their distinctiveness.

On the other hand, conventional packaging, though seemingly simple, offers a world of possibilities for label design. With a broader surface area, you can play with design elements, ensuring your brand's story is told just as you envision.

So, where's the best spot for your label? The body of the jar, perhaps, to showcase your brand prominently? Maybe the lid—offering a sneak peek into the luscious honey beneath? Or a seal on the lid, doubling as a guarantee of the product's authenticity? For those looking to make a statement, a wrap-around label might be the way to go. It provides ample space for design and essential information and wraps your jar of liquid gold in your brand's essence.

A well-thought-out cutout or a unique shape can elevate the look, making your product stand out on the shelves. The key is to find that perfect balance between the container's shape and the label's design, so that they complement each other.

Step 2: It's All About the Material

Ever thought about how a suitable dress material can make or break your look? Well, the same goes for your honey labels. It's not just about a catchy design; your chosen material can elevate your honey from being "just another jar" to "must-have golden goodness!"

- **White Honey Labels:** Picture this: a pristine canvas ready to showcase any design or hue you fancy. With a white film base, these labels are all about contrast. Whether for bold typography or a delicate image, everything stands out beautifully against that white backdrop.

- **Clear Honey Labels:** Now, if you're proud of that golden nectar and want the world to see it, these are your best bet. Printed on transparent film, they give your honey jar a polished, almost invisible look. It's like giving your customers a sneak peek into the jar, with the essential information subtly wrapped around.

- **Metallic Honey Labels:** Are you feeling a bit fancy? Dive into the world of metallics. Printed on a glimmering silver base, these labels have a reflective charm. Ideal for your premium range, they shout luxury and elegance.

Hang on—there's more! Ever peeked at what your competitors are up to? It's a great way to gather ideas, but always remember, *your* honey is one-of-a-kind, and your label should reflect that.

The Finishing Touches:

Think of these as accessories to your outfit.

- **Gloss Laminated Labels:** For those who love a bit of drama, these labels shine and shimmer, making every detail pop.

- **Matte Laminated Labels:** If subtlety is your style, the matte finish offers a soft, sophisticated touch.

- **Soft Touch Laminated Labels:** It's luxury at your fingertips. Smooth, velvety, and utterly irresistible.

- And if you're in the mood to go all out, sprinkle in some **gold foil** magic. It's like adding a splash of gold to your favorite outfit. It's the ultimate luxe touch, perfect for highlighting logos or unique elements.

Step 3: Crafting the Perfect Content for Your Honey Labels

While a sharp design might catch the eye, the content truly resonates. Think of it as the narrative behind your brand that speaks to every customer that handles your product.

- **Colors:** Have you ever noticed how honey labels bask in soft, pastel shades? It's like they're trying to mirror nature's gentle palette. But here's a thought: imagine the rich amber of your honey set against a deep, mysterious black. Bold? Absolutely. But it's these unexpected choices that can make your product pop. And if you're feeling whimsical, why not throw in a splash of vibrant hues? It's like giving your honey its own personality.

- **Fonts:** Let's think about fonts. Sending a message is more important than merely being aesthetically pleasing. But remember, clarity is king. You don't want customers straining their eyes. Keep the text bold, legible, and oozing with style. And a little advice from the pros? *Two* fonts are plenty. Any more, and you risk clutter. Also, play with contrasts. It ensures your message doesn't just blend into the background, but stands tall and proud.

- **Images:** Ah, the power of pictures. It's like a visual handshake, introducing your honey to the world. A delicate acacia bloom on your label could be the perfect image if you're selling acacia honey. Or perhaps a honeycomb's intricate patterns, or a beehive's charm. These visuals aren't just decorations; they're telling stories.

Step 4: Navigating the Labyrinth of Compliance in Honey Labeling

Alright, let's dive right in. You've got this delicious golden nectar and are eager to share it. But before you allow your creativity to run wild with label designs, there's a crucial step: ensuring your labels are on the right side of the law. It's not just about *looking* good; it's about *being* good, too.

First off, a quick shoutout to our friends at the FDA. They ensure everything we eat, including honey, is safe and properly labeled. Whether your honey is homegrown or imported, the FDA's guidelines, rooted in the Federal Food, Drug, and Cosmetic Act (FD&C Act) and the Fair Packaging and Labeling Act, have covered you.

Now, let's break down the essentials, shall we?

- **Honey Type:** While a jar's golden glow might hint at its contents, it's always best to spell it out. Not everyone's a honey guru, after all. If you're peddling something unique like creamed honey, shout it from the rooftops—or at least make it clear on the label.

- **Source:** Blossom, nectar, or honeydew? It's not just a fun choice; it's a crucial distinction. And believe me, honey enthusiasts can be picky.

- **Floral Source:** Whether your honey hails from orange blossoms or wildflowers, naming its floral origin adds authenticity and charm.

- **Origin Details:** Where did this sweet treat come from? A little geographical shoutout never hurts.

- **Identity Statement:** The United Nations' Codex Alimentarius sets the gold standard here. If it's labeled "Honey," it better be 100% natural. But here's a little insider tip: not all supermarket honey is pure. If yours is a blend with corn syrup, just be upfront about it. Honesty is *always* the best policy.

- **Nutritional Lowdown:** A nutritional breakdown is a must-have since honey is food, after all. It's not just informative; it's the law.

- **Ingredient Insights:** Have you got raspberry-flavored honey? Make sure it's clear on the label. It's all about setting the right expectations.

- **Weighty Matters:** List the net weight sans the jar. Clarity is your best friend whether you're going metric or sticking to U.S. measurements.

- **Extra Info:** A production year or bottling date is a neat touch. And if you're batching your honey, a lot number is super handy. Oh, and don't forget your name, address, and website—your fans will want to know where their new favorite honey came from!

Throughout this chapter, we've delved deep into the intricacies of hive profitability, gauged the number of hives one can realistically manage, and mastered the subtle art of honey pricing. And remember—beekeeping offers more treasures than just honey. Beekeeping also involves understanding your initial costs, ongoing maintenance, and the best places to showcase and sell liquid gold. And let's not forget the importance of crafting that perfect label, which tells the story of your dedication and passion. As you buzz forward, let these insights be your compass. Here's to every drop of honey you and your fuzzy friends produce, and every success that awaits you in beekeeping. Dive in; the hive is calling!

CONCLUSION

You've made it through the book (or you are peeking at the end!) and now you should be ready to start the whole beekeeping process. Keeping bees is about managing and assisting an entirely natural process. It's an unwritten, sincere contract between you and the bees. The deal is that you provide stability, consistency, care, and watchfulness that should prevent a natural disaster from striking, as it often does in the wild.

The return? Well, there are two returns.

The first is the surplus honey which, in well-managed hives, should be considerable, delighting you and your friends and customers too. But the *real* return is the satisfaction that you're helping out in this highly important natural process.

To fully appreciate this, just imagine for a moment what the world would be like without bee pollination. There are other pollinators, but bees are up there and leading the pack. In many ways, the honey is really a side issue (might be hard to consider it this way when you taste the honey you've helped your bees to produce); the real value is the pollination of the flora, a vital part of nature at work.

In fact, there's not much more that's *so* important—especially today with the need for carbon-capturing plants while the human population continues to grow. A reduction in bee numbers threatens major sources of food; you can do your part to reverse this while also having fun developing a hobby that absorbs you while you learn.

And then, of course, there's still the honey, the royal jelly, the beeswax, the propolis—with all these products' special features and attributes.

Keeping bees in your backyard is about "returning to nature" (a cliché but true!) and applying human intelligence into the mix. That way, you're playing a key role, preparing for potential disasters, managing the hives you have to safeguard, and perhaps increasing them in time.

There's a lot to consider before even constructing your first hive. Do you have a little spare space, time, and cash for investment? It doesn't take *much* of these, but you will need a little. Have you checked with the neighbors and any local authorities who may be involved?

Don't forget to be checked for allergies to bee stings as this could be make or break for your beekeeping activities.

Right, you've covered the basics and decided to go ahead. Put down your newly-acquired protective clothing, sit down with pen and paper, and plan how to proceed. We've covered vital aspects to underwrite your success as a beekeeper covering water supplies, drainage, warmth, and accessibility.

Together, we've covered the types of honey and the relationship of flavor with the dominant flora in your area. Do a rough timetable as well—assemble equipment in the winter ready for a spring start-up when your newly-acquired bees should be arriving.

Time to stress the obvious now—as a beginner, you need to start with a Langstroth hive, they're much simpler and easier—why make it harder, particularly in the early years? There's plenty of time to explore the other hives later on in your beekeeping life.

One step at a time and you'll gain confidence as you go along; too much too soon and you might feel out of your depth.

You need to understand the basic biology of bees, so we've covered it earlier in some depth. How bees operate, what they do, and their life cycle matter a *lot* to the thoughtful beekeeper. It's not an onerous pastime but a little thought, knowledge, and planning will make the difference between success and failure.

We have also covered common problems, ailments, and diseases—explaining not just what they are and what we know about them—but providing practical steps to *avoid* them altogether, or to minimize their effect. A key part of this is regularly inspecting the hives under your care, but with knowledge of what you're looking for.

Beekeeping for Beginners should be kept at hand, and dipped into whenever you start something new in your beekeeping activities. It's not intended to be "put away" after reading once; it's designed to be a *reference* book, a 21st century handbook to successful beekeeping.

In 2011 there were 81.41 million hives and by 2021 there were about 101.6 million beehives in the world. You can join the movement!

Finally, there's the honey, the immediate end game. We've looked at the types of honey and discussed the harvesting. This is what you can share, at the end of the day ...

Honey

... and helping nature, along the way, to maintain crops and flora. That's quite a noble aspiration for all beekeepers. You can be one of them, one step at a time.

Your Feedback Helps Us All Bee Better: Please Leave a Review!

Thank you so much for buzzing through *Beekeeping for Beginners*! I hope you found the guide a valuable resource for becoming a successful beekeeper. Your feedback is incredibly important to me and to fellow aspiring beekeepers. If you could take a few seconds to leave a review on Amazon, I would be truly grateful. Your insights help me improve and guide others in choosing the right guide for their beekeeping adventure.

Printed in Great Britain
by Amazon

44989351R00169